Disabled Students in Higher Education

This item ha

Widening access to higher education has become a top priority for governments in the UK and around the world. As a university degree increasingly becomes an essential gateway to professional employment, the under-representation of disabled people studying at this level underlines a massive social injustice that still exists in today's education system.

The authors of this timely publication have closely analysed rates of participation by, and the experiences of, disabled students in higher education over a two-year period. They compare the responses of eight different universities to new anti-discriminatory practice, contrasting their social profiles, academic missions, support for disabled students and approaches for the implementation of change. It is this approach to making changes that comes under particular scrutiny, with a close examination of the universities' interpretation of 'reasonable adjustments', and the extent to which they have modified their facilities and teaching accordingly. Student case studies are used throughout to illustrate the real impact of institutional responses to the legislation.

Insightful and ground-breaking, this book raises the questions that policy-makers, vice-chancellors and government officials are reluctant to ask. It will make fascinating reading for students of education, social policy, politics and disability studies, and for those working towards accredited university teacher status.

Sheila Riddell is Professor of Inclusion and Diversity at the University of Edinburgh. **Teresa Tinklin** is an independent researcher based in Sheffield. **Alastair Wilson** is Senior Research Fellow in the Faculty of Education, Strathclyde University.

Disabled Students in Higher Education

Perspectives on widening access and changing policy

Sheila Riddell, Teresa Tinklin and Alastair Wilson

Routledge
Taylor & Francis Group

LONDON AND NEW YORK

First published 2005 by Routledge
2 Park Square, Milton Park, Abingdon, Oxon OX14 4RN

Simultaneously published in the USA and Canada
by Routledge
270 Madison Ave, New York, NY 10016

Routledge is an imprint of the Taylor & Francis Group

© 2005 Sheila Riddell, Teresa Tinklin and Alastair Wilson

Typeset by Graphicraft Limited, Hong Kong
Printed and bound in Great Britain by TJ International Ltd, Padstow,
Cornwall

British Library Cataloguing in Publication Data
A catalogue record for this book is available from the British Library

Library of Congress Cataloging in Publication Data
A catalog record for this book has been requested

ISBN 0–415–34078–0 (Hbk)
ISBN 0–415–34079–9 (Pbk)

Contents

Illustrations

Tables

Acknowledgements

We would like to extend our thanks to members of the advisory group of the ESRC project *Disabled Students and Multiple Policy Innovations in Higher Education*, who gave us an enormous amount of support and assistance during the course of the research. In particular, we owe a big debt of gratitude to Professor Alan Hurst and Paul Brown, who have worked in this area for many years and have made a huge contribution to the development of policy and provision for disabled students. Throughout the project, they gave us the benefit of their insight and depth of knowledge.

On a personal note, we would like to thank our family and friends who, as always, have supported us through the highs and lows of fieldwork and writing.

Finally, a big thank you to all the students and staff who took the time to share their views with us. In writing about the wide range of experiences, we hope we have struck the right balance between optimism for the future and realism about the barriers which still have to be overcome.

Sheila Riddell, Teresa Tinklin and Alastair Wilson,
Edinburgh, October 2004

Abbreviations

ADA	Americans with Disabilities Act
A levels	General Certificate in Education Advanced Level
BPD	Borderline Personality Disorder
BSL	British Sign Language
CNAA	Council for National Academic Awards
CSV	Community Service Volunteers
DA	disability adviser
DAG	Disability Advisory Group
DDA	Disability Discrimination Act
DEA	disability employment adviser
DfEE	Department for Education and Employment
DfES	Department for Education and Skills
DLA	Disability Living Allowance
DO	disability officer
DRC	Disability Rights Commission
DS	disabled students
DSA	Disabled Students Allowance
EU	European Union
FE	Further Education
HE	Higher Education
HEFCE	Higher Education Funding Council for England
HEFCW	Higher Education Funding Council for Wales
HEI	Higher Education Institution
HESA	Higher Education Statistics Agency
Highers	Scottish Qualifications Agency Higher Level
HMC	Headmasters' and Headmistresses' Conference
HNC	Higher National Certificate
HND	Higher National Diploma
HUCS	Heads of University Counselling Services
ILF	Independent Living Fund
ILT	Institute for Learning and Teaching
IT	information technology

JSA	Job Seekers' Allowance
LEA	Local Education Authority
MH	mental health
MHSW	mental health support worker
MHT	mental health tutor
MSP	Member of the Scottish Parliament
NCIHE	National Committee of Inquiry into Higher Education
NDT	National Disability Team
OECD	Organisation of Economic Cooperation and Development
OPCS	Office for Population Censuses and Surveys
OU	Open University
PA	personal assistant
PC	personal computer
QAA	Quality Assurance Agency
RAE	Research Assessment Exercise
RNID	Royal National Institute for the Deaf
SAAS	Student Awards Agency Scotland
SE	Scottish Executive
SEN	Special Educational Needs
SHEFC	Scottish Higher Education Funding Council
Skill	National Bureau for Students with Disabilities
SRC	Student Representative Council
SSS	Student Support Services
TLA	Teaching Learning and Assessment
TQA	Teaching Quality Assessment
UCAS	Universities and Colleges Admissions Service
UG FTE	Undergraduate Full Time Equivalent
UPIAS	Union of Physically Impaired Against Segregation
UUK	Universities UK
VP	Vice Principal
VST	visual support tutor

Chapter 1

Setting the scene

Disabled students and multiple policy innovations in higher education

Introduction

Widening access to higher education has reached the top of the UK political agenda. It is seen as a positional good and as the passport to better paid work. The White Paper *The Future of Higher Education* (DfES, 2003) noted that those who have received any form of higher education, including sub-degree courses, earn 50 per cent more than those who have not. Honours graduates earn 64 per cent more than those without an honours degree. Furthermore, obtaining a degree from some universities brings much greater financial returns than others. Conlon and Chevalier (2002) found a 44 per-centage point difference between graduates from institutions at extreme ends of the graduate pay scale. Because participation in higher education, particularly attendance at elite institutions, is so closely linked to subsequent earnings and life chances, there is increasing competition for places on certain courses and within particular institutions. Modest efforts to encourage disadvantaged students to enter traditional universities are resisted by independent schools and there are debates about the extent to which the government should directly intervene by making funding contingent on the attainment of widening access targets. The higher education White Paper (DfES, 2003) underlined the theme of widening access to higher education in the interests of social justice and economic competitiveness. In 2004, the Higher Education Bill scraped through its second reading with a majority of five. The legislation attempts to reconcile moves to widen access, through the creation of a new Office for Fair Access and bursary system, with the implementation of a hypothecated graduate tax, which some fear will deter students from poorer backgrounds.

In line with the increased political focus on higher education, there is a growing body of research investigating trends in participation in higher education and the experiences of 'non-traditional' university students (see, for example, Archer *et al.*, 2003; Furlong and Forsyth, 2003). Disabled students are now recognised as an 'under-represented' group, and, for the first time in December 2002, HEFCE published data on the extent of their participation. However, they are still somewhat marginalised within official policy documents, for example, the recent White Paper simply noted that the extension of the Disability Discrimination Act to education prohibited discrimination against disabled students. It is not clear whether the Office for Fair Access will focus on students from poorer backgrounds, or whether targets will be set for increasing the number of disabled students in higher education. Despite the growing interest in higher education on the part of both policy-makers and researchers, there have to date been no large-scale studies of patterns of participation and experiences of disabled students in higher education. The vast majority of studies conducted have been evaluations of funding initiatives or small-scale studies often based in one institution. This book, which draws on data from an ESRC funded study entitled *Disabled Students and Multiple Policy Innovations in Higher Education*, attempts to locate provision for disabled students within the much broader field of access studies and the sociology of education.

The study was conducted by researchers at the universities of Glasgow and Edinburgh between 2001 and 2003. Its aim was to analyse rates of participation by and experiences of disabled students in higher education, in the light of wider policy agendas affecting the sector. Key policies affecting higher education, we surmised, were likely to include widening access, managerialism and marketisation. Both quantitative and qualitative methods were employed, since we wanted to compare patterns of participation as reflected in categorical data with students' experience of negotiating an independent identity within higher education. Did the official UCAS categories of disability, or the social relational account suggested by the social model of disability, play any part in their negotiation of self? In addition, did their relationship to the concept of disability have a bearing on their construction of social networks and social capital, which is a critical part of university life?

A particular focus of the book is the impact of anti-discrimination legislation on institutional practice and student experience. Part 4 of the Disability Discrimination Act 1995 (as amended) (DDA), which came into force in September 2002, made it unlawful to discriminate against disabled students or prospective students in the provision of educational services, including pedagogy, the curriculum and assessment (see below for further discussion). Like other equality legislation, the Act is based on the liberal idea that education may reduce inequality experienced by disabled people if discriminatory practices can be eliminated. Such views would of course be challenged by Marxian writers such as Bourdieu (1989), who portray the dynamic of class struggle as determining access to various forms of capital, which may be economic, cultural, social or symbolic. In this book, we compare the response of eight different universities to the legislation, contrasting their social profiles and academic missions, support for disabled students and approaches to the implementation of the DDA in terms of their interpretation of the concept of reasonable adjustments. Student case studies are used to illustrate the impact of institutional response to the legislation on student experience. In particular, we focus on contrasting interpretations of the notion of 'reasonable adjustments' and the extent to which universities have modified their approaches to teaching and learning.

There have been major changes in the nature and mode of operation of British higher education institutions over the past two decades. The number of students more than doubled in the ten-year period between the mid-1980s and the mid-1990s, whilst the unit of resource fell by a third. The middle classes benefited disproportionately from this expansion (Archer, 2003), and continued to dominate the old universities and, to a lesser extent, the post-92 universities.[1] In 1999, for example, they made up 80 per cent of participants in pre-92 universities and 67 per cent of participants in post-92 universities. As Reay (2003) pointed out, it is difficult to identify 'working class space' in higher education since in even the most accessible institutions the majority of students are middle class (for example, working-class students make up 41 per cent of undergraduates at the University of Bolton, 41 per cent at London Metropolitan, 45 per cent at Teesside and 45 per cent at Wolverhampton). Despite the continuation of middle-class dominance, the university body is more heterogeneous than ever before, with a growth in the number of mature and part-time students in higher education as well as those from minority ethnic and working-class backgrounds. Disabled students have also benefited from the expansion, although this group continues to be under-represented, making up about 5 per cent of home students, well below the proportion of disabled people in the population (about 16 per cent of the working-age population, although this is skewed towards older age groups and includes people with, for example, severe learning disabilities who would be unlikely to qualify for higher education under current selection arrangements) (Riddell and Banks, 2001).

Although patterns of participation in relation to social class, gender, ethnicity and geographical location have been widely discussed (e.g. Paterson, 1997; Osborne, 1999; Archer et al., 2003; Hayton and Paczuska, 2002), the participation rate of disabled students has often been omitted from the analysis. Despite growing interest in higher education as an important arena in the distribution of life chances (Slowey and Watson, 2003), we know little about the daily lives and experiences of students and the ways in which HEIs act as sites which reproduce or disrupt existing social inequalities (Field, 2003). Furthermore, little is known about the interaction of policies focusing on marketisation and managerialism and those promoting widening access and social inclusion. To address these gaps in the literature, the research sought:

---

1 A number of former polytechnics and higher education institutions were accorded university status in 1992.

- to examine how policies on wider access for disabled students interact with multiple policy innovations in higher education and to analyse the effects of both sets of policies on the experiences of students with particular impairments;
- to compare the development of policy and practice affecting disabled students in England and Scotland and in different types of institution, including ways in which institutions have interpreted and implemented national policies, and to assess how local and national policies are experienced by disabled students;
- to assess the impact of wider access policies on participation levels of disabled people by integrating them into existing analyses of participation by disadvantaged groups;
- to inform the development of higher education policy and practice, particularly in relation to disabled students, by providing an independent analytical perspective on recent developments.

Disabled students pose particular challenges to higher education not only in terms of gaining physical access to buildings, but also in relation to much broader access issues concerning the curriculum, teaching and learning and assessment. For these reasons, they may be seen as a litmus test of the ability of higher education to include a diverse range of learners, an essential part of the objective of transforming the UK into a knowledge society (DfES, 2003; Scottish Executive, 2003).

The policy and legislative context

We have already alluded to the background changes in higher education which have taken place over the last two decades, which form an essential part of the backcloth against which the development of policy and provision for disabled students has taken place. Prior to 1993, higher education was largely inaccessible to disabled people and any adjustments made were at the good will of staff and students (Barnes, 1991; Leicester and Lovell, 1994). A few institutions had limited provision for disabled students; for example, Kalikundis House at the University of Sussex was adapted for students with multiple disabilities, who were supported by personal assistants and student volunteers. However, such initiatives were the exception rather than the rule, and the general assumption was that university was not the place for disabled people.

In 1993, following the creation of Skill (the National Bureau for Students with Disabilities), a voluntary organisation dedicated to promoting access to higher education for disabled people, the Scottish and English Higher Education Funding Councils (SHEFC and HEFCE) were persuaded to offer special initiative funding to institutions to improve their provision for disabled students. In England, the funding was used to support particular initiatives in selected institutions, whereas in Scotland it was distributed more evenly across institutions. In 1994, SHEFC established the post of National Coordinator, whereas the English equivalent, the eQuip team, was not established until 1997. Special initiative funding has continued in England, and, at the time of writing, projects are focused on improving access to the curriculum and assessment. In Scotland, the Teachability Project, led by the University of Strathclyde, receives support from SHEFC and supports institutions and departments which are auditing their curricula, pedagogy and assessment practices in order to make them more inclusive. The funding councils have now moved towards mainstreaming funding for disabled students. Premium funding was introduced in 1999–2000 in England and 2000–1 in Scotland. The funds are paid on the basis of the number of students within the institution claiming Disabled Students Allowance (DSA). This new way of allocating funds is mirrored in the premium funding allocated to institutions on the basis of the number of students recruited from low-participation neighbourhoods, and is intended to acknowledge that there is a cost to the institution of recruiting and retaining 'non-traditional' students. On the one hand, these measures could be seen as pathologising 'non-traditional' students. On the other hand, those institutions attracting relatively large numbers of 'access' students maintain that this activity should be financially incentivised, just as research is incentivised by the Research Assessment Exercise.

Despite these moves to inject cash at an institutional level, funds continue to be channelled to individual students through the DSA, which was established in 1990. Following an assessment, the DSA is paid directly to the student to cover costs incurred as a result of the disability, the costs of any special equipment and the costs of non-medical personal help with study. The DSA was originally means-tested and only payable to students qualifying for a local authority award. Following the publication of the Dearing Report (NCIHE, 1997a), means-testing of the DSA was abolished and it was extended to all students. It might be argued that the DSA reflects an individualised view of impairment as residing within the student, which is somewhat at odds with social model thinking. Premium funding, on the other hand, reflects the need to remove institutional barriers and therefore could be seen as more attuned with the thinking of the disability movement. In Chapter 4, the implications of these different funding streams in different institutions will be further explored.

As noted earlier, there have been considerable difficulties in getting the needs of disabled students incorporated into mainstream higher education policy and practice. The reviews of higher education carried out by the Dearing and Garrick committees (NCIHE, 1997a, 1997b) did not initially include disabled students in their terms of reference (Hurst, 1996). However, due in part to pressure from the voluntary organisation Skill, a number of disability-related recommendations emerged from these reports, including the need to fund learning support in higher education institutions, the need for the Institute for Learning and Teaching (ILT) to include the learning needs of disabled students in their programmes and the extension of the DSA (Hurst, 1999).

The Quality Assurance Agency's *Code of Practice for Students with Disabilities* was published in 1999 and implemented in 2000. Its 24 precepts were intended to ensure that 'students with disabilities have a learning experience comparable to that of their peers'. Institutions were also encouraged to adapt it to their 'own needs, traditions, cultures and decision-making processes'. Since December 2002, HEFCE has published benchmark data relating to disability, indicating the percentage of disabled students in each institution and comparing participation with comparable institutions.

There are ongoing debates about whether devices associated with new public management (Clarke and Newman, 1997), such as equality audits and target-setting, are capable of promoting social justice goals (Clarke *et al.*, 2000; Exworthy and Halford, 1999). Critics of the new management maintain that regimes which are intended to foster accountability and transparency may simply be used to limit the creativity of professionals, distort performance by encouraging minimal compliance with targets and ultimately breed a climate of mistrust (Power, 1997). On the other hand, proponents of the new management maintain that effective public services can only be delivered when appropriate goals and values are identified and targets used to assess progress. In higher education, there has been particular resistance to management regimes from the pre-92 universities. The quality inspection process, introduced in the early 1990s through teaching quality assessment, followed by subject review and institutional audit, was bitterly resisted by the traditional universities, but generally accepted by the post-92 universities, which had been used to closer scrutiny and regulation by the Council for National Academic Awards (CNAA). Subject benchmarking, also a product of the early 1990s, was resisted strongly in the pre-92 universities on the grounds that the government was trying to introduce a national curriculum into higher education. Farwell (2002) noted that 'the benchmark monster turned out to be toothless', with most subjects producing a set of bland outcomes to which any degree course in the country would be able to conform. Other areas arousing opposition from some quarters of the old universities included modularisation and requirements for the teaching of generic skills, particularly those associated with employability. In many of these debates, the elite institutions maintained that their academic freedom was being eroded and that a 'dumbing down' of higher education was taking place. In understanding the impact of measures such as the QAA's Code of Practice on Provision for Students with Disabilities, it is important to take account of the fundamental opposition within the pre-92 universities to any manifestation of new managerialism.

In addition to management regimes, legislation has been used to make discrimination against disabled students unlawful. Here, too, there are debates about the potential of disability equality legislation to enhance the position of disabled people in the UK (Gooding, 2000; Meager and Hurstfield, 2005). The Disability Discrimination Act was seen as of great symbolic importance in recognising the political claims of disabled people. However, there is continued unease within the disability movement about the definition of disability within the Act (see discussion above), the justifications for failing to make reasonable adjustments or providing less favourable treatment, and the extent to which the legislative route is an effective way for disabled people to achieve justice. The research therefore examined the early impact of Part 4 of the DDA on the higher education sector and considered the future potential for legislation to bring about significant social change for disabled people.

The legal duties of higher education institutions towards disabled students have increased over time. The Further and Higher Education (Scotland) Act 1992 required further and higher education institutions to have regard to the needs of disabled students. Similar measures applied in England. Education was originally exempt from the Disability Discrimination Act 1995, although Part 4 required institutions to publish disability statements indicating policy, provision and future plans for disabled students. The DDA was amended by the Special Educational Needs and Disability Discrimination Act 2001, whose provisions were implemented in 2002. The new Part 4 DDA made it unlawful to discriminate against disabled students. Discrimination was defined as a failure to make reasonable adjustments or providing less favourable treatment to a student for a reason relating to their disability without justification. Institutions were expected to carry out anticipatory adjustments, rather than simply responding in an *ad hoc* way to the needs of individual students. The bulk of our fieldwork took place as institutions were gearing themselves up to comply with the legislation. Early responses to the legislation at policy level are discussed in Chapter 3 and the implications for teaching, learning and assessment are considered in Chapter 5.

The international context

It is important to have a sense of where the UK stands internationally in relation to the development of services for disabled students. The USA was the first western state to introduce comprehensive anti-discrimination legislation. The Americans with Disabilities Act (ADA) 1990 provided the legal basis for equal opportunity and access for disabled people. The law prohibits discrimination on the basis of disability in employment, state and local government, public accommodations, commercial facilities, transportation and telecommunications. Universities were covered by the Act from the start, in contrast with the British Disability Discrimination Act which excluded education until 2001. The definition of disability in the ADA is broader than that of the DDA (see earlier discussion). Thus the ADA states:

> An 'individual with a disability' means any person who has a physical or mental impairment which substantially limits major life activities, who has a record of such an impairment, or who is regarded as having such an impairment.
>
> (USC, 1990: para. 12102(2))

The DDA, by way of contrast, does not cover individuals who are regarded as having a limiting long-term impairment. The ADA developed as an extension of the civil rights legislation which was introduced much earlier to counter discrimination against Afro-Americans and is clearly aligned with the US tradition of individual rights. From the start, regulatory bodies were set up to ensure compliance, again in contrast with the situation in Britain, where the DRC was not set up until 1999.

The majority of cases brought to court under the ADA have involved discrimination in dismissal from employment and relatively few cases have been brought in relation to education. Nonetheless, scrutiny of US university websites indicates that provision for disabled students is well embedded and systematic. For example, the University of California – Berkeley website clearly sets out the university's duties under the ADA. It makes clear that the university has a responsibility to assist a disabled student in accessing auxiliary aids and services, if the absence of aids and services would result in the student being excluded. The university would assist the student in obtaining these from the State vocational rehabilitation service, but if this were not possible the university would provide the funding. In addition, academic requirements should be modified to ensure that they do not discriminate against disabled students. These might include:

> ... changes in the length of time permitted for the completion of degree requirements, substitution or waiver of specific courses required, and adaptation in the manner in which specific courses are conducted. For example, a campus may permit an otherwise qualified student who is deaf to substitute music history for a required class in music appreciation, or the campus could modify the way in which the music appreciation course is conducted for the student who is deaf.
>
> (www.berkley.edu/students)

The ADA has become a model for other countries introducing anti-discrimination legislation. In Australia, the Commonwealth Disability Discrimination Act outlaws discrimination on the grounds of disability in many arenas including education and training. Disability Standards for Education were issued under the Act and are legally binding. Adams (2001) undertook a study tour in Australia to study the lessons to be learnt there for higher education institutions in Britain prior to the implementation of Part 4 of the DDA. The following key points emerged:

- The major identified 'gap' in provision in Australia was the quality of advice, information and support given to academic staff.
- The majority of legal cases taken against institutions were directly related to teaching and learning issues through direct discrimination in not allowing access to courses, the inability to make reasonable adjustments to teaching and learning and the absence of materials in alternative formats.
- Pockets of best practice existed in relation to the production of flexible learning resources, but these were not well disseminated to other institutions.
- Disability was treated as a social welfare issue and policies in relation to disabled students were not linked to other widening access strategies.

In Europe, the development of support for disabled students is somewhat patchy and whereas most countries have some anti-discrimination legislation for disabled people, often in relation to employment, few have comprehensive anti-discrimination legislation in place akin to the Disability Discrimination Act. However, the situation in Europe is changing and of particular significance are the European Employment Directives, which establish six grounds in relation to which discrimination may occur. These are gender, race, disability, religion or belief, age and sexual orientation. Many European countries have anti-discrimination legislation in place in relation to some areas, but not others. For example, in Britain it is unlawful to discriminate in employment in relation to gender, race and disability, but not the other three strands. It is also the case that some anti-discrimination legislation applies to some fields of social policy, such as employment, but does not apply in others, such as education. It is likely that in the future, the social policy fields in which anti-discrimination legislation applies will be extended, so that areas such as education and health, as well as employment, will be covered.

In order to develop a common approach across the EU, it is evident that member states will have to harmonise their understandings of such key concepts as disability and discrimination (Thusing, 2003). In Germany, for example, a disability is deemed to exist when someone suffers a more than 50 per cent and permanent, but not necessarily employment-related, condition. Someone who is temporarily ill is not deemed to be disabled. The ADA and the DDA also specify that an impairment must be significant, long term and have a 'significant' effect on an individual's ability to perform normal day-to-day activities. However, in Britain and America an impairment would not be quantified as it is in Germany. In addition, both countries now recognise that a person with an asymptomatic, but nonetheless significant, long-term condition, such as HIV, should be covered by the legislation, on the grounds that such conditions will certainly affect the individual's ability to perform normal day-to-day activities in the future. Symptom-free HIV would not be recognised as a disability under anti-discrimination legislation in Germany, but it would in France. Interestingly, the ADA and the DDA exclude certain conditions although they are often regarded as mental impairments. These include paedophilia, exhibitionism, kleptomania and pyromania. Such exceptions, however, are absent from European law.

The Bologna process envisages that common policies and practices will be established across the EU in order to facilitate the movement of students between one institution and another and to ensure that similar standards are enforced in institutions awarding higher education qualifications in different parts of Europe. A small body of literature is beginning to emerge in relation to legislation, policy and practice for disabled students in European higher education institutions. For example, Shevlin *et al.* (2004) describe provision for disabled students in Ireland, where a very low proportion of students are recorded as having a disability (less than 1 per cent). However, this did not include students with hidden impairments such as asthma, diabetes and epilepsy. As in Britain, students with dyslexia are the largest group and the main difficulties appear to be the lack of reasonable adjustments in relation to teaching and learning as well as physical access. Whilst the majority of students believe the main problems to be attitudinal, staff blame lack of physical access and technical aids and equipment. Overall, the charity discourse, which has traditionally dominated social care in Ireland, continues to infuse higher education. It is hoped that the new Education for Persons with Disabilities Act will place duties on institutions to make reasonable adjustments to their approaches to teaching and learning in order to facilitate the inclusion of disabled people. In Finland, the Law of Support for Disabled People came into force in 1988, but an article by Poussu-Olli (1999) indicates that much remains to be done in the way of improving access, developing flexible approaches to teaching and learning and knowing which students are disabled. At the time of writing, there was no registration process on the grounds that this might stigmatise disabled students, again exemplifying some key contrasts in thinking in different parts of the western world.

Further fascinating differences between six European countries in their approaches to provision for disabled students were evident in a report presented to the Higher Education Reform Network Conference in January 2004 (Woessner, 2004). Variations were apparent in the locus of responsibility for supporting disabled students. For example, in Sweden, universities are legally obliged to set aside funds for this purpose, whereas in Poland, universities are not required to allocate any resources. In Britain, as discussed earlier, there are three sources of funding. First, resources are channelled from the Scottish Student Support Agency or the local authority to the individual student through the Disabled Students Allowance; second, the funding councils allocate premium funding to institutions on the basis of the number of students claiming the Disabled Students Allowance; and finally, universities are expected to provide auxiliary aids and services for students who could not obtain support through any other route (e.g. disabled students from overseas). The proportion of disabled students in other parts of Europe appears to be much lower than in British institutions. Even in relatively rich countries like Sweden, only 1.6 per cent of students are recorded as disabled and in Eastern European countries such as Latvia, the proportion is less than 1 per cent. According to the country report for Latvia, there are no blind students in higher education because of lack of technical support and an unsuitable learning environment. Many countries do not hold any official statistics on the number of disabled students.

To summarise, it is evident that countries which have had comprehensive anti-discrimination legislation in place for the longest period of time (the USA, Australia and, more recently, the UK) have made most progress in provision for disabled students, although difficulties in making reasonable adjustments to teaching and learning and providing adequate staff support seem to be ubiquitous. In Europe, few countries have comprehensive legislation to protect the rights of disabled people and clear definitions of disability. Official statistics on the proportion of disabled students in higher education and evidence on institutional support reveal a very patchy picture. However, change is taking place. The European Employment Directives are instituting a common approach to ensuring the rights of disadvantaged groups in employment, and this approach is likely to be applied in other social policy fields. In addition, the Bologna process is seeking to harmonise higher education provision, including approaches to equalities, across the European Union. At a grassroots level, the collection of papers edited by Hurst (1998) demonstrated both the national specificity of approaches to provision for disabled students and also the commonality of the problems encountered. Common dilemmas included whether to concentrate resources in centres of excellence, as opposed to spreading them more thinly through all institutions, and whether to target support on the individual student or on the institution. There is clearly a need for more comparative research over coming years to monitor the extent of international progress.

Theoretical context

Thirty years ago, access to higher education was restricted to a narrow group of socially advantaged students in the richest parts of the world. Globalisation is associated with increasing competition between institutions and students for positional advantage in the higher education market.

As noted by Eggins (2003), the effects of globalisation in higher education are complex:

> On the one hand is the pull towards co-operation, social cohesion, social harmony, transparency, equity and to enabling greater numbers to participate in higher education. On the other hand are the financial issues, the neo-liberal agenda that calls for competition, free trade, the dominance of the market. The flows of change move first one way, then in another: equity, inequality, convergence, divergence; change, non-change; inclusion, exclusion; the global, the local.
>
> (Eggins, 2003: 8)

Throughout the book, we consider the part played by higher education in both creating and challenging social disadvantage, in transmitting ideas about fairness in access to institutional resources and in playing a key part in the formation of individual identities. Some of the key ideas which thread their way through the text are discussed below.

Higher education: reproducing or disrupting social structures?

Traditionally, sociology of education has focused on schools and their role in the creation or disruption of existing patterns of social inequalities. A notable exception is the work of Bourdieu, whose book *The Inheritors*, co-authored with Jean-Paul Passeron, was first published in France in 1964. *The Inheritors* draws on national statistics and data from surveys and case studies of arts faculty students in Lille and Paris. The central argument is that, whilst middle-class students regard access to higher education as their natural heritage, for working-class students passage through higher education represents a constant struggle because of the dislocation between institutional norms and values and their own cultural endowment. The institution reinforces privilege by simply ignoring it; all students are subjected to exactly the same treatment, despite the fact that some students experience higher education as a highly familiar cultural milieu, whereas others live with a permanent sense of dislocation and isolation. The universities subsequently assume that certain forms of behaviour are evidence of superior academic ability, thus creating a slippage between merit and privilege. Bourdieu's work is reflected in a number of studies of widening access to higher education (see, for example, Reay, 2002, 2003; Reay *et al.*, 2001; Macrae and Maguire, 2002). These authors stress the awareness of risk which accompanies working-class students' passage through higher education, compared with the relative absence of risk for middle-class students. In investigating the experiences of disabled students from a wide range of backgrounds in different types of higher education institutions, we wished to study the way in which their received cultural endowment, or habitus to use Bourdieu's terminology, articulated with the cultural norms of the institution in which they were studying. Furthermore, we wished to explore the extent to which students' cultural endowments were a product of their identity as a disabled person, or reflected a range of social characteristics such as social class, gender, ethnicity, sexual orientation and so forth.

In addition, we wished to explore the extent to which social capital appeared to play a part in shaping disabled students' experiences of higher education. Interest in the concept of social capital by policy-makers and researchers has increased over the past few years (see Field, 2003, and Baron *et al.*, 2000 for further discussion). Broadly speaking, social capital refers to the social norms and networks which act as the glue promoting social solidarity. For early proponents of social capital theory, such as Coleman (1988–9) and Putnam (1995), social capital was independent of, but linked to, the generation of economic capital. The thesis of both was that social capital in the west was in decline. Coleman regarded the participation of women in the workplace as a serious challenge to social capital. Working women would be unable to devote sufficient time to overseeing their children's academic and social development, thus middle-class families with two working parents might be high on economic capital but low on social capital, thus creating problems for the future. Putnam, in his emblematic work *Bowling Alone* (2000), used membership of voluntary societies as indicators of stores of social capital and concluded that, at least in the USA, there was evidence of terminal decline, with poorer communities having much less civic engagement than their more affluent neighbours. These ideas have suggested to government that, to achieve the regeneration of communities in decline, there is a need not only for economic assistance but also for community development. Some critics have suggested that the turn to social capital may be seen as a rejection of economic solutions to community problems (Blaxter and Hughes, 2000; Fine, 1999). Other critics have argued that the pattern of decline evident in the USA is not repeated in Europe (Field, 2003), and that Putnam has used old-fashioned measures of social capital which simply reflect the fact that more women are working. The types of civic engagement in which women are involved, such as organising the school run or sharing childcare, are not included in the analysis, and therefore the decline on social capital is over-stated (Morrow, 1999).

Whilst there is a tendency to see social capital as a 'good thing', a number of writers have pointed out that it may also have a 'dark side' (Putnam, 2000; Field, 2003). Bourdieu (1986), in particular, focused on the use of social capital to safeguard the privileges of the middle class, citing the golf club as an example of a site where social networks were likely to operate as a form of exclusion for some and advancement for others. For Bourdieu, social capital seems to be conceptualised as something which is possessed by the middle class. Putnam (2000), on the other hand, in his more recent work developed the idea of different types of social capital which might be used by different groups for different purposes. Bridging capital was likely to be used in order to make vertical connections to people and organisations outwith the immediate circle of friends and family and could, therefore, be used as a means of 'getting on'. Bonding social capital, by way of contrast, described the links between people in constrained circumstances, and, whilst it was useful for people in 'getting by', it was unlikely to help individuals to move beyond their established social position. For poorer people, bonding social capital might be damaging because it was likely to impede wider social engagement and might underpin various forms of nepotism. Riddell, *et al.* (2001) applied these ideas in their study of people with learning difficulties and lifelong learning. They concluded that people with learning difficulties had access to bonding, but not bridging, social capital. They were linked into their communities as consumers of special education and recipients of support from welfare services and voluntary organisations. Bonds with family were particularly strong, with the result that they were stuck in the ascribed roles of permanent child or orphan.

In the case study element of this research, our aim was to focus on the daily lives of disabled students in higher education to understand the cultural dynamic in their interaction with the institution and other students. We wished to explore the types of social capital which disabled students brought with them to the institution and the types of social networks they were able to develop during their time in higher education, which would accompany them in their later experiences in the labour market.

Conceptualising social justice in relation to disabled students

As noted above, Bourdieu was concerned about the ways in which cultural norms and values are deployed in constructing discourses of social justice and equality. During the course of the research project, we wished to explore the salience of a range of theories of social justice and their implications for widening access to higher education for disabled students (see Goodlad and Riddell, 2005, for discussion of theories of social justice in relation to disabled people). According to Miller, social justice provides a rationale for 'how the good and bad things in life should be distributed among the members of a human society' (1999: 1). Social justice may be conceptualised in relation to the distribution of social goods such as education, hence our concern with rates of participation of disabled students in higher education and their social profile with regard to gender, social class and ethnicity. We also wished to explore the amount and quality of support in different institutional contexts since this may also be regarded as a key resource. Social justice is also concerned with cultural claims, associated with the 'politics of recognition' or 'identity politics' (Fraser, 1997). We therefore investigated how disabled students constructed their own identity and were constructed by significant others during the course of their daily lives and in their experiences of teaching, learning and assessment.

In addition, we explored the overall approach of different institutions to promoting social justice for disabled students and other under-represented groups. Conceptions of social justice are based on values, both in relation to beliefs about what constitutes a social good and how social goods and burdens should be distributed. It is evident that the social value of higher education has been increasing, with mounting competition amongst the middle class for entrance to the 'best' universities (Ball, 2003). We were therefore concerned to examine the values which came into play when decisions were made on admitting disabled students to higher education, and the subsequent distribution of learning support resources. We considered the extent to which disabled students' needs were recognised during the admissions process and during their subsequent academic career. Schools, at least theoretically, base their distribution of learning support resources on the idea of need, with those experiencing the greatest difficulties receiving the most generous support. Universities, on the other hand, particularly those in the pre-92 grouping, have tended to operate with the idea that all students should receive the same input, so that their academic performance may be graded on the basis of merit. As Bourdieu argued:

> The sociology of educational institutions and, in particular, of higher educational institutions, may make a decisive contribution to the frequently neglected aspect of the sociology of power which consists in the science of the dynamics of class relations. Indeed, amongst all the solutions provided, throughout the course of history, to the problem of the transmission of power and privileges, probably none have been better dissimulated and, consequently, better adapted to societies which tend to reject the most patent forms of hereditary privileges, than that provided by the educational system in contributing to the reproduction of class relations and in dissimulating the fact that it fulfils this function under the appearance of neutrality.
>
> (Bourdieu, 1972, quoted in Jenkins, 1992: 110)

According to Bourdieu, then, treating all students the same is a certain means of ensuring that established inequalities both persist and are legitimated. It was therefore important to explore the extent to which the internal distribution of resources was based on notions of need or merit, and how these were understood in practice. Finally, whilst all institutions were obliged to at least pay lip service to the ideas of widening access, we wished to explore the way in which different types of institutions operationalised the idea of equality, in particular the extent to which they emphasised procedural justice, equality of outcome or equality of status.

Disability and identity

Within social science, there is currently much interest in the ways in which individuals develop and negotiate their sense of self over the life course. Classical social science saw identity as being stable and shaped by an individual's position within wider economic and social structures. Theorists of late-modernity (for example, Beck, 1992; Lash and Urry, 1993) have questioned the notion of an essential self, emphasising instead the self as a social construct, constantly defined and redefined in a range of social contexts. These views have been criticised for placing too much weight on individual agency, although Beck has emphasised that poorer people face 'an abundance of risk', whereas the socially advantaged may use their resources to protect themselves from some of the dangers which form part of the backcloth of working-class lives.

Disability Studies, the academic wing of the disability movement, has developed rapidly over the past decade and the project of theorising disability is still underway. Thomas (2002) underlines the social relational kernel at the centre of the social model of disability. She refers to the definition of disability developed by the Union of Physically Impaired Against Segregation (UPIAS). According to this definition, disability 'is the disadvantage or restriction of activity caused by a contemporary social organisation which takes little or no account of people who have [impairments] and thus excludes them from the mainstream of social activities' (UPIAS, in Oliver, 1996a: 22). The disability movement has drawn a distinction between disability, which refers to social restriction, and impairment, which refers to a mental or physical deficit. A key idea is that impairment does not necessarily result in disability, and in an ideal society, where all barriers were removed, disability would cease to exist. At the same time, disability activists have wished to build a strong movement based on a common identity and sense of shared oppression, and have therefore tended to draw boundaries between disabled people (those who have impairments) and non-disabled people (those who do not). This creates a paradox, since the key idea of the social model of disability is to challenge the notion that there is a fixed group of people who are disabled simply as a result of having an impairment.

Recently, there has been a growing challenge to the idea of disability as a fixed and unitary category (see Riddell and Watson, 2003; Corker and Shakespeare, 2002). Contributors to the collection of papers edited by Riddell and Watson noted the tensions between different groups of disabled people. For example, groups of people with learning difficulties and deaf people believed that the mainstream disability movement did not fully understand the nature of the specific barriers they faced and was not empowered to speak for them. Indeed, deaf people did not regard themselves as disabled at all, but rather as a linguistic minority. Contributors to the Corker and Shakespeare collection reflect on the implications of postmodernity for the disability movement. The editors conclude that it is no longer feasible to hang on to the idea that disability represents some sort of essential characteristic. Rather, a disabled identity may be used for strategic and political goals, and juggled with other competing facets of identity such as those associated with gender, social class and ethnicity.

Just as Disability Studies is distancing itself from essentialist thinking, various pieces of policy and legislation are cementing the idea of disability as a fixed and bounded category. For example, the Disability Discrimination Act 1995 (as amended) (see below for further discussion) states that an individual is disabled if he or she has a mental or physical impairment which has a substantial and adverse long-term effect on his/her ability to perform normal day-to-day activities. This definition has been criticised by social modellists on the grounds that it reflects medical model understandings based on ideas of individual deficit rather than social barriers. Nonetheless, as the DDA is extended this definition is being used increasingly and is being reflected in the types of questions asked in large-scale surveys. The Disability Bill, modelled on the Race Relations Amendment Act and announced in the Queen's Speech of November 2003, places a duty on public bodies to positively promote equality for disabled people. This implies that all public bodies will have to monitor participation rates of disabled people in employment, education and access to goods and services, and the DDA definition will be used. In order to bring a case under the DDA, the complainant has to first prove that they are disabled under the terms of the Act, and it is evident therefore that disabled people are being encouraged to think of themselves in these categorical terms. It is also the case that, when applying to university, students are invited on their University and Colleges Admissions Service (UCAS) form to select a medical category of impairment. The Disabled Students Allowance is also allocated following a medical or psychological assessment designed to locate the students within a particular medical category.

There are thus a range of bureaucratic and administrative arrangements which promote a medicalised concept of disability. In order to claim legal protection or state benefits, the disabled student must locate themselves within such a definition, thus implying a degree of acquiescence. At the same time, the government has announced the establishment of a single equalities body which will incorporate a human rights commission. This implies a new generic approach to equalities, with the possibility that future legislation will reflect broad equality principles in place of the discrete definitions of existing legislation. Despite these new directions, currently disabled students are forced to operate within a system which understands disability in terms of mental or physical deficit. The research wished to investigate the implications of these categories for the construction of student identity. This was a particularly important part of the research, since identity formation represents such as an important aspect of university experience. For some students, new opportunities for social mobility may be created, whereas for others, far from opening up new possibilities, higher education may reinforce their existing social position as the risks, including those of debt, outweigh the benefits.

Whereas the funding councils have endorsed the idea that more disabled students should be included in higher education, it is important to recognise that there is a persistent strand of opinion, articulated by writers like Furedi (2004), which maintains that disability is a social construction which is used by those who are feeling weak and vulnerable to claim victim status, thus removing responsibility for tackling the normal problems of life. Furedi refers to the increase in conditions such as dyslexia, attention deficit disorder, social phobia and co-dependency, and argues that professionals collude with grassroots movements to create needs and dependency. He notes that:

> Throughout the Anglo-American world, universities report a massive increase in the number of students seeking counselling. For example, both Columbia University and the State University of New York reported a 40 per cent increase in the number of students seeking on-campus help for depression, and anxiety, as well as schizophrenia, bipolar, obsessive-compulsive and panic disorders in 2002.
>
> (Furedi, 2004: 108)

According to Furedi, the growth in recognition of disabled students within higher education is damaging because it diminishes the individual's sense of agency and exaggerates the risks associated with normal life events. The evidence presented in this book does not support the argument that students are being unhelpfully pathologised. Nonetheless, the argument is an important one because, in some senses, it is an extension of the disability movement's argument that disability is largely socially constructed. These questions are returned to in Chapter 8, which considers the way in which a range of students are engaged in the active negotiation of identity through their experiences of higher education.

Structure of the book

Having reviewed the policy and theoretical context of the study, we briefly present the overall structure of the book.

Chapter 2 reports on patterns of participation in higher education based on an analysis of data gathered by the Higher Education Statistics Agency. We examine the representation of disabled students in higher education in different institutional contexts and also make cross-border comparisons between England and Scotland. The social characteristics of students in relation to nature of impairment, social class, gender and ethnicity are discussed. The categories employed in this type of analysis are critiqued.

We argue that, whilst it is possible to raise major objections to their meaning and validity, nonetheless they do hold up some type of mirror to social reality.

The following chapter provides insight into developments at the level of institutional policy, drawing on interviews with senior managers and on a questionnaire survey distributed to all providers of higher education in England and Scotland. Most institutions were taking steps to improve their provision for disabled students. At the same time, there was an awareness throughout the sector of the pressures posed by a general decrease in institutional funding, increase in accountability through the QAA and the RAE, the general expansion in student numbers and the widening access/ participation agenda. Traditional and new universities appeared to experience these pressures differently, and, we argue, this has salience for the experience of disabled students.

In Chapter 4, the analysis moves down a level to probe the policies and practices within particular institutions in relation to the provision of support for disabled students, learning support more generally and the widening access agenda. We explore the extent to which institutions were locating their services within academic departments, or whether the disabled students advisory service was located as an addendum of welfare provision. Some examples of innovative practice in particular institutions, in relation to, for example, students with mental health difficulties, are highlighted. In order to understand provision for disabled students, it is essential to take account of the wider university culture, and the understandings this fosters of concepts such as 'need', 'merit' and equality.

The focus of Chapter 5 is the conceptualisation of 'reasonable adjustments', as demanded by the DDA, in relation to the curriculum, pedagogy and assessment. Disabled students may provide a lens for viewing universities' capacity to respond and adapt to needs of 'under-represented' groups. The nature of the adjustments made by institutions was quite limited in practice, and students with dyslexia were seen as posing a particular challenge to academic standards, particularly in the pre-92 universities. The approach to teaching and learning in the college of further and higher education, which featured in one of our institutional case studies, was contrasted with that of the universities. The learning support ethos of the college was much closer to that of a school, in which the underlying understanding is that students' learning needs should be met through the targeting of resources on those with the greatest need. This was in direct contrast with the universities, particularly the pre-92 institutions, where there was a more general assumption that all students should be treated the same.

Chapter 6 addresses the politics of support in relation to disabled students. The relationship between service providers and disabled people has been identified as of major importance by the disability movement. Discourses of 'care' have been challenged and the values and practices of independent living have been promoted. However, in order to achieve independence (or, in Shakespeare's terminology, inter-dependence), disabled people have to control the services they receive, specifying the tasks to be performed and paying directly those who provide support services. This chapter focuses on arrangements for the provision of services to disabled students. These may take the form of academic support, such as note-taking, sign language interpretation and scribing in examinations, or personal assistance. Support may be required in academic, social and living environments and may be paid for by the individual student through the Disabled Students Allowance, by the institution or by social services. The power relations underpinning different arrangements for the provision of support are discussed and the extent to which students with the highest support needs are being empowered by the current system is considered.

In Chapter 7, attention focuses on the experiences of students with mental health difficulties in higher education. It is argued that, as a result of the rapid changes in higher education over the past decade, they have become much more changeable and stressful places for both students and lecturers. Institutional responses to students with mental health difficulties are analysed, and we discuss the measures which might reduce levels of anxiety. Furedi's argument, that institutions are complicit in creating dependency and vulnerability, is considered.

Chapter 8 returns to the issue of the negotiation of identity within higher education institutions and the part played by disability in the project of the construction and maintenance of self. Students' accounts are used to identify salient facets of identity which may or may not include disability. The extent to which disabled students are able to forge new identities within higher education is considered, and we explore the social networks which are available to disabled students.

In the concluding chapter, we draw together the various theoretical, political and empirical strands of the book and consider their implications for future policy and practice for disabled students. The focus on widening access has drawn attention to the position of disabled students, but the impact of access policies has often been blunted by their intersection with the agenda of management and performativity. Key themes of the book are returned to, including the types of social justice being pursued in different institutions, the struggles of disabled students for representation and respect and the uses of social capital within higher education.

Chapter 2

Patterns of participation of disabled students in higher education

Strategies for researching access to higher education

Educational research in the postwar period was informed by the political arithmetic tradition. The establishment of the welfare state prompted researchers to focus their efforts on investigating the extent to which it was succeeding in its goals of creating a more equal society. To undertake this research, ways had to be found of measuring social class, and father's occupation was used as a proxy indicator. Whilst such measures could only be regarded as rough approximations, their use in a range of studies led to their reification. For example, Glass (1954) reported that from 1928 to 1947, 8.9 per cent of all boys from non-manual backgrounds entered university compared to 1.4 per cent of all boys from manual backgrounds. The provision of full fees in 1960 along with the post-Robbins expansion of higher education led to a rise of 50 per cent in university entrance between 1963 and 1968, and by 1989 the number of university entrants had risen by 150 per cent. However, researchers continued to document the persistence of social class inequality in rates of participation by students from particular social groups (Blackburn and Jarman, 1993; Egerton and Halsey, 1993; Tinklin and Raffe, 1999).

Research on rates of participation fed into policy developments on access to higher education by 'under-represented groups'. The Robbins Committee (DES, 1963) was followed 30 years later by the Dearing and Garrick Reports (NCIHE, 1997a, 1997b). Government documents on lifelong learning (Scottish Executive, 1999; DfEE, 1998, 1999b) called for wider access for students from socially disadvantaged groups, supported by funding council initiatives (HEFCE, 1998; SHEFC, 1998). Social class remained the main focus of analysis, with gender, ethnicity and disability attracting rather less attention. HEFCE began publishing performance indicators on the participation of under-represented groups in 1998, focusing on participation of students from different social backgrounds and ages, 'efficiency' measured by the proportion of students completing a course and research output. From 2002, performance indicators in relation to disabled students and employment outcomes were published. The performance indicators do not cover gender and they only address ethnicity in relation to employment outcomes (see HEFCE, 2002). Primacy continues to be attached to measures of inclusion related to social class; information is published on pupils from state schools or colleges, low-participation neighbourhoods and social classes IIIM, IV and V. The disability indicator is based on the number of students receiving the Disabled Students Allowance. The funding councils make additional premium payments to institutions based on social class and disability indicators. The benchmarks published in relation to each indicator are based on the performance of other comparable institutions in the sector and are intended to signal to institutions whether they are performing better or worse than expected.

Critiques of the categorical approach

It is evident that both research and policy on access to higher education have by and large been informed by the categorical or neo-realist approach criticised so extensively by postmodern writers, although some researchers have adopted a much more reflexive and critical approach. For example, Archer (2003), whilst working with traditional conceptualisations of social class, provided an excellent critique of the way in which such measures are developed and deployed. She questioned the accuracy and validity of the measures of social class employed by the University and Colleges Admissions Service (UCAS), which underpin the performance indicators developed by the Higher Education Statistics Agency (HESA). For example, she noted that all those who are economically inactive are classified as 'other', and in certain parts of the UK numbers thus classified may be as high as 50 per cent of the population. The categories were defined with men rather than women in mind, and do not accommodate easily families where mother and father have different occupations. In addition, as the service sector expands, more jobs are likely to be classified as IIINM, but in terms of substance, pay and degree of autonomy, these may differ little from jobs in the old manufacturing sectors. Furthermore, the categories are based on the assumption that the young person retains the social class of their family until they have an independent job. However, with the collapse of the youth labour market in the late 1970s, there has increasingly been a delay in the young person having an occupational location independently of their parents, although the family social class designation may not reflect accurately their present social circumstances. The category assigned to the young person may therefore have little subjective validity.

Similar criticisms of accuracy and meaningfulness have been made in relation to the measurement of ethnicity (Modood and Acland, 1998) and disability (Riddell and Banks, 2001). Indeed, categories used to measure disability may fly in the face of social model thinking. For example, in order to assess participation in higher education by disabled students, UCAS forms invite students to allocate themselves to one of the following categories: dyslexia, unseen disability, blind/partially sighted, deaf/hard of hearing, wheelchair user/mobility impaired, personal care support, mental health difficulties, multiple disabilities, other disability. Whilst these categories attempt to characterise an individual in relation to their impairment, recent writing in the field of disability studies (Riddell and Watson, 2003, and Priestley, 2001) underlines the wide range of identity positions held by disabled people, which are influenced but not determined by their impairment, generational and cultural locations.

The use of categorical data has been criticised for defining an individual in relation to only one of their characteristics (see, for example, Abberley's (1992) critique of OPCS categorisation of disability), which may have little subjective validity. Opponents of categorisation, drawing on the work of theorists such as Bourdieu (1990) and Williams (1961, 1977), maintain that social class, disability, gender and ethnicity should be seen as negotiated and fluid identities. In addition, categorical data, employed as a tool of managerialist culture, are criticised by those opposed to the growth of the 'audit society' (Power, 1997). However, categorical data may also be used in pursuit of social justice goals (see, for example, Scottish Executive, 2000), and monitoring of institutional performance against equality indicators is promoted by the Equality Commissions and Government Social Inclusion Units. A number of innovative studies of access to higher education, rather than seeing these approaches as mutually exclusive, have adopted multiple strategies, using fixed categories to analyse statistical patterns of participation, whilst also exploring the way in which particular groups of students negotiate their identities within particular institutional contexts (see, for example, Archer 2003). Our research on access to higher education by disabled students attempted to adopt this eclectic approach, and in the following sections we present and critique our strategies and findings.

In this chapter we present analyses of the Higher Education Statistics Agency (HESA) dataset. The aim of the analysis was to examine patterns of participation and outcomes in higher education by disabled students. Whilst accepting the limitations of this mode of analysis, we believe that, in conjunction with the other more qualitative methods used, it nevertheless provides an interesting backdrop to the qualitative data.

Data and definitions

The dataset used for this analysis was supplied by HESA. It covers all enrolments in higher education institutions as at 1 December 1999. Because a student can enrol on more than one programme of study, the number of enrolments exceeds the actual number of students. The total number of enrolments (henceforward referred to as students) in the dataset for Scottish and English institutions was 1,895,775.

The dataset does not cover students enrolled on higher education courses in colleges of further education. It would have been interesting to have incorporated these students into the analysis, in particular because FE in Scotland provides a greater share of higher education than in England, and because these institutions have a better record on access for those from under-represented social class groups. However, we have been informed that data available on enrolments in FE do not include accurate information on disability, because a significant number of colleges do not return information on numbers of disabled students.

It should be borne in mind that the HESA data on disabled students will not provide a complete picture of the numbers of disabled students. This is because only those students declaring a disability on the UCAS form or at registration are recorded. Anyone declaring a disability after these points, or who chooses not to declare a disability to their institutions, will not be recorded.

In this chapter, higher education institutions have been divided into three groups: pre-92 institutions, post-92 institutions and non-university HEIs. The decision to divide up universities in this way was based on the notion that new and old universities have different histories in terms of governance, funding and degree-awarding powers. Numbers of institutions in each category are shown in Table 2.1.

Non-university HEIs perhaps comprise the most diverse category, as they include colleges teaching specialist subjects, such as art, nursing and music, as well as more general colleges of higher education. They will be referred to as HEIs throughout the rest of the chapter.

The Open University (OU) has been excluded from the main analysis because it has a significantly higher proportion of disabled undergraduates compared with other institutions (5.9 per cent, compared with approximately 4 per cent in other institutions). In the HESA data, the OU is classified as an English institution, in spite of the fact that it has a sizeable base in Scotland. This skews the analysis by country, inflating the English figures upwards. For this reason, the OU has been excluded from the main analysis. However, where appropriate, separate figures are included for the OU, to illustrate its unique position in the sector.

All analyses reported are based on cross-tabulations, using chi-square tests to ascertain whether differences between groups were significantly

Table 2.1 The number of HE institutions in each category

	Pre-1992 institutions	Post-1992 institutions	Non-university HEIs
England	51	36	45
Scotland	8	5	5

different. Only those that were significant at the p<0.05 level (i.e. there was less than a 5 per cent likelihood that they occurred by chance) are reported in the text.

Analysis of higher education statistics for England and Scotland

The HESA dataset suggests that the proportion of disabled students in higher education increased between 1995–6 and 1999–2000 (Table 2.2). However, it should be borne in mind that these figures include only those students willing to declare a disability on the UCAS form or at registration. It is likely that this apparent increase is due in part to increased incentives to disclose an impairment, particularly for students with dyslexia. Nowadays, students declaring dyslexia may be entitled to buy a computer through the DSA, which will help them with grammar and spell-checking, and to extra time in examinations.

Overall, a higher proportion of undergraduates disclosed a disability compared with postgraduates (see Table 2.2). This could be because postgraduates do not complete a UCAS form and may not be asked about their disability status. Postgraduates may also be less aware of support available, including the DSA, and therefore have less incentive to disclose a disability. For this reason, subsequent sections of this chapter refer mainly to undergraduates because the numbers of known disabled students are more reliable.

For undergraduates, all types of institution in England had significantly higher proportions of known disabled students than Scottish institutions. However, the differences were not that great. Similarly in this respect differences between pre- and post-92 universities were not large, with the percentage of disabled students being fairly close to 4 per cent in both sectors. HEIs had higher proportions of disabled students than universities (6.1 per cent in England and 5.3 per cent in Scotland). This was largely due to the fact that they had more students with dyslexia and unseen disabilities than universities.

Table 2.2 Percentage of first year UK-domiciled HE students known to have a disability by level of study 1995/6–1999/2000

	1995/6	1996/7	1997/8	1998/9	1999/2000
All first year students	3.1	3.5	3.8	3.9	3.9
First degree	3.7	4.4	4.7	4.9	4.8
Other undergraduate	3	2.9	3.3	3.4	3.5
Postgraduate	1.7	2	2.4	2.6	2.9

Source: HESA.

Table 2.3 First year UK-domiciled undergraduates known to have a disability by type of impairment 1995/6–1999/2000

	1995/6	*1996/7*	*1997/8*	*1998/9*	*1999/2000*
Total known to have a disability	15,754	19,337	20,486	22,469	22,290
Dyslexia	17.9%	19.9%	23.1%	25.5%	32.7%
Unseen disability	48.6%	42.8%	45.1%	39%	29.7%
Blind/partially sighted	3.9%	3.8%	3.4%	3.3%	3.5%
Deaf/hard of hearing	7.1%	6.4%	5.9%	5.8%	5.8%
Wheelchair user/mobility impaired	4.9%	7.1%	4.1%	4.6%	4.4%
Personal care support	0.2%	0.2%	0.3%	0.2%	0.3%
Mental health difficulties	1.8%	2.5%	2.2%	2.8%	3.3%
Multiple disabilities	3.6%	4.9%	5.1%	6.7%	7.3%
Other disability	11.9%	12.4%	10.7%	12.1%	13%
Total first year undergraduates	448,199	491,474	479,329	522,887	525,140
Not known/sought	56,517 (12.6%)	29,746 (6%)	20,970 (4.4%)	17,829 (3.4%)	31,860 (6%)

Source: HESA.

Nature of impairments of disabled students

Table 2.3 shows that students with dyslexia made up a larger share of all disabled students in 1999–2000 than in 1995–6. The increase in the proportion of disabled students with dyslexia corresponds with a decrease in the proportion known to have unseen disabilities (e.g. diabetes, ME). This relates to an actual drop in the numbers of students with unseen disabilities. In 1995–6, they formed the largest group, but were replaced by students with dyslexia in 1999–2000. There were small increases in the proportions of students with multiple disabilities and mental health difficulties and very small declines in the proportions of students with mobility difficulties or with sensory impairments.

Table 2.4 shows that, in England, HEIs had attracted a higher proportion of students with dyslexia than universities had, while in Scotland new universities lagged behind both old universities and HEIs in this respect, although this was accounted for by their unusually high proportion of students with unseen disabilities.

A separate analysis of the OU revealed that they had, by far, the highest proportion of students with multiple disabilities (59.2 per cent, compared with between 2 per cent and 5 per cent in other institutions), and the lowest proportion of students with dyslexia (7.7 per cent), confirming its unique

Table 2.4 Percentage of known disabled students with different impairments by type of institution and country (undergraduates only)

	England			Scotland		
	Pre-1992 universities (N = 19,579)	Post-1992 universities (N = 22,597)	HEIs (N = 6,768)	Pre-1992 universities (N = 3,532)	Post-1992 universities (N = 1,580)	HEIs (N = 464)
Dyslexia	27.8	33.1	40.1	29	25.7	29.7
Blind, partially sighted	3.9	3.2	2.4	2.8	3	–
Deaf, hard of hearing	6.3	5.3	3.9	5.3	4.9	–
Wheelchair user, mobility difficulties	4.3	4	3.1	3.2	3.2	–
Personal care support	0.2	0.3	–	–	–	–
Mental health difficulties	2.2	1.9	1.6	2.5	–	–
Unseen e.g. diabetes, epilepsy, asthma	40.5	36.5	36.2	42.7	50.8	47.6
Multiple disabilities	3.1	4.4	3.4	2.1	2.7	–
Other disability	11.6	11.3	9.3	12.1	8.6	9.3

Note: Cells with fewer than 20 cases are represented with a '–'.

position in the higher education sector in respect of provision for disabled students.

Proportion of disabled students in receipt of the Disabled Students Allowance

Approximately one-quarter of disabled undergraduates in England and one-fifth in Scotland were known to be in receipt of the Disabled Students Allowance (DSA) (Table 2.5), and only a small fraction of postgraduates (3.7 per cent overall). There are issues about the accuracy of the data on DSA, however, highlighted by the recent introduction of premium funding for disabled students in Scotland, which was based on number of students

Table 2.5 Known disabled undergraduates in receipt of the DSA by type of institution and country

	Pre-1992 universities	Post-1992 universities	HEIs
England	2,219 (23.4%)	2,901 (21.6%)	1,370 (34.7%)
Scotland	424 (25.7%)	65 (12%)	–

Note: Cells with fewer than 20 cases are represented with a '–'.

in receipt of DSA. Figures supplied to HESA on DSA were shown to provide a poor proxy for the actual number of disabled students in some institutions, because they had failed to supply accurate information. We anticipate that the accuracy of the data in subsequent years will have improved. However, for the purposes of this analysis, the figures should be treated with some caution.

In England, HEIs had the highest proportion of students receiving the DSA. Students with most types of impairment were more likely to be in receipt of the DSA than those studying at universities. In Scotland, traditional universities had by far the highest proportion of DSAs, with HEIs reporting fewer than 20 DSAs in total.

A separate analysis of the relationship between impairment and DSA (not shown) revealed that, in England, students with dyslexia and those with sensory impairments, mobility difficulties and multiple disabilities were most likely to receive the DSA in all sectors. A breakdown was not possible in Scotland, because of the small numbers in each cell.

Subjects studied by disabled students

It was not possible to analyse subject studied by type of institution and country, because the numbers in each cell were too small. So a combined analysis was carried out, comparing the participation of disabled students with that of non-disabled students, looking at the relationship between type of impairment and subject studied across institutions and countries (Table 2.6). (Personal care support is excluded because there were too few students per subject area to do a meaningful analysis.)

What stands out from this table is the high proportion of students with dyslexia on creative art and design courses. Also a high proportion of students with sensory impairments, mobility difficulties and mental health difficulties were studying combined courses (or had an invalid course code in the data). Disabled students were generally under-represented in veterinary science, agricultural subjects and information science, and strongly represented in business and administration and social sciences.

Table 2.6 Subject studied by impairment (undergraduates only) (%)

	No known disability	Dyslexia	Blind, partially sighted	Deaf, hard of hearing	Mobility difficulty	Mental health difficulty	Unseen disability	Multiple disabilities	Other disability
Medicine/Dentistry	2.3	1.1	1.6	1.2	–	–	2	–	1.2
Allied to medicine	13.4	7.6	6.4	10	4.3	4.6	10.2	5.6	7
Biological Sciences	5.3	6	4.5	4.2	4.7	5.8	6.9	5.5	5.8
Veterinary Sciences	0.3	0.2	–	–	0	0	0.1	0	–
Agriculture and related	0.8	2	–	0.7	0.9	–	1.4	–	0.9
Physical Sciences	4	5.5	4.4	4.2	2.6	3.6	5.2	4.8	4.6
Mathematical	1.2	0.7	1.3	1.1	–	–	1.5	–	1.1
Computer Science	5.6	6.3	7.6	6.1	7.9	5.1	5.2	7.3	5.8
Engineering and Technology	7.3	9.2	6.7	5.6	3.5	5	6.8	7.3	5.9
Architecture, Building and Planning	2.4	3.1	1.6	1.8	1.7	–	2.2	1.6	2.2
Social, Economics, Political	7.3	8.5	10	8.4	12.1	7.5	7.5	11.1	9.7
Law	3.2	1.3	3.7	2.4	4.2	2.9	3.6	4	3.7
Business and admin	11.8	8.9	10.4	7.5	6.7	3.8	9.7	9.5	9.3
Librarianship and Information Sciences	1.4	1.4	1.2	1.2	1.7	–	1.9	2.3	1.7
Languages	5.8	2.2	5.7	5.6	6.1	9.1	5.9	3.7	5.6
Humanities	3.4	4.4	4	5.6	6.1	8.3	3.9	6	5.9
Creative Arts and Design	6.6	17.6	6.5	8.7	7.2	11.8	8.8	10.6	8.9
Education	4.6	3.5	3.5	4.2	2.7	–	4.8	2.5	3.4
Combined/invalid code	13.2	10.3	20.3	21.3	26.1	25.8	12.5	16.4	17.2

Pre-entry qualifications

The majority of undergraduate students in all types of institution had entered with A levels or Highers (Table 2.7). However, new universities and HEIs also had a sizeable number of students with 'other HE' qualifications (e.g. HNCs/HNDs). Where this was the case, disabled students were more likely than non-disabled students to have A levels/equivalent than 'other HE' qualifications. Those entering via Access courses formed a small minority overall (between 1.9 per cent and 6.6 per cent), with disabled students more likely to enter via this route than non-disabled students in England, but not Scotland.

Disability in relation to other social variables

Initiatives to widen access to higher education to under-represented groups have typically not included disabled students. For this reason, we were keen to examine the 'social profile' of disabled students in terms of their gender, ethnicity and socio-economic status, comparing this with that of non-disabled students.

As discussed in Chapter 1, identity is rarely based on a single aspect of an individual's being, but is a complex amalgam of shifting parts. Different aspects of identity may be foregrounded at different stages in the life course, and may shift in prominence at points of transition. Identities are negotiated with significant others and may be contested or denied. In this chapter, our concern is with categorical aspects of individual identity. In the following sections, we consider the inter-relationship between students' disability status and their gender, ethnicity, social class and age.

Disability and gender

Disabled students were more likely to be male than non-disabled students (male: disabled students 49 per cent, non-disabled students 44 per cent, all 44.5 per cent[1]) (Figure 2.1). This was largely explained by the fact that males were more likely to have dyslexia than females and those with dyslexia made up the largest group of those known to have an impairment.

Disability and ethnicity

Overall, disabled students were less likely to have come from minority ethnic groups than non-disabled students. There were more non-white students (both disabled and non-disabled) in English than in Scottish institutions

---

1 Significantly different at the p<0.001 level using chi-square test.

Table 2.7 Highest pre-entry qualifications by disability, type of institution and country (undergraduates only) (%)

England

	Pre-1992 universities		Post-1992 universities		HEIs	
	No known disability (N = 374,058)	Known disability (N = 1,441)	No known disability (N = 438,566)	Known disability (N = 21,764)	No known disability (N = 97,919)	Known disability (N = 6,530)
Postgraduate	2	2.1	0.9	0.6	0.7	0.4
Other HE	11.5	10.8	18.8	14.2	20.2	10.7
A level/Highers	69	68.2	50.8	55.3	60.5	66.8
Access course	1.9	3.2	3.6	6.2	4.4	6.6
Other	4.1	4.4	8	8.6	7.8	10.2
No formal qualification	3	3.5	3.2	3.4	2.8	3.1
No information	8.6	7.7	14.7	11.6	3.6	2.3

Scotland

	Pre-1992 universities		Post-1992 universities		HEIs	
	No known disability (N = 72,936)	Known disability (N = 3,329)	No known disability (N = 37,252)	Known disability (N = 1,532)	No known disability (N = 7,382)	Known disability (N = 440)
Postgraduate	1.2	1.2	0.6	–	0.5	–
Other HE	10.1	10.8	27.3	21.1	25.1	21.6
A level/Highers	70.9	75.3	55.3	62.1	64.3	68.4
Access course	2.5	3.8	1.2	1.4	2	–
Other	1.7	1.6	2.9	2.3	3.4	5.2
No formal qualification	2.6	1.4	2.5	3.1	–	–
No information	11	5.9	10.2	10.1	4.6	–

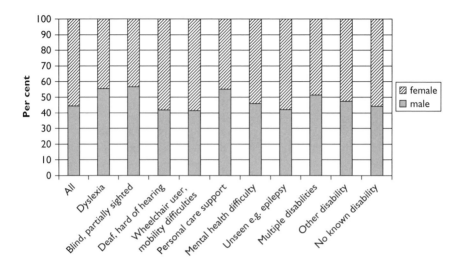

Figure 2.1 First year, full-time, UK-domiciled undergraduates (Scotland and England only) by gender and disability (N = 266,494).

(non-white England: disabled students 12 per cent, non-disabled 18 per cent, all 17.7 per cent;[2] Scotland: disabled students 3.3 per cent, non-disabled 4.4 per cent, all 4.3 per cent[3]). Figure 2.2 shows the breakdown by ethnic background of disabled and non-disabled students for England. The numbers were too small to repeat the analysis for Scotland.

Disability and social class

Data on the socio-economic status of students were problematic, because information was missing for 66.3 per cent of students. The following analysis can only serve as a guideline, therefore. Information relates to the occupation of the applicant's parent/guardian or, where entrants are aged 21 or over, the occupation of the person contributing the highest income to the household.

In pre-92 universities, there were no marked differences in participation of disabled and non-disabled students by social class (Table 2.8). In new universities and HEIs disabled students were slightly more likely to have come from the more advantaged end of the spectrum than non-disabled students.[4]

2 Significant at the p<0.01 level using chi-square test.
3 Marginally significant at the p<0.1 level using chi-square test.
4 Significant at the p<0.01 level using chi-square test.

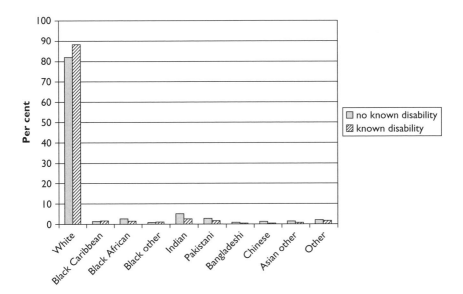

Figure 2.2 First year, full-time, UK-domiciled undergraduates (England only) by disability and ethnic background (N = 221,376).

Disability and age

In all sectors disabled students were less likely to enter higher education at the earliest opportunity (18 years or less) and more likely to go in slightly older (between the ages of 19–24) (see Table 2.9). Also they were generally less likely to enter as mature students (over the age of 25).

Level and mode of study by disability

Disabled students were more likely than non-disabled students to be studying for a first degree rather than another undergraduate qualification (Table 2.10). This was true across the board.

Disabled students were more likely to study full time and less likely to study part time than other students, in all sectors except pre-92 universities in England, where the proportions were fairly similar. These data suggest that only those disabled students who are well qualified and motivated are likely to gain access to higher education at the moment. Students on sub-degree courses may have failed to get the entry requirements for a full degree programme and may be regarded as more marginal. It appears that many disabled students may be deterred from embarking on an HE course unless they feel confident that they are going to obtain a degree.

Table 2.8 First year, full-time, UK-domiciled undergraduates (Scotland and England) by disability, social class and type of institution (%)

	Pre-92			Post-92			Non-university HEIs		
	No known disability (N=67,713)	Known disability (N=2,816)	All (N=70,529)	No known disability (N=40,691)	Known disability (N=2,273)	All (N=42,964)	No known disability (N=15,850)	Known disability (N=1,046)	All (N=16,896)
Professional	21	22	21	11	13	11	10	13	11
Managerial, technical	47	48	47	41	41	41	43	47	43
Skilled-non-manual	12	12	12	15	15	15	15	15	15
Skilled-manual	12	12	12	20	17	19	19	15	19
Partly skilled	6	6	6	11	11	11	10	9	10
Unskilled	1	1	1	3	3	3	2	2	2

Note: Columns do not sum to 100 because of rounding.

Table 2.9 Age of students by disability, type of institution and country (undergraduates only) (%)

England

	Pre-1992 universities		Post-1992 universities		HEIs	
	No known disability (N = 368,513)	Known disability (N = 18,581)	No known disability (N = 437,219)	Known disability (N = 21,739)	No known disability (N = 97,569)	Known disability (N = 6,519)
18 and under	15.4	11.5	10.6	8.5	11.4	8.6
19–24	58.4	60.3	54.5	59.2	55	64.9
25–39	13.4	11.9	25	22.2	21.8	16.8
Over 40	12.8	16.4	9.9	10	11.9	9.6

Scotland

	Pre-1992 universities		Post-1992 universities		HEIs	
	No known disability (N = 72,804)	Known disability (N = 3,328)	No known disability (N = 37,242)	Known disability (N = 1,532)	No known disability (N = 7,380)	Known disability (N = 440)
18 and under	22.1	18.4	19	17.8	17.7	19.8
19–24	56.3	62.1	49.3	57.1	55.3	60.7
25–39	11.8	10.1	24	17.6	18.7	13.6
Over 40	9.8	9.4	7.7	7.5	8.4	5.9

Table 2.10 Level of study by disability, type of institution and country (undergraduates only) (%)

England

	Pre-1992 universities		Post-1992 universities		HEIs	
	No known disability (N = 423,531)	Known disability (N = 19,579)	No known disability (N = 485,797)	Known disability (N = 22,597)	No known disability (N = 104,591)	Known disability (N = 6,768)
First degree	76.8	79.8	73.5	81.8	74.5	85.2
Other undergraduate	23.2	20.2	26.5	18.2	25.5	14.8

Scotland

	Pre-1992 universities		Post-1992 universities		HEIs	
	No known disability (N = 81,206)	Known disability (N = 3,532)	No known disability (N = 39,975)	Known disability (N = 1,580)	No known disability (N = 8,235)	Known disability (N = 464)
First degree	83	89.7	76.5	85	86.5	91.8
Other undergraduate	17	10.3	23.5	15	13.5	8.2

Table 2.11 Proportions of disabled and non-disabled students obtaining first degrees by country and sector (%)

England

	Pre-92	Post-92	HEI
Known disability	91.5	79.2	80.3
No known disability	89.2	72.1	72.7

Scotland

	Pre-92	Post-92	HEI
Known disability	97.4	80.3	88.8
No known disability	95.3	72.8	88.5

Qualifications obtained by disabled and non-disabled students

As Table 2.11 demonstrates, the success rate of disabled students at first degree level was higher than that of non-disabled students in all types of institution, except for Scottish HEIs.

These differences were significant at the $p<0.01$ level using chi-square tests.

Degree classification obtained by disabled and non-disabled students

Despite the fact that disabled students were more likely to be registered for and obtain an undergraduate degree than any other qualification, there was evidence that the classification of their degrees was lower than those obtained by non-disabled students. In all types of institution in England, disabled students were significantly less likely to obtain 2.1s and firsts than non-disabled students and significantly more likely to obtain 2.2s and third class degrees. In Scottish pre-92 universities, there were no significant differences in the class of degrees obtained by disabled and non-disabled students. In post-92 institutions, the degree classifications of disabled students appeared to be more widely distributed than those of non-disabled students, with a significantly higher proportion obtaining first class honours, 2.2s and thirds ($p<0.05$).

Conclusion

In this chapter, we deliberately adopted a categorical approach to investigating the social characteristics of disabled students in higher education.

The salience of the nature of a student's impairment emerged strongly from the data. Certain types of impairment (dyslexia and hidden impairments) are by far the most common. Other types of impairment, such as mental health difficulties, appear to be reported less frequently amongst the student population than the general public. However, the context in which an impairment is disclosed is significant. People with mental health difficulties make up the largest group of people on sick leave and among Incapacity Benefit claimants. In this case, a significant mental health difficulty may justify taking time off work. However, at university the benefits of declaring a mental health difficulty are very small, and the risks very great in terms of jeopardising future career prospects. It is likely that many more students have mental health difficulties than are known to the university. An alternative possibility is that the mental health of students is much better than that of the rest of the population. Since the majority of students come from socially advantaged groups, and mental health is very closely associated with social class, this may also be the case.

Impairment is strongly associated with subject studied. Overall, disabled students are more likely to study arts, social science and business subjects, and this is reflected in differences in the employment sectors they move into after graduation. Students with dyslexia, in particular, gravitate towards art and design courses.

The links between disability and other key social variables are also apparent. There are no significant differences between the social class of disabled and non-disabled students. Pre-92 universities are dominated by the children of social classes 1 and 2, and this is the case for both disabled and non-disabled students. However, there are significant associations between gender (more disabled students are male), ethnicity (disabled students are less likely to come from minority ethnic groups) and age (disabled students are likely to be slightly older).

Subtle differences between England and Scotland also emerge from the data. Overall, there is a higher proportion of disabled students in English than Scottish institutions. There are far more ethnic-minority disabled students south of the border. Despite Scotland's view of itself as more egalitarian than England, its pre-92 universities are just as elite as those of England, reflected in the social class background of disabled and non-disabled students alike.

Despite the limitations and frustrations of the data, the analysis throws up many intriguing patterns and associations which are interrogated through the use of case studies in the following chapters.

Chapter 3

Policy and provision for disabled students in higher education

The current state of play

Background

The Higher Education Funding Councils for England and Scotland (HEFCE and SHEFC) began to provide funding to improve provision for disabled students in 1993. Prior to that higher education was largely inaccessible to disabled people. Barnes (1991), in a review of education for disabled people, found that the majority of British colleges and universities were inaccessible and many were unwilling or unable to provide the necessary support services to make them accessible. Leicester and Lovell (1994) in a study of equal opportunities practice carried out between 1990 and 1992 in British universities found a relative lack of awareness of disability as a form of oppression and correspondingly little disability awareness in departmental practice and provision. Those disabled students who did go to university in the early 1990s received *ad hoc* support to enable them to access higher education, which was very much dependent on the good will of staff and students. For example, a rota might be created of students willing to carry a student in a wheelchair up and down a flight of steps in order to reach a particular classroom. Or a politicised disabled student might blaze a trail through a particular course by being vocal about instances of discrimination, in effect educating the educators (Hall and Tinklin, 1998).

A study of the experiences of disabled students in Scotland carried out in academic year 1996–7 (Tinklin and Hall, 1999) indicated that, although there were some signs of improvement in provision for disabled students, barriers remained in entrance to higher education, the physical environment, access to information and low levels of awareness among staff. Good experiences for students depended largely on the attitudes, experience and personal knowledge of particular members of staff, rather than on institutional policies, and provision varied greatly between academic departments within institutions. Disability officers were employed in every institution and, while they were warmly praised for their efforts by students, they were often trying to effect change at an institutional level with no senior management support and with full case loads of students, while employed on part-time, temporary contracts. One commented that 'I can only chip away at the mountain at the moment' (Hall and Tinklin, 1998: 74). Conditions were far from ideal. Some disabled students were entitled to the Disabled Students Allowance (DSA), which, depending on an assessment of needs, paid for equipment, such as computers, specialist software and tape recorders and the employment of support workers, such as personal assistants, sign language interpreters and note-takers. Some students receiving the DSA, however, were being individually equipped to get round institutional obstacles that ideally should have been removed. For example, one student, who used a wheelchair, was given money to employ a fellow student to help her negotiate closed fire doors, find books in the otherwise inaccessible library and use the photocopier, which was too high for her to use herself.

Until 2001, when Part 4 of the Disability Discrimination Act (DDA) was amended, it was not illegal for providers of higher education to discriminate against disabled people. (The change in the law was brought into force in September 2002.) The Further and Higher Education (Scotland) Act 1992 required further and higher education institutions to have regard to the needs of disabled students. The Disability Discrimination Act of 1995 made it unlawful for providers of services to discriminate against disabled people, but did not apply to education. Part 4 of the Act, however, did place a duty on the higher education funding councils to require higher education institutions to publish Disability Statements containing information on existing policy and provision, future activity and policy development for disabled students. The first of these statements was produced early in 1997 and, in Scotland, they were seen as having had a positive impact on raising awareness of disability issues among senior management in higher education (Hall and Tinklin, 1998). The amendment to Part 4 of the DDA makes it unlawful for further and higher education institutions to discriminate against disabled people and goes further, requiring them to be 'prepared in advance' for such students rather than relying solely on reactive and *ad hoc* arrangements.

There is evidence that disabled students are now being recognised more fully as a group experiencing particular disadvantage. The Higher Education Statistics Agency (HESA) includes disabled students in its annual statistical report. The introduction of premium funding for disabled students indicates a recognition of the need to mainstream disability provision. Disabled students are now included in performance indicators relating to widening participation. In addition, evaluations of policy and provision for disabled students throughout Great Britain in the late 1990s (HEFCE/HEFCW, 1999; Brown *et al.*, 1997; Hall and Tinklin, 1998) indicated that:

- All institutions had a Disability Statement.
- Arrangements were largely in place for addressing disabled students' needs in examinations.

- The majority of institutions had application and admissions procedures relating to the needs of disabled students.
- Ninety-five per cent of institutions in England and Wales and all institutions in Scotland had a disability officer. This was a part-time post in some institutions and a relatively new post in most English/Welsh HE institutions.
- The extent and quality of provision for disabled students varied across and within institutions.

Developments in provision for disabled students have been made in a demanding context. Higher education has been through a period of major change since the mid-1980s. The number of students more than doubled in the ten-year period between the mid-1980s and the mid-1990s, whilst the unit of resource fell by more than a third (NCIHE, 1997a). Devices such as the Research Assessment Exercise (RAE) and quality assurance regimes encouraged universities to compete with each other for the brightest staff and students, and staff and institutional performance was managed through the publication by the funding councils of performance indicators and benchmark statistics. The New Labour government established widening participation to higher education as one of its policy priorities and premium funding was instituted in relation to the number of students from under-represented groups in particular institutions. At one level, these changes produced a higher education system which, according to the OECD, was the most efficient in the developed world. On the other hand, academics perceived a decline in their condition of employment and academic freedom (Halsey, 1995).

This chapter draws primarily on the findings of the survey of further and higher education institutions which was carried out between March and August 2002. The aim of the survey was to gain an overview of current policy and practice for disabled students, and to understand how policy and practice for disabled students was influencing or influenced by other institutional priorities. The survey also enabled an examination of differences between Scotland and England and between different kinds of institution. Questionnaires were sent to all higher education (HE) institutions in England and Scotland, including the Open University, and those further education (FE) colleges with a reasonable number of HE students. This chapter concentrates on responses from the HE sector, since institutional missions, funding arrangements, policies and practices are quite different in HE and FE. A full report of the findings, including responses from FE colleges is available in Tinklin et al. (2002).

Response rates were reasonably good (Table 3.1), with over three-quarters of Scottish and just over half of English higher education institutions responding. The questionnaire was sent to institutional principals with a request that it be filled in by a member of senior management, with assistance

Table 3.1 Questionnaire response rates (%)

	No. sent*	No. returned	Response rate
HE Scotland	19	15	79%
HE England	136	75	55%

* Excluding those returned uncompleted because of merger or change of status.

Table 3.2 Level of seniority of main respondents (%)

	HE England	HE Scotland
Senior manager	51	60
Middle manager	23	20
Academic	4	0
Support staff	17	20
Other/no answer	5	–

Table 3.3 Number of institutions by type and country

	Pre-92 universities	Post-92 universities and non-university HE institutions
England	30	45
Scotland	8	7

from a specialist disability officer if necessary. This was because the questions did not relate solely to provision for disabled students, but asked about the broader policy context as well. In practice, the majority of questionnaires were filled in by senior or middle managers, with assistance in about one-third of cases, from disability-related or student services staff (Table 3.2).

Throughout the chapter higher education institutions have been divided into two groups: 'pre-92 universities' and 'post-92 universities and other HE institutions' (Table 3.3). The decision to divide up institutions in this way was based on the notion that old universities have different histories in terms of governance, funding and degree-awarding powers and it is therefore interesting to assess whether their responses were different to those of other institutions. The abolition of the binary divide was intended to produce greater uniformity between institutions. However marked differences remain between the academic culture of the pre-92 universities, emphasising the acquisition of knowledge in traditionally defined subject areas, and the post-92 universities, where the acquisition of vocational knowledge and transferable skills was emphasised. Bennett *et al.* (1999) note that attempts

Table 3.4 Percentage of respondents citing these factors as among the three most significant influences on general policy-making and provision in their institutions in the past five years (open-ended question)

	England		Scotland	
	Pre-92 universities	Post-92/ other HEIs	Pre-92 universities	Post-92/ other HEIs
General decrease in funding	47	36	25	57
General increase in accountability/ quality assurance	23	44	75	29
RAE	47	7	50	14
General expansion in student numbers	23	20	13	29
Wider access/ participation	23	18	0	43
DDA 1995	17	18	25	0
Staffing changes/issues	13	4	13	14

to introduce the teaching of core skills into pre-92 universities were met with considerable resistance, since these were seen as alien to the traditional knowledge-based culture (Dunne *et al.*, 1997). New universities, with their better record at attracting students from 'under-represented groups', were also more used to teaching non-traditional students and often already had learning support services in place, whereas pre-92 institutions had to establish these to meet the needs of the expanding student population (Wolfendale and Corbett, 1996). The relatively small number of institutions in Scotland made it impracticable to separate post-92 universities from other HE institutions.

The wider policy context

In order to understand the wider policy context within which provision for disabled students was being developed, respondents were asked to list the three factors which they believed had had the most significant impact on general policy-making and provision in the past five years in their institutions. Reflecting the major changes that have been taking place, the most significant factors were seen as the general decrease in funding, the increase in accountability including the requirements of the Quality Assurance Agency (QAA) and the RAE, the expansion in student numbers and the wider access/participation agenda (Table 3.4). The RAE had been more of a concern to pre-92 universities than other institutions and the general in-crease in accountability had particularly affected traditional universities in Scotland. The general decrease in institutional funding and the increase in staff workloads were seen as having inhibited the development of provision for disabled students by the majority of institutions (figures not shown), while special initiative and premium funding for disabled students and the DDA 1995 were seen as having supported developments. The requirements of the QAA, including subject review, and the RAE were not seen as having inhibited developments for disabled students directly; however, they would have contributed indirectly by increasing workloads. This was corroborated through our case studies. For example, analysis of the four institutional case studies carried out in Scotland indicated that lecturers, particularly in pre-92 institutions, felt that academic freedom had been eroded through a range of managerialist measures, giving them less time and freedom to respond to the needs of disabled students (Riddell et al., 2002). The QAA code of practice for students with disabilities was generally seen as having had some influence, but not a great deal, on the areas to which it related.

Widening access/participation had been one of the three most significant factors impacting on general policy and provision in about one-fifth of English institutions, over four out of ten Scottish new universities and other HE institutions, but no older Scottish institutions. This could be because widening participation has had a lower profile in Scotland than in England, where parliamentary questions have been asked on the subject and a high-profile complaint has been brought against Oxford University. In spite of the fact that Scottish pre-92 universities did not list widening participa-tion among their three most significant influences in the past five years, most institutions – Scottish and English – were actively recruiting students from under-represented groups, in particular those from low participation neighbourhoods and social classes IIIM–V (Table 3.5) and overall Scottish institutions reported more active recruitment initiatives than English ones. Significant numbers of institutions, both north and south of the border, also reported active recruitment of disabled people. This came as a surprise, since we were not aware of such initiatives and our key informants had clearly described a disconnection between policies aimed at widening access and those aimed at access for disabled students. According to them, policy for disabled students had tended to focus on retention rather than recruit-ment, with institutions fairly cautious about actively recruiting disabled students because of the financial implications of providing them with support (Wilson et al., 2002).

Table 3.5 Institutions with specially funded initiatives aimed at actively increasing recruitment from under-represented groups (%)

	England		Scotland	
	Pre-92 universities	*Post-92/ other HEIs*	*Pre-92 universities*	*Post-92/ other HEIs*
Social classes IIIM–V	77	76	100	100
Those from low-participation neighbourhoods	77	71	100	100
Those with non-traditional qualifications	53	53	75	86
Students from state schools	57	31	75	86
Minority ethnic groups	63	40	38	43
Disabled people	37	53	63	71
Mature students	47	47	75	71

Current policy and provision for disabled students

There were signs of a marked improvement in staffing and structures for disabled students in 2002 compared with 1996–7. Most institutions had at least one disability officer, with administrative support and a designated senior manager with responsibility for disability matters (Table 3.6). More than seven out of ten disability officers had permanent posts. Some had a budget, others, especially in Scottish new universities and other HE institutions, did not. This tended to be wholly discretionary in Scotland, but not in England. The majority of institutions had committees with a particular remit for disability issues, but these did not tend to have direct control over a budget. Institutions varied on whether they had staff representatives in each department/college with responsibility for disability issues – this tended to be a Scottish rather than an English practice – and whether they had disabled student representatives on relevant committees. However, they did tend to consult the student representative body and individual disabled students about disability-related developments. Consultation with disabled students groups varied, but such groups did not exist in all institutions.

To provide an up-to-date picture of provision for disabled students, respondents were asked to rate their institutions against the criteria adopted by HEFCE and HEFCW in 1999 as defining 'base-level provision'. One of the main aims of HEFCE's 1999 funding initiative (£2m per annum

Table 3.6 Staffing and institutional structures for the development of disability-related policy and provision (%)

	England		Scotland	
	Pre-92 universities	Post-92/ other HEIs	Pre-92 universities	Post-92/ other HEIs
Employ a disability co-ordinator/adviser/officer	97	93	100	86
Is this a permanent post?	72	87	75	71
Administrative support provided for disability service	73	78	100	57
Disability officer has a budget	69	64	88	29
Budget wholly discretionary	55	55	71	100
Senior manager with responsibility for disability issues	77	82	100	71
Committee with a particular remit for disability issues	90	73	88	57
Committee has a budget	10	7	0	14
Staff reps in each department or college with responsibility for disability issues	47	38	75	71
Disabled student reps on relevant committees	63	49	88	57
Student representative body consulted about disability-related developments	90	84	100	71
Individual disabled students consulted in an *ad hoc* way	87	89	100	86
Disabled students group consulted	50	47	75	57

for three years, HEFCE, 1999) was to help English institutions with little experience or provision for disabled students to move towards 'base level', which was clearly specified as a *minimum* level of provision, rather than best practice. Most of the criteria are listed in Table 3.7. Additional criteria, not listed, but asked about elsewhere in the questionnaire, were to have a permanently employed disability officer (or several depending on the size of the institution), with adequate administrative support, a senior manager with responsibility for disability and an estates strategy that ensures the

Table 3.7 Extent to which institutions met base-level provision

% answering 'meets' or 'meets and surpasses' (In brackets: % answering 'partially meets')	England		Scotland	
	Pre-92 universities	Post-92/ other HEIs	Pre-92 universities	Post-92/ other HEIs
Comprehensive disability statement	97 (3)	87 (7)	100	86 (14)
Admissions policy and procedures that specifically address the needs of disabled students	83 (10)	78 (16)	63 (25)	86 (14)
Monitoring of statistics about application/enrolment rates for disabled students	67 (13)	47 (42)	25 (63)	57 (43)
Arrangements for the assessment of individual student needs	80 (20)	89 (7)	100	100
These arrangements being well publicised	73 (23)	73 (22)	75 (25)	72 (29)
Target times for completion of arrangements for assessing individual needs	37 (50)	42 (40)	50 (38)	43 (0)
Provision of services to meet assessed needs	70 (13)	56 (36)	50 (50)	57 (43)
Arrangements to monitor the provision of support services that have been agreed following professional assessment	50 (27)	51 (38)	50 (38)	43 (14)
Access to networks of trained support workers	53 (37)	56 (33)	100	29 (43)
Code of practice on confidentiality of information	60 (20)	56 (29)	38 (25)	43 (43)
Clear internal communication and referral policies	53 (40)	56 (36)	63 (25)	57 (43)
An institution-wide policy and procedure covering exams and assessments, which addresses the needs of disabled students	70 (27)	73 (22)	50 (38)	57 (29)
Staff development programmes covering information about disabled students and support available to them	50 (40)	56 (36)	25 (63)	29 (43)
The inclusion of these staff development programmes in induction and training of new staff	43 (50)	45 (31)	63 (25)	29 (29)
Procedures to regularly monitor the impact and effectiveness of policy and provision for disabled students	60 (20)	45 (33)	13 (38)	29 (43)

needs of disabled people are considered in the design and refurbishment of the physical environment.

Table 3.7 shows that most institutions had a comprehensive disability statement, admissions procedures that addressed the needs of disabled students and arrangements for the assessment of individual student needs. Percentages of institutions meeting the other criteria tended to be fairly low or to vary across types of institution. Areas needing further development in most institutions included monitoring of statistics and services for disabled students and staff development. In spite of previous findings (HEFCE/ HEFCW, 1999) that indicated that most institutions had procedures largely in place that addressed the needs of disabled students in examinations and assessment, only about three-quarters of English and about half of Scottish institutions reported that they had such procedures in place institution-wide. About half the English institutions had access to networks of trained support workers. The picture was more mixed in Scotland with all older institutions and only just over one-quarter of other institutions having such networks in place. Only about half the institutions (somewhat more in Scotland) had clear communication and referral policies and about six out of ten in Scotland and four out of ten in England had codes of practice on confidentiality. While this suggests that there is room for much further development, it is encouraging to note that, where institutions did not fully meet criteria, significant numbers of them often stated that they partially met them (Table 3.7).

Model of provision available

While the findings reported in the previous section suggest signs of progress, there is a risk that the emphasis in provision for disabled students remains too much on providing students with *individual* support to access an otherwise inaccessible 'mainstream' system, which remains largely unchanged. In this model the emphasis is placed on student support and individual funding through the DSA to provide the necessary assistance, which is seen as 'extra' to what is viewed as 'normal'. From this perspective, individual students are provided with support to get round or over barriers in the institutional environment. The alternative perspective, informed by the social model of disability, would say that it is the environment that needs to change, in order that barriers to disabled students are tackled and removed. Tinklin and Hall (1999) identified barriers to disabled students in four main areas: the physical environment, entrance to higher education, accessing information and levels of staff awareness. In practice, it is likely that some elements of both approaches are needed. However, there is a risk that the emphasis remains too strongly on individual support, especially when that provides a functional solution, and not enough on more fundamental institutional change. The change in legislation puts the emphasis on

Table 3.8 Reference to the needs of disabled students/applicants in policy documents

% with written policy/ % stating that policy explicitly refers to DS or written policy for DS covers this area	England		Scotland	
	Pre-92 universities	Post-92/ other HEIs	Pre-92 universities	Post-92/ other HEIs
Student recruitment	73/64	51/60	75/75	86/86
Admissions	80/80	84/80	75/76	100/85
Teaching and learning	83/54	87/53	38/38	86/85
Examinations and assessments	80/70	89/80	88/88	86/85
Estates and buildings	77/60	69/68	75/88	57/58
Accommodation	70/64	56/62	75/63	57/72
Staff development	87/63	78/46	50/38	86/29
Student support services	57/67	67/64	63/75	71/85
Other services (e.g. library)	60/57	71/63	50/51	57/57
Complaints	83/45	84/31	88/38	86/28
Quality assurance	77/46	80/42	63/63	100/85
Monitoring and evaluation	53/44	64/36	50/51	71/72
Equal opportunities	83/77	89/76	88/88	100/100
Provision of information for applicants and students	70/67	49/60	38/88	71/86
Strategic plan: % explicitly referring to disabled students	67	53	100	57

institutions being prepared in advance for disabled students, which in practice would eradicate some disabled students' 'special' needs. For example, a student with a visual impairment who needs copies of handouts and overheads in advance of classes would no longer have this 'special need' if this were adopted as standard practice for all students. At the same time, some disabled students' needs are unique and would be impossible to anticipate, which means that a level of individual assessment and support would still be necessary.

Ideally policy and provision for disabled students should be embedded into all institutional procedures in all areas of institutional operation. However, responses to the questionnaire indicated that this was not the case. There was evidence that, where written policies existed, the majority of them either referred explicitly to disabled students or the area was covered by a written policy for disabled students (Table 3.8). This was true for recruitment, admissions, examinations and assessments, estates and buildings, accommodation, student support services, equal opportunities and the

Table 3.9 Proactive–reactive continuum

	England		Scotland	
% proactive: all relevant staff prepared in advance to work with disabled students, taking account of individual needs as appropriate *(In brackets: % reactive: ad hoc arrangements made depending solely on individual students' needs)*	*Pre-92 universities*	*Post-92/ other HEIs*	*Pre-92 universities*	*Post-92/ other HEIs*
Admissions	27 (7)	22 (7)	13 (0)	43 (14)
Teaching and learning	10 (20)	2 (13)	0 (13)	0 (14)
Examinations and assessments	30 (10)	24 (4)	13 (0)	29 (14)
Estates and buildings	27 (3)	16 (7)	13 (13)	14 (14)
Accommodation	33 (3)	29 (7)	13 (0)	14 (14)
Staff development	20 (7)	11 (11)	13 (0)	14 (14)
Student support (e.g. welfare)	47 (7)	47 (2)	38 (0)	43 (0)
Other services (e.g. library)	27 (3)	27 (4)	25 (13)	29 (0)

provision of information. The area of complaints was a notable exception. Areas where responses were more mixed included teaching and learning, staff development, monitoring and evaluation and quality assurance. Disabled students were explicitly referred to in institutional strategic plans in all Scottish pre-92 universities and in about five to six out of ten institutions otherwise.

While this suggests that disabled students have been written into institutional policies in a significant number of areas, the questionnaire also provides evidence that, in practice, provision for disabled students has largely remained the province of student support services. Percentages of institutions considering themselves prepared in advance to work with disabled students were fairly low in all areas of institutional practice, except for student support services (Table 3.9), in which about four out of ten respondents considered their institutions to be prepared in advance. Our key informants were clear that disability issues needed to be mainstreamed across institutions and that further and significant progress for disabled students could only be achieved, in particular, through a greater emphasis on developing learning and teaching policies and procedures within academic departments. Table 3.9 suggests that institutions are far from meeting the requirements of legislation to be prepared in advance for disabled students. However, very few institutions considered their provision to be completely

Table 3.10 Institutions' future plans with regard to disabled students

% definite written plans/ % time limit set to meet this objective	England		Scotland	
	Pre-92 universities	Post-92/ other HEIs	Pre-92 universities	Post-92/ other HEIs
Remove all possible barriers in the physical environment	77*/40	51*/29	63/13	57/71
Raise awareness among all academic staff of the needs of disabled students	83/13	71/22	75/13	86/29
Raise awareness among all non-academic staff	80/10	73/22	75/13	71/29
Ensure provision meets requirements of legislation	73/20	67/20	88/0	71/14
Provide all information for students/applicants in accessible formats	70/13	67/22	63/0	86/29
Identify and remove all barriers to accessing the curriculum	43/0*	42/13*	50/0	71/14
Embed policy and provision for disabled students into all institutional procedures	67/3	62/13	75/0	71/14

* Significantly different at p<0.05 level, using chi-square tests: the two types of English HEI were compared, as were the two types of Scottish HEI. Asterisks indicate which columns are significantly different from each other.

ad hoc and reactive in any of the areas studied. In fact, about one-third of institutions rated their provision as '2' on a continuum of '1 proactive: prepared in advance' to '5 reactive/*ad hoc*', once again suggesting signs of improvement.

Most institutions had plans to mainstream disability. However, few had set time limits for meeting this objective (Table 3.10). The majority of institutions had definite written plans to raise awareness among all staff of disability issues, to ensure that they met the requirements of new legislation, to provide all information for students and applicants in accessible formats and to embed policy and procedures for disabled students into all institutional procedures. Fewer institutions (but still over half) had written plans to remove all possible barriers in the physical environment. Only about four out of ten English, but more Scottish, institutions had plans to identify and remove barriers to accessing the curriculum, once again highlighting teaching and learning as a particular area of concern.

While it is heartening that the majority of institutions are aiming to mainstream disability, there is clearly a long way to go before this objective is achieved. At the time of the survey, although disabled students had been written into institutional policies in a significant number of areas, in practice support for disabled students remained largely the province of student support services, with the emphasis, as yet, remaining largely on providing individual support rather than on more fundamental institutional change.

Teaching and learning

The findings of the questionnaire and of the key informant interviews clearly highlight teaching and learning as an area of particular concern. Table 3.9 showed that the percentages of institutions considering themselves prepared in advance to work with disabled students in the area of teaching and learning were particularly low compared with other areas. While progress has been made in most institutions in the areas of admissions, examinations and assessments and student support, teaching and learning is an area where significant change is still needed. Disability officers expressed the difficulty of influencing developments in this area, since teaching and learning is regarded as the domain of academics. Academics in our case studies expressed the difficulty of providing 'extra' support for disabled students, in a context in which they were experiencing mounting pressure and increasing workloads. Ideally, of course, support for disabled students should not be seen as 'extra', but a routine part of everyday practice. Adjustments such as providing lecture notes in electronic format in advance were seen as problematic because students might not then attend lectures or because some lecturers did not routinely use notes and this would require a substantial change in practice. Concerns were expressed about lowering standards through providing extra support or alternative means of assessment. In addition, some academics thought equality meant treating everyone in exactly the same way, and this also represented a significant barrier to the development of provision for disabled students (Riddell et al., 2002).

The Teachability Project (Teachability, 2002), which began in Scotland and is currently being introduced in England, provides a resource to facilitate a review of teaching and learning by academics, with a view to making departments better prepared to work with disabled students, thereby improving teaching practice for all students. The idea is to engage academics in discussion of their current practice, highlighting exclusive practices and identifying areas for change. Significantly the first step in the process is to discuss the *core requirements* of a subject or discipline, since it is only once these have been established that alternative means of assessment can be identified, which do not compromise standards. For example, language specialists need to decide whether a core requirement of their discipline is that students be able to speak the language, in which case students with

Table 3.11 Responses to the DDA Part 4

% answering 'already done or underway'	England		Scotland	
	Pre-92 universities	*Post-92/ other HEIs*	*Pre-92 universities*	*Post-92/ other HEIs*
Set up a working group	63	73	63	100
Put on agenda of relevant committee	73	87	63	71
Seek legal advice	30	33	50	43
Attend national seminars	90	98	75	100
Gather relevant information	93	93	100	100
Review policies and procedures	83	76	75	86
Change practices	53	44	50	71
Give advice to staff	73	76	88	86
Appoint more disability-service staff	43	29	63	57

speech impediments might be excluded, or indeed whether the core requirement is that students be able to communicate in the language, in which case alternative means of expression can be found. This process raises fundamental questions about the privileging of the written word in British higher education, which effectively disadvantages significant numbers of students with dyslexia. The report of the Teachability Project in Scotland concludes that the goals of the new legislation, i.e. to create

> ...a sector in which the teaching and learning needs of disabled people are anticipated, ... in which academic staff are knowledgeable about and able to put in place 'reasonable adjustments' and where disabled students are not treated unjustifiably less favourably than their peers ... must be acknowledged to be a challenging goal, the achievement of which will require major institutional commitment.
>
> (Teachability, 2002: 29)

Legislative changes

One might have expected that the change in legislation would have provoked significant activity in higher education institutions. Our findings certainly suggest that institutions had taken note of the amendments. Over 90 per cent of respondents reported having a good understanding of the changes and their implications for higher education. In response to the changes, however (Table 3.11), institutions were most likely to have undertaken information gathering and review activities and less likely to have actually changed practices, although most had definite plans to do so.

Although the legislation has potentially far-reaching implications, there are a number of conditions which potentially weaken its impact depending on how they are interpreted. For example, in deciding what adjustments are reasonable, responsible bodies may take the following factors into consideration:

- the need to maintain academic and other prescribed standards;
- the financial resources available to the responsible body;
- grants or loans likely to be available to disabled students such as the DSA;
- the cost of taking a particular step;
- the extent to which it is practicable to take a particular step;
- the extent to which aids or services will otherwise be provided to disabled people or students;
- health and safety requirements;
- the relevant interests of other people including other students.

Indeed our key informants reported only 'a little nervousness' among senior management about the legislation. It was seen as limited in extent with lots of 'get-out clauses' and its exact interpretation remains ambiguous until case-law is established. They suggested that institutions would respond with a 'risk assessment' exercise, in which discriminatory practices would be knowingly retained, especially where they were difficult or costly to change, where the risk of anyone taking them to court was seen as minimal. A review of the impact of similar legislation in Australia, brought in in 1992 (Adams, 2001), indicated that:

- the legislation had resulted in increased awareness of disability issues and the formalisation of existing provision;
- few cases of discrimination had reached court and most were settled out of court;
- the majority of cases related to teaching, learning and assessment.

Conclusion

There were definite signs of progress in provision for disabled students, taking place within a demanding context. The general decrease in institutional funding, increase in accountability through the QAA and the RAE, the general expansion in student numbers and the widening access/participation agenda were all seen as having had a significant impact on general institutional policy-making in the past five years. All of these factors had directly or indirectly influenced the development of policy and provision for disabled students. However, almost all institutions had staffing and structures in place to support the development of provision for disabled students. Where they did not fully meet the criteria for base-level provision, significant numbers reported 'partially meeting' them. There were also signs that institutions were moving away from a completely *ad hoc* reactive approach to dealing with the needs of disabled students. While few could claim to be prepared in advance to meet the needs of disabled students, there were signs of movement away from the reactive end of the continuum. Disabled students had been written into policies on admissions, assessments, estates and buildings and, in some cases, strategic plans. Most institutions had definite written plans for further development, which suggested that they intended, in the long-term, to mainstream disability. While all of these signs of progress are encouraging, there are many areas that still need much further development. Areas needing particular attention include teaching and learning, monitoring and evaluation, staff development and quality assurance.

Monitoring and evaluation of statistics and services for disabled students is an area that clearly needs further development. Institutions did consult student representative bodies and individual disabled students about developments, but systematic evaluations of policy and practice for disabled students were generally lacking. Until institutions consult their disabled students directly they will remain ignorant of the difficulties and barriers faced by disabled students as they go about their daily business. They will not know which areas need particular attention or development and members of staff remain unaccountable for their practice. Monitoring of this kind would highlight the gap between policy and practice that was evident in our case studies, with, for example, students having to repeatedly ask for adjustments, such as handouts in advance, that were promised to them at the start of their courses.

Teaching and learning remains an area of particular concern, with respondents emphasising that the kind of culture change required to really make a difference in this area will take a very long time. The difficulties faced by disabled students simply provide a catalyst that enables the least effective parts of higher education to be more clearly seen. Disabled students present a challenge to higher education staff to question traditional notions about teaching and learning. If higher education takes up the challenge, then this could represent a significant improvement in practice for all students.

At the moment, the emphasis in provision for disabled students remains too much on providing disabled students with individual support to get round institutional barriers, rather than on more fundamental institutional change. The intention to mainstream disability remains a rather vague notion at the moment, with no time limits set on achieving any of its component parts. The recent introduction of premium funding for disabled students heralds a shift in funding council policy towards mainstreaming disability. As yet, however, disability remains a fairly distinct policy area, mainly addressed by student support services staff and its relocation, particularly in teaching and learning, will demand a significant commitment on the part of all institutions.

Chapter 4

Institutional ethos and support for disabled students in higher education

Introduction

In this chapter we begin the task of exploring the impact of institutional ethos and culture on the widening access agenda and the experiences of disabled students in particular. Culture is likely to permeate many aspects of the institution, including the background of students and staff, the historical legacy, geographical and physical features, organisation of student support services and response to external initiatives including those associated with widening access and performance management. Before considering the characteristics of the eight institutions in which we worked, we consider briefly why institutional culture plays a key role in the production or subversion of social inequalities.

Higher education institutions as creators and distributors of social capital

As we noted in Chapter 1, higher education institutions are designed to fulfil the neutral task of equipping students with the knowledge and skills needed for their future working lives. At the same time, they operate as sites for the accumulation and distribution of social capital. As discussed earlier, there is a strong association between social class background and entry to higher education for disabled and non-disabled students, with students from professional and managerial backgrounds, regardless of their disability status, being over-represented in traditional universities. According to Bourdieu, the experience of middle-class students in higher education is likely to reinforce and legitimate their privileged position, since their social class endowment is likely to be reinforced, whilst that of working-class students is likely to be ignored or rejected. Middle-class students are thus likely to find a sense of familiarity with institutional expectations, whilst these are likely to feel strange and unfamiliar to students from poorer backgrounds. At an institutional level, we wished to understand the extent to which universities were accommodating the needs of diverse student groups. In addition, we wished to explore the inter-section of institutional understandings of disability and social class.

Higher education institutions as arbiters of social justice

In Chapter 1, we noted that the concept of social justice is capable of a number of interpretations and much of this interpretative work is likely to happen at institutional level. Higher education institutions within the UK are officially independent of government, although they depend on the state for the majority of their funding. The Scottish Executive and the Department for Education and Skills convey in broad-brush terms the priorities which they wish to see pursued, and the funding councils convey these to higher education institutions. Rather than informing institutions of policy priorities, the funding councils cooperate by creating a financial climate in which certain activities are incentivised and others discouraged.

Social inclusion and widening access have been major concerns of the New Labour administrations in both England and Scotland and financial premiums have been attached to the recruitment of students from low participation neighbourhoods and disabled students. However, individual institutions vary in response to these initiatives and convey powerful messages in their understanding of social justice through decisions on internal resource distribution. For example, the amount of money allocated to student support services reflects institutional commitment to redistribute resources in favour of those experiencing barriers to participation. On the one hand, higher education institutions generally function as part of a meritocratic system; therefore distribution of some resources on the basis of need may be seen as running counter to wider institutional values. On the other hand, in institutions where widening access is part of their core agenda, spending money on support services may be justified in financial terms as a key strategy to increase student retention.

In addition to their role in resource allocation, institutions transmit important messages with regard to the politics of recognition or identity. Institutional practices may reinforce the 'middle class as norm' message, or alternatively may validate a much wider range of identities. In relation to disability and identity, institutions may encourage the presence of disabled students by active recruitment policies, by encouraging students to disclose disability and by supporting groups of disabled students to organise into active groups with a remit to challenge the institution. The active promotion of shared identity among disabled students may of course be perceived as double edged, since politicised disabled students are likely to be much more demanding of resources.

To summarise, institutional culture plays a major role in determining the backcloth against which disabled students and other non-traditional groups experience a sense of either validation or marginalisation. In this chapter we begin the task of exploring the impact of institutional ethos and culture on the widening access agenda and the experiences of disabled students in particular. Key features of the eight institutions in which we worked are summarised in Table 4.1. Some important aspects of their approach to disability are discussed below.

Key characteristics of the institutions

Scottish University 1

A medium-sized post-92 institution with approximately 14,000 undergraduate students, Scottish University 1 described itself as a friendly local institution, geared to helping students find work in a range of vocational areas such as business and management, professions allied to medicine, nursing, social work, engineering and journalism. Scottish University 1's buildings were all new or relatively new and, compared with other universities in the city, the estate was relatively accessible. The university had little student accommodation and most students lived at home or commuted in from the surrounding area. Scottish University 1 had the largest enrolment of part-time undergraduates in Scotland and had made significant efforts to attract students from non-traditional backgrounds, often through a further education articulation route. Research funding represented a relatively small proportion of the recurrent grant from the Scottish Higher Education Funding Council. As shown in Table 4.1, Scottish University 1 attracted a high proportion of students from socially disadvantaged backgrounds (36 per cent from social class IIIM, IV, V), but also had much higher non-completion rates than pre-92 universities, with 22 per cent of students failing to continue or qualify. Despite having a relatively accessible modern campus, Scottish University 1 had a very low proportion of disabled students declaring disability on their UCAS form (2 per cent), and a particularly low proportion of students with dyslexia.

Scottish University 2

A traditional pre-92 university with a strong research base, Scottish University 2 had about 16,000 undergraduates and 4,000 postgraduates. Its building varied from the ultra-modern, which generally conformed with access requirements, to Victorian buildings which were very poor on access. The worst buildings were those built in the late 1960s and 1970s, which had features such as lifts which stopped at only a small number of floors, thus making access extremely frustrating. The university was proud of its record on widening access (21 per cent of undergraduates from social class IIIM, IV and V and 85 per cent from state schools) and had been identified by the *Times Higher Education Supplement* as being a member of an 'access elite',

Table 4.1 Characteristics of case study institutions

Institution/ type of institution	Campus description	Learning support/disability office staff	Disability policy/planning
Scottish University 1 Post-92. UG FTE: 12,329 Disabled: 251 (2.3%) DSA: 0.9% State school: 96%	Relatively new city-centre campus with reasonable accessibility but difficulties remain. New build programme set to make vast improvement.	Large learning support structure with links to disability officers – staffing 2 FTE DO, 1 FTE admin support worker, dyslexia support worker.	Disability recognised at a high level but policy implemented in *ad hoc* manner. Equal Opportunities Working Group established.
Scottish University 2 Ancient. UG FTE: 17,998 Disabled: 617 (3.9%) DSA: (1.2%) State school: 60%	Largely Victorian with many older buildings inaccessible.	Temporary disability officer in SEN service.	Little contact between Effective Learning Service, Counselling Service and Disabled Students Service. Formerly little involvement of senior management, but staffing crisis prompted renewed commitment to developing effective service. New Disability Advisory Committee established.
Scottish University 3 Ancient. UG FTE: 5,070 Disabled: 282 (6.6%) DSA: 1.2% State school: 60%	Many old and listed buildings. Serious barrier to many potential disabled students.	1 disability officer, dyslexia support coordinator and new appointment to support students with MH difficulties.	Disability advisory group (DAG) chaired by senior manager convened to inform on disability issues.
Scottish College 1 HE: 2,500 Disabled: 4% Most deprived area: 36%	3 main campuses with number of community learning centres. Mixture of 1960s and newer buildings accessibility fair to good.	Learning support has 20 FTE P/T lecturers in 3 schools. Specific support for deaf and visually impaired students. Students have personal support plan.	Head of learning support is a VP and on senior management committee.

DDA response	Impact RAE/QAA	Approaches to teaching and learning	Recent developments
Expectation by DO that DDA would make inroads into improving teaching and learning. Cost of full access seen as prohibitive.	VP believed research income as of only marginal importance in relation to teaching. Concerns of affordability of all aspects of QAA precepts but major effort made to comply.	Some innovation in lecturing with instant subtitles in process of being developed. Some lecturers have strong political commitment to inclusion.	Functions of the disability adviser separated into different posts. Post 1 – casework, Post 2 – staff development & policy. Additional staffing to be provided via premium funding.
Limited training offered to academic/ administrative staff. Cost of physical accessibility deemed prohibitive.	QAA report critical. DO felt RAE had negative impact on widening access agenda. Research prioritised.	Innovation in medical faculty. Problem based learning easier for dyslexic students.	After end of research period, new senior DO appointed with responsibility for high-level policy. Two other DOs to be appointed.
Senior management believed improvements for disabled students good for all students.	Disability Advisory Group formed in response to SHEFC review of QAA code. RAE seen as positive in bringing more cash to university.	Some resistance to giving out lecture materials in advance, seen as attacking traditional methods.	Restructuring underway after strategic planning review, moving from ad hoc structures to more managerial approach across the board.
DDA not viewed by VP as particular concern. Some anxiety re access to buildings. Emphasis on 'inclusiveness' rather than specifically disability.	Not applicable.	Small class sizes <20 generally facilitate better lecturer response.	None – but continued ethos of inclusion.

Table 4.1 (continued)

Institution/ Type of institution	Campus description	Learning support/disability office staff	Disability policy/planning
English University 1 Pre-92. UG FTE: 6,200 Disabled: 222 (3.9%) DSA: 0.9% State school: 80%	Main campus relatively new in compact area outside city centre – recent audit on physical access financed by HEFCE. Largely accessible but some buildings inaccessible.	1 DO, 1 FTE support worker, dyslexia support worker.	Limited to impact of DO – no direct route to senior management. DO argues this is necessary and that she has sole responsibility for disability issues.
English University 2 Post-92. UG FTE: 10,639 Disabled: 341 (3.9%) DSA: 0.7% State school: 97%	2 main campuses with newer one particularly accessible – some older buildings inaccessible to wheelchair users but these in process of being upgraded.	1 FTE disability services manager with 1 FTE support worker 1 FTE administrator – named disability support tutor in each school.	Disability Working Group established – involved senior managers and was working out in detail institutional responses to the legislation.
English University 3 Post-92. UG FTE: 17,162 Disabled: 650 (3.8%) DSA: 1.2% State school: 93%	3 main campuses – new buildings are fully accessible but older buildings inaccessible. 73% general purpose teaching rooms – accessible.	Extensive – disability support service coordinator, DO, administrator, mental health development officer, mental health support worker, 2 dyslexia support specialists.	Head of student support services committed to developing disability agenda and strong representative in senior management – disability advisory group reports directly to Vice-Chancellor's Equal Opportunities Advisory Group.
English University 4 Ancient. UG FTE: 12,313 Disabled: 202 (1.6%) DSA: 1.5% State school: 60%	Very diverse campus with mix of old and new buildings. Access for those with mobility impairments restricted.	All students primarily the responsibility of academic departments but with support of Access Unit when required. Tradition of Deaf Studies.	Autonomy of academic departments restrictive in terms of planning but group formed to consider DDA Part 4 implications.

DDA response	Impact RAE/QAA	Approaches to teaching and learning	Recent developments
Limited to DO's personal efforts – some senior management concern. Support for staff training – limited. DO feels personal negotiation, not anticipation, remains effective means of support.	Effort by DO to help departments implement parts of code of practice – far from complete at present.	DO role to educate academic staff – some departments have appointed disability reps.	Extensive access audit carried out with recommendations being implemented.
DO felt DDA would effect change in academic practice. Capacity of university to meet legal requirements limited by resource availability.	Senior manager felt that the QAA and RAE were disciplinary mechanisms used unfairly against new universities.	Central point for collection of lecture notes ineffective – increased use of web by some departments.	Developing close support between local health and social work teams to support students with mental health problems.
Senior manager – DDA would not affect everyday practice as complaints likely to be dealt with internally – staff to take more responsibility.	Senior manager concerned that RAE had distracted academic staff from supporting disabled students due to time constraints. QAA Code useful in highlighting issues.	Teaching and learning experience of disabled students dependent on identifying themselves. Problems with low disclosure (particularly mental health problems).	Developing mental health support, access centre status.
University has established a working group to consider the implications of the DDA Part 4 with disabled people having strong representation.	Director of the Access Unit believed DDA could deliver some principles of the QAA. Pressures of RAE affected time available for individual students.	Deaf students permitted to use BSL in exams.	Disability co-ordinators to be appointed in each academic department.

a group of universities with high rates of access for students from non-traditional backgrounds coupled with high quality teaching and research. At 17 per cent, the university had a relatively high drop-out rate for a pre-92 university. The proportion of disabled students (4 per cent) was slightly below the national average. Many students were recruited from the urban conurbation surrounding the university and around half of undergraduate students lived at home during their studies.

Scottish University 3

Scottish University 3 was a pre-92 university in a small town with a relatively small undergraduate body (about 6,000 students on first degree courses). The majority of university buildings were old and many were listed; this was identified by staff at all levels as presenting a major barrier to the recruitment of disabled students. Scottish University 3 had a small number of mature students and a high intake from the independent school sector and from England. A low proportion were from working-class backgrounds (15 per cent) and drop-out rates were low (10 per cent). Overall, 6 per cent of students disclosed a disability, considerably above the national average. There was a stated commitment within the Strategic Plan to widen access and include more students from non-traditional backgrounds. It was argued by a senior manager that the absence of an industrial hinterland made it very difficult to recruit students from socially disadvantaged backgrounds. Linking arrangements with local colleges and schools had been established to try to remedy this, but staff were wary of lowering academic requirements for students from non-traditional backgrounds, fearing a dilution of standards. A new part-time evening degree programme was seen as contributing to the wider access programme. The university concentrated on a limited range of subject areas which tended to be highly academic rather than vocational.

Scottish College 1

In Scotland, just over 20 per cent of higher education provision takes place in further education settings, with students normally taking the first two years of a degree in college before transferring to university for the last two years. Scottish College 1 had pioneered higher education in a further education setting, with 50 per cent of its provision in higher education. Twenty thousand students, including 5,000 full-time students, were enrolled each year. Of these, 3,800 were studying at HE level. The college had a number of campuses, some of which had been built recently using a combination of public and private funds. Links had been established with a network of community learning centres. The college was located in an area of multiple deprivation and 36 per cent of students, including HE students, were from deprivation category 5 based on the Scottish Deprivation Index. For twenty years, the college had been given additional funding by the Scottish Executive to provide higher education to deaf students, who continued to be attracted to the college because of the existence of a well-established deaf community. The social inclusion agenda underpinned all of the college's work and staff regarded disabled students as a core part of the student population, rather than a new group of students making additional and unfunded demands.

English University 1

This was a small pre-92 university recruiting 80 per cent of students from state schools and 23 per cent from social classes IIIM, IV and V. Drop-out rates after year of entry were low at 7 per cent. Approximately 4 per cent of students disclosed a disability on their UCAS form. The main campus was relatively new and in a compact area outside the city centre. Buildings were generally accessible but there were some exceptions and building works taking place at the time of the research compromised access. The university had secured a relatively high position in the league tables of higher education institutions, and was investing considerable efforts in retaining this position, possibly detracting attention from the social inclusion agenda. The university taught traditional arts, social science and science subjects, and was part of a consortium developing a new medical school.

English University 2

English University 2 was identified in the *Times Higher Educational Supplement* as part of an 'access elite'. A post-92 institution, English University 2 had about 10,500 undergraduates, of whom 97 per cent were from state schools. Thirty-five per cent were from social class IIIM, IV and V and HESA statistics indicated that 3.9 per cent were recorded as having a disability. Fifteen per cent dropped out after their year of entry. The university had two main campuses, the newer one having better access for students with physical disabilities. The university was in competition with a significant number of neighbouring institutions in the locality, and felt challenged by a number of pre-92 universities which were venturing into the 'access market'. The following few years were envisaged as a period of retrenchment rather than expansion. Vocational subjects dominated the curriculum.

English University 3

English University 3 was another post-92 institution identified as a member of an 'access elite'. Of its 17,000 undergraduates, 93 per cent were from state schools and 26 per cent from social classes IIIM, IV and V. Eleven per cent of students failed to continue or qualify after their year of entry. According to HESA data, about 4 per cent of students disclosed a disability. English University 3 had three campuses with a mix of old and new buildings, the former presenting problems for access. The curriculum spanned vocational and more traditional subjects.

English University 4

English University 4 recruited 60 per cent of its undergraduate intake from state schools and 11 per cent from social classes IIIM, IV and V, giving it an overwhelmingly upper-middle-class social profile rather like that of Scottish University 3. Only 1.6 per cent of students were disabled. Retention rates were very high, with only 5 per cent of students failing to complete or qualify after their year of entry. The university had a mixed estate, with some very old and inaccessible buildings. English University 4 occupied a high league table position, and there were mixed views among staff as to whether widening access was a rational agenda to pursue given the university's position and history (see below for further discussion). The university's curriculum was typical of a traditional academic institution, with the full range of arts, social science and science subjects and a large medical school.

To summarise, it is evident that the eight institutions had very different social profiles, curricula and academic missions. The proportion of students recruited from state schools varied from 97 per cent to 60 per cent and the proportion of students from working-class backgrounds ranged from 35 per cent (Scottish University 1) to 10 per cent (English University 4, Scottish University 3). As we noted in Chapter 1, it is hard to find any university with a 'fair' representation of working-class students. In the urban area surrounding Scottish University 1, 50 per cent of the population are classified as working class, so that even the most working-class university in our case studies is failing to accurately reflect the social class composition of its geographical location. The association between the proportion of working-class students and drop-out rates was noticeable, and this was highlighted in the case of Scottish University 2, a pre-92 university with relatively high working-class intake accompanied by a relatively high drop-out rate. The proportion of disabled students ranged from 1.6 per cent (English University 4) to 6.6 per cent (Scottish University 3), both of which were pre-92 universities. In the following sections, we consider issues in relation to the organisation and resourcing of support services for disabled students, the links with other widening access programmes, the relationship between dedicated disability services and academic departments and the impact of managerialist regimes in higher education.

Nature of support for disabled students

Organisation and staffing of disabled students service

The composition and organisational structure of the disabled students advisory service in the different institutions is summarised in Table 4.1. Following funding council initiatives in the 1990s, disabled students support services were established in all universities in England and Scotland. Posts which were originally short term became established and administrative support was provided as the remit of disabled students advisers expanded from support for individual students to strategic development at institutional level. The level of support relative to the number of students varied greatly; for example, Scottish University 3 was better resourced in relation to the number of disabled students than Scottish Universities 1 and 2. This was partly because premium funding in Scottish University 3 had been ploughed back into additional part-time support posts. In both English and Scottish institutions, the support of a senior manager with an interest in the area appeared to have been critical in its successful development. Disabled students services tended to be located within student services, and this was seen as problematic by some advisers who felt that a welfare approach stood in the way of establishing a mainstream service:

> Well it's the professional model versus the medical model, really. Putting it in welfare services had medicalised it whereas if you have a social model, then it's a teaching and learning issue. If all universities were fully accessible and it was incorporated in teaching and learning, it wouldn't be a welfare issue.
>
> (Disability adviser, English University 1)

English institutions often had more generous levels of staffing in their disabled students support services as a result of HEFCE special initiatives for disabled students. Over a number of years, institutions had bid for money to fund projects developing particular types of services or provision. Some institutions had been particularly successful in attracting additional funds. For example, English University 3 had received support for projects in three successive HEFCE bidding rounds and as a result employed a disability support service coordinator, a disability officer, an administrator, a mental health support worker and two dyslexia advisers. They were also creatively pooling students' DSA money to fund dyslexia and mental health adviser posts, i.e. by each student getting funding for one hour per week with an adviser. The university was managing this money and using it to pay salaries.

Institutions varied in their degree of support for students with particular impairments. English University 4 and Scottish College 1 had established traditions of attracting deaf students, and both employed staff who were users of British Sign Language. Other universities had begun to appoint advisers specialising in support for students with mental health difficulties and dyslexia (Chapters 5 and 7 provide accounts of how this type of support was experienced by students).

Scottish College 1 provided a model of learning support provision which was markedly different from that available in the universities. The college had nine faculties, one of which was dedicated to learning support, indicating the overall importance of this area in the college's mission. The Faculty of Learning Support had more than 1,000 student full-time equivalents, although only a minority of these were enrolled for higher education programmes. Twenty full-time special needs lecturers with particular specialisms were employed, backed up by a pool of part-time lecturers. This meant that the college could provide specialist support for blind and deaf students as a matter of routine. The college operated within a discourse of need, based on the assumption that as much learning support should be channelled to disabled students as was required to help them succeed. Unlike the universities, the college did not view learning support as a finite resource which had to be rationed on the grounds of finance or fairness. Post-92 universities were generally ahead of pre-92 universities in their development of support for disabled students and learning support more generally. The disabled students adviser in English University 3 explained that advice had been consciously sought from neighbouring FE colleges in setting up its provision. This was less likely to be the case in pre-92 universities, although after the end of the research period we learnt that Scottish University 2 had recruited a special needs adviser from FE.

Engagement with academic departments

It was evident that in every institution, apart from Scottish College 1, there was a degree of tension between academic departments and the disabled students support service. In all cases, the ambition of the disabled students adviser and the senior manager was to shift responsibility for the provision of teaching and learning support away from the disabled students advisory service and towards academic departments. However, it was evident that these initiatives were achieving only limited, if any, success. English University 2 had named disability coordinators in all schools with a specified time allocation to undertake the job, but even here it was felt that more work was needed to develop the role. In other institutions, less progress had been made. A senior manager noted that disability advisers might have 'wildly unrealistic expectations' of what could be delivered in departments, given the range of pressures on lecturers' time. At English University 4, the tensions produced by delegating responsibility to departmental level was described thus:

We got to the stage where each department had to have someone to look after women, someone to look after overseas students, somebody to look after disabled students and someone to look after mature students. In small departments, together with the requirement to fill out performance forms for the QAA and the RAE, it was producing real aggro . . . We have been thinking about having one person in each department who has a sort of conglomerate portfolio for all the waifs and strays.

(Senior manager, English University 4)

A common pattern was for guidance to be sent from the disabled students advisory service to the course coordinator with regard to the adjustments required by an individual student. However, it appeared that information was often not conveyed to the relevant tutor, or the adjustments were not carried out. This resulted in the disabled students having to engage in separate negotiations with each member of staff they encountered during the course of their university career (see Chapter 5 for further discussion).

Links with widening access and effective learning services

It was evident that coordination of widening access initiatives varied greatly across institutions and this was influenced by the conceptualisation of social inclusion in their mission. The senior manager in Scottish College 1 described the centrality of social inclusion thus:

Well, I mean widening access in its broadest sense so you're talking about the social inclusion partnership areas, low achievers and people with poor basic skills but not just that group. It's access in its broadest terms. People with learning difficulties, disabilities, all kinds of social problems. We have links locally and further afield with external agencies. We're very well engaged with councils and community learning and planning processes so there is that kind of contact to make sure that links and partnerships are in place.

(Senior manager, Scottish College 1)

In other universities, pursuing a social inclusion agenda fitted less neatly with the institution's historical mission and involved political conflict. In English University 4, for example, the principal had announced his intention to recruit students from more diverse backgrounds, and this had prompted an angry reaction from the Headmasters' and Headmistresses' Conference (HMC), representing the interests of the independent school sector, who feared that state school pupils might be admitted with lower grades. In summer 2003, the HMC suggested independent school pupils should not apply to English University 4 until it could demonstrate that 'its procedures are fully documented, fair, objective, transparent and consistently applied'. *The Times Higher Education Supplement*, 20 February 2004, reported a subsequent drop in applications and a university spokesperson indicated that the 'shortlived and inappropriate' boycott by some independent schools might well have had an impact on recruitment from this sector. The HMC view was that there was no boycott – 'In the final analysis, it is the consumer who makes the choice'. According to the senior manager at the university, the main outcome of the widening access initiative was an increase in the recruitment of 'good middle-class children' from state schools rather than young people from working-class backgrounds.

In all the institutions, the major target group for widening access initiatives appeared to be young people from working-class backgrounds. Sometimes, initiatives geared towards this group took no account of the fact that such students might also be disabled. It was reported, for example, that summer schools sometimes took place in inaccessible settings. In addition, initiatives branded as 'effective learning' services sometimes refused to take account of the needs of disabled students. For example, in Scottish University 2 it was reported that the effective learning service questioned whether it should give support to students with mental health difficulties, since they were the responsibility of the counselling service. Moves to widen access for disabled students have to date been less politically controversial than those geared towards altering the social class balance of students in university, although it was evident that none of the case study universities were engaged in actively recruiting greater numbers of disabled students.

Funding issues

The funding of support for disabled students was seen as of critical importance in all institutions, with constraints on funding seen as a major barrier to implementing the Disability Discrimination Act effectively (see below for further discussion). A key difference between English and Scottish institutions was the use made of the Disabled Students Allowance, which was paid to between 0.7 and 1.5 per cent of students in the case study institutions. All the English universities ran a scheme whereby the institution employed a number of support workers, such as note-takers and personal assistants. Once the DSA assessment had taken place, the university supplied the student with an appropriate support worker according to their needs. The student authorised the university to retain the funds which were claimed retrospectively from the local authority. The disabled students in the English institutions were thus relieved of the responsibility of employing their own workers, and the university was able to build up a pool of skilled and trained support workers. Sometimes, pooled DSA funds were used to pay for some of the service infrastructure or to employ an additional disabled students adviser specialising in a particular area such as mental health difficulties. In English University 2, the disabled students adviser was running a certificate in support for disabled students accredited by the Open College, thus contributing to the development of a more professionalised service for the future. Improving services in this way, it was believed, would free disabled students and enable them to focus on their course of study:

> . . . at the end of the day, you are here as a student to do a course or whatever and then all these things, like liaising with your lecturers about your needs, can very easily become the focus and distract from actually doing the course and getting on with it.
> (Disabled students adviser, English University 3)

In the Scottish universities, on the other hand, arrangements for the employment of support workers was much more *ad hoc*. In Scottish University 2, for example, Community Service Volunteers were used. The aim of people participating in this scheme was to increase their confidence and employability, rather than to offer a professional service. Students felt that those employed often lacked basic employment skills such as punctuality, and note-takers were rarely knowledgeable about the subject area. The disabled students adviser in Scottish University 1 argued that if the university were to take over the employment of support workers, this would disempower the student because they would no longer be regarded as the employer. There are parallels here with the debates around direct payments for disabled people, with fears that moves by local authorities to take over the running of support services will domesticate the scheme so that it ceases to have a radical and empowering effect (Riddell *et al.*, 2005).

There were also differences between the institutions in the way in which the premium funding had been used. In some institutions, it had all been allocated to the disabled students service and used to employ existing or new staff. In other universities, it had been absorbed into central funds. One disability adviser had spent some time trying to track what had happened to the funds, since she felt that their use should be transparent and they should be spent only on services for disabled students. Something of a paradox existed here. Whereas most senior managers and disability officers were seeking ways to mainstream services for disabled students by locating them in the domain of teaching and learning, the universities with the most effective provision appeared to have well-resourced and dedicated provision. This suggests that a dual-pronged approach may be necessary, with support directed at the individual student whilst at the same time changes are made to the wider institutional environment. However, the channelling of individualised payments into collective provision is worth noting, since in the future it might herald a reduction in services aimed at the individual, with an increase in generic support services provided across the institution.

Impact of managerialist regimes

As we noted in Chapter 3, the Research Assessment Exercise (RAE) was regarded as having a major impact particularly in pre-92 institutions and this finding was reinforced by the institutional case studies. There was disagreement about the extent to which the RAE had deflected attention away from teaching. For example, a senior manager at English University 4 commented:

> There is no doubt that the emphasis on research in the RAE, and the university's determination to be a top research university has meant that the interest in and attachment to teaching has been reduced a bit.
> (Senior manager, English University 4)

A contrasting view was presented by the senior manager in Scottish University 3, who argued that the RAE was not at odds with the desire to improve provision for disabled students:

> I don't think the RAE has had any impact other than positive on our ability to respond to these issues, because RAE success is equated with financial success and it gives a bit more monetary flexibility . . . we are here to do teaching and research and if we prosper through doing these things excellently then we have got more flexibility to respond to these issues.
> (Senior manager, Scottish University 3)

Two respondents from post-92 universities also felt that their institutions had been unduly drawn into the RAE competition, with attention deflected from teaching as a result. The senior manager in Scottish University 1 was of the view that in the old universities, research subsidised teaching because tutorials were often undertaken by postgraduate and postdoctoral students. In new universities, however, staff spent a lot of time and energy chasing very small amounts of money, without realising the negative impact this had on their teaching efforts.

The emphasis on quality assurance, which dominated much of the 1990s, was seen as having a lesser impact on the position of disabled students. It was noted that the QAA's Code of Practice on provision for disabled students had only a minor impact, since its publication coincided with the political decision to introduce a much 'lighter touch' to quality assurance. Most lecturing staff, it was pointed out by the disabled students adviser in English University 3, would be completely unaware that such a document even existed.

A further manifestation of the audit culture, the publication of league tables based on a range of data including research and teaching quality assessment scores and student drop-out rates, were seen as being highly influential on institutional behaviour. In particular, the publication of data on student retention was seen as having a negative impact on the social inclusion agenda, since socially disadvantaged students were much more likely to drop out of their course. Universities were therefore conscious that recruiting high numbers of working-class students was likely to be damaging to their league table position. This may go some way to explaining the finding presented in Chapter 2 that disabled students in pre-92 universities are from similarly privileged backgrounds to non-disabled students.

Finally, students' growing awareness of their power as consumers was seen as having a double edged effect on universities' willingness to recruit disabled students in greater numbers. In Scottish University 3, an official complaint by a disabled student with regard to her treatment resulted in a major enquiry which found that a number of lecturers displayed negative attitudes which needed to change. By way of contrast, a senior manager in English University 2 described a long-drawn-out dispute between a disabled student and the institution. The student had physical impairments and mental health difficulties and was involved in criminal activity. Dealing with the complaint was time-consuming and raised fears that the institution would be unable to cope if a number of such cases occurred simultaneously:

> I suppose you can construct the worst case scenario that somebody is admitted to the institution without declaring a significant mental health problem or major disability problem. They find themselves in totally unsuitable accommodation and/or in a programme of study for which they are clearly unprepared and in respect of which members of staff, with the best will in the world, are unable to make adjustments.
>
> (Senior manager, English University 2)

The implications of these comments was that institutions should be wary about admitting students whom they might find difficult to manage, particularly in the light of the growing importance of consumerist and rights agendas.

Impact of the Disability Discrimination Act

Informants were asked for their views of the future impact of Part 4 of the Disability Discrimination Act. Different accounts were given, with some universities believing that they could deal with the new legal requirements relatively easily, since minimal compliance was not difficult, whilst others alluded to the difficulties institutions were likely to experience.

The problems of resourcing accessible provision throughout the institution were seen as a major problem. The senior manager in Scottish University 1, for example, wondered how it was possible to justify spending £46,000 on a fume cupboard for a student in Chemistry who was a wheelchair user. The senior manager in English University 4 noted that it was possible to install a 'deaf friendly' fire alarm in the Deaf Studies Centre, but that this could not be afforded across the university. The university already had a pending law case brought by a deaf member of staff who felt that the university should provide sign language interpreters for all its public lectures, and this too was seen as involving prohibitive costs.

The boundaries of reasonable adjustments in assessments were also regarded as potentially problematic (see Chapter 5 for further discussion). The senior manager at English University 2 described a recent case where a student with epilepsy who experienced stress had been permitted to take an examination paper at home in unsupervised conditions. This arrangement had been reached without any external approval and appeared not to have been rigorously thought through. This, it appeared, was an example of 'over-compensation' which gave the student an unfair advantage over other students. The senior manager in Scottish College 1, on the other hand, explained the position adopted within her institution:

> ... you can't start watering down courses and just saying 'Oh well'. But I think you can look at alternative methods that a person can be engaged in, such as making a presentation orally or whatever.
>
> (Senior manager, Scottish College 1)

The overall impression within the case study institutions was that the demands of the DDA were potentially considerable, but if the condition of reasonableness was taken seriously then little change would be needed.

Institutional culture and the construction of disability

It was evident that institutions were involved in active negotiation with their students with regard to the nature and meaning of disability. At a very basic level, the wider institutional context had an impact on which students were likely to disclose a disability or think of themselves as disabled in the first place. For example, the senior manager of Scottish University 1 noted that it was difficult to get students within this post-92 institution to identify themselves as dyslexic, since those who came from socially disadvantaged schools might not have received a prior diagnosis. Obtaining a DSA assessment involved a considerable amount of bureaucracy and the benefits of declaring dyslexia might not be clear to the individual student. However, the institution suffered as a result of this reluctance, since less money entered the institution through the DSA and premium funding routes. Conversely, institutions which advertised widely the support they offered for students with, for example, mental health difficulties had larger numbers of students disclosing this disability.

The operation of admissions policies was a further mechanism by which disabled students could be either encouraged or discouraged from pursuing an application and disclosing a disability. Institutions all maintained that admission was based on academic grounds alone. However, interviews with disabled students advisers often happened on the same day as academic interviews, and sometimes a disabled students adviser was invited to attend such an interview. Senior managers acknowledged that institutions could operate a 'cooling out' effect, stressing the difficulties which the student would encounter at the university and urging them to consider taking up a place elsewhere. As noted above, staff were aware of the costs which might accrue to the institution by admitting a disabled student with high support needs, and it was therefore unsurprising that some degree of caution was emerging. The operation of the cooling out effect was confirmed by our student case studies, and as a result students sometimes chose to underplay the significance of their impairment in order to obtain a place.

Respondents at institutional level described the type of disabled student who could be readily accommodated and those who were likely to be seen as 'difficult'. The director of the access unit at English University 4 commented:

> My own view is that because of its overall ethos the University tends to deal better with those students who are nearest to the norm and the further away the student is from the norm the more difficult it is for other students and the more informal university if you like to deal with it.
>
> (Director of access unit, English University 4)

At English University 2, the senior manager described the university's 'nightmare scenario':

> It was a blind student who, not only was he blind, but he was clearly an alcoholic and mentally unstable. Well he was extremely objectionable and kept on trying to secure every conceivable means of support whilst at the same time clearly not doing any work and making a nuisance of himself around the campus and regularly wrecking his room . . . I can't remember how we finally got rid of him but it went on and on and on.
>
> (Senior manager, English University 2)

The accounts provided by institutional informants distinguished between the type of disabled student who would be welcomed (personable, hardworking, claiming DSA, making modest demands on institutional resources) and the type who would be rejected (litigious, lazy, making 'unreasonable' demands on the time of lecturers or support staff, not claiming DSA). These understandings are likely to have an impact both on the type of disabled student recruited and subsequently the range of behaviours signalled as acceptable.

The pressures on disabled students to define themselves as different from other students but at the same time to seek acceptance by conforming to institutional norms was underlined by the disabled students adviser at English University 3:

> There is that ongoing dilemma . . . you want to be a student of the university with the same sort of rights as other students and to do that you do have to speak up for your rights more and be more involved and stand out a bit. But then you don't want to [be] labelled as the disabled student, the disabled person, because there's that balance of equality . . . But by virtue of wanting to get more equality you do tend to have to stand out more because you're the one who's saying 'Can I have this in large print, can I sit here?'
>
> (Disabled students adviser, English University 3)

Conclusion

This chapter illustrates the way in which the culture of universities shapes the context in which disability is constructed and students negotiate their identity. Data on social characteristics of students at the eight case study institutions underlined their diversity but also drew attention to some common patterns. Pre-92 universities attract a much higher proportion of middle-class students, although even in the most accessible universities working-class students are under-represented. Whilst the government encourages widening access initiatives, the use of student retention data creates perverse incentives, so that institutions recruiting more socially disadvantaged students are then penalised for higher drop-out rates. This goes some way to explain the fact that disabled students tend to share the social class profile of other students in the institutions where they are studying. Universities in England and Scotland thus play a powerful role in consolidating rather than challenging middle class advantage.

With regard to widening access initiatives, it is evident that the focus continues to be on recruiting more students from socially disadvantaged areas, with far less attention paid to disabled students. Many initiatives fail to acknowledge that poorer students are more likely to be disabled, given the well documented links between social class and disability (Riddell, forthcoming). A major anxiety about recruiting more disabled students in many institutions centres on the cost implications and legal compliance issues. It appears that disabled students are welcome within institutions as long as they do not require a refocusing of resources, including both physical adaptations and staff time.

With regard to meeting the needs of disabled students, it is evident that services have developed markedly over the past ten years, but continue to be located within a welfare discourse. Mainstreaming support for disabled students in academic departments remains an aspiration in most institutions, and departmental autonomy means that this cannot be imposed from above. The Research Assessment Exercise appears to have reinforced the prioritisation of research over teaching, although this is less so in the post-92 institutions. The College of Further and Higher Education provided a model of support for learning imbuing all aspects of institutional activity, and it appears the post-92 universities have been attempting to incorporate this approach into their own practice. Pre-92 universities still employ a discourse of merit rather than need in making judgements about how resources should be distributed, and are reluctant to devote more funding to students who are regarded as less worthy.

Finally, institutions convey clear messages about the types of disabled students they wish to recruit. Those who are able to adopt the existing institutional ethos are most readily absorbed, whilst those who reject these norms are marginalised and are likely to be excluded. There is thus considerable pressure on disabled students to conform to the institutional habitus, defining themselves as the same as rather than different from others. However, unless disabled students emphasise their difference in a strategic manner, they are unlikely to achieve institutional recognition either culturally or in terms of resource distribution.

Chapter 5

The construction of 'learning difficulties' and 'reasonable adjustments' to teaching, learning and assessment

Introduction

This chapter focuses on understandings of learning difficulties in higher education, the types of barriers encountered by students with a range of impairments in different institutional settings, and the actions taken in different institutions and disciplines to remove obstacles to learning. This is particularly important in the context of Part 4 of the Disability Discrimination Act 1995 (as amended) (DDA). Like other equality legislation, the Act is based on the liberal idea that education may reduce inequality if discriminatory practices can be eliminated. The legislation, however, goes beyond the prohibition of less favourable treatment. More radically, institutions are required to make reasonable adjustments to counteract the inequality which disabled people may experience. Furthermore, the adjustments must not simply be in response to problems encountered by individuals; rather, institutions must anticipate the barriers which are likely to impede disabled students' progress and remove these before they become a problem. Whilst tackling physical barriers may be contentious in terms of the amount of money involved in relation to the number of students who will benefit, altering teaching and assessment approaches for particular students is likely to be far more contentious, since questions of fairness and the maintenance of academic standards inevitably arise.

The chapter begins with a discussion of the ways in which learning difficulties are understood and responded to in higher education. Since the largest group of disabled students have dyslexia, we then explore recent scientific evidence as well as understandings of the concept employed by advocacy and professional groups, drawing on a recent review conducted by the National Research and Development Centre for Adult Literacy and Numeracy (Rice and Brooks, 2004). Finally, we present brief case studies of dyslexic students and contrast these with institutional responses to students with a range of other impairments. These cases are drawn from the in-depth study of 48 students, which involved in-depth interviews with the students and lecturing and support staff. In addition, each student was asked to identify a number of academic and social contexts which exemplified their experience of higher education, and these were observed with the student's permission (see Appendix, pages 158–90, for a summary of the student case studies).

Part 4 of the Disability Discrimination Act and the construction of 'reasonable adjustments'

As noted earlier, the provisions of Part 4 of the DDA relating to university policy came into force on 1 September 2002. The duty on responsible bodies to make reasonable adjustments involving the provision of auxiliary aids and services applied from 1 September 2003 and the duty to make adjustments to physical features or premises came into force on 1 September 2005. The *Code of Practice for Providers of Post-16 Education and Related Services* (DRC, 2002) explained the new duties, giving practical examples to illustrate the legal terminology clearly. Our research was therefore being conducted at the time when institutions were gearing up for the change. Although the legislation has potentially far-reaching implications, there are a number of provisos which potentially weaken its impact. For example, in deciding what adjustments are reasonable, responsible bodies may take a number of factors into consideration (see Chapter 3). The notion of 'reasonableness' is evidently a somewhat slippery concept which may be interpreted differently in a variety of contexts. There are also major ambiguities in relation to who is covered by the DDA and whether the Act's definition includes people with less severe forms of dyslexia. The key question here is whether an individual's condition has a significant and adverse effect on his or her ability to perform normal day-to-day activities. The wording of the legislation implies that an individual whose impairment has only a trivial effect would not be covered by the Act, and only a court can decide whether an individual is disabled under the terms of the legislation. Institutions are unlikely to query a diagnosis of dyslexia, but, as we shall see below, there is considerable variation in the tests used to diagnose dyslexia, which are not always administered by chartered psychologists. In the following sections, we illustrate the importance and variability in understandings of what adjustments are reasonable and, conversely, what adjustments might be too costly, contravene academic standards or compromise the interests of other students.

Constructing disability, 'learning difficulties' and dyslexia in higher education

In Chapter 2, we discussed the growth of dyslexic students as a proportion of disabled students in higher education, increasing from 18 per cent in 1995/6 to nearly 33 per cent in 1999/2000. Since then, there has been a further increase in dyslexic students as a proportion of the total, and in 2003/4 they accounted for 40 per cent of all disabled students. The analysis of HESA statistics demonstrated that dyslexic students are significantly more likely to be male and middle class, in line with a Scottish study of school pupils identified as having dyslexic-type difficulties (Riddell *et al.*, 1994). Dyslexic students in higher education pose particular challenges to academic staff because their difficulties are not visible and they may not therefore elicit an immediately sympathetic response compared with students with visible impairments.

Academic staff may also be uncertain about the nature of dyslexia and how to respond to individual students who approach them. This is not surprising, given the lack of scientific consensus around the topic. Rice and Brooks (2004) conducted a systematic review of the evidence on the nature, incidence, diagnosis and treatment of dyslexia in adults and concluded:

> While research into dyslexia generates all of the excitement of the California Gold Rush it also stirs up much of the heat and dust. For a number of years, it has been 'commonplace to bemoan the state of confusion and disagreement in the field' (Stanovich, 1988). A prominent researcher has referred to 'the competitive viciousness that so characterises the dyslexia eco-system', describing it as 'an explosive mixture of high numbers of the affected, high parental emotion, yet poor understanding of the condition, hence poor definition and unreliable methods for judging the outcome of treatments' (Stein, 2002).
>
> (Rice and Brooks, 2004: 13)

As a result of this, research on dyslexia must be regarded as 'tentative, speculative and controversial' and diagnosis procedures must be regarded as unreliable, since 'the standard diagnostic criteria for diagnosing dyslexia cast much too wide a net' (Rice and Brooks, 2004).

Many of the disagreements surrounding dyslexia concern its causes and, following on from this, appropriate forms of assessment and pedagogy. The study conducted by Riddell *et al.* (1994) investigated the perspectives of Scottish parents, voluntary organisations and professionals. Voluntary organisations and some doctors tended to believe that dyslexia was inherently different from other forms of learning difficulty. They believed that dyslexia was physiological in origin, advocated the use of psychometric assessment designed to identify discrepancies in ability and promoted particular teaching methods which were best delivered by specially trained teachers. Educational psychologists, education officers and teachers, on the other hand, believed that children with specific learning difficulties (their preferred term) did not represent a discrete group but were part of a continuum, with a diverse array of abilities and difficulties attributable to environmental and individual factors operating interactively. According to this perspective, there was no absolute dividing line between children with 'common or garden' learning difficulties and others. The preferred form of assessment was classroom observation of difficulties in order to devise a range of teaching strategies, to be implemented by the class or learning support teacher, without the need for intervention by an educational psychologist. Faced with a refusal to acknowledge dyslexic children as a discrete group with specific problems and teaching needs, parents often became extremely frustrated, and adopted a range of strategies including engaging independent psychologists to conduct assessments and, in England but not in Scotland, taking appeals to the Special Educational Needs Tribunal.

A decade later, and in relation to adults rather than children, it appears that the battle lines continue to be drawn along similar lines. This may in part reflect an impasse in the fundamental research which should underpin practitioner action. Rice and Brooks (2004) note that there are major design flaws in many studies, particularly in relation to their use of control groups. In order to test the hypothesis that dyslexic pupils or adults are different from other groups with reading difficulties, two control groups are needed, one made up of people in the 'normal' population and one made up of people with reading difficulties who have not been diagnosed with dyslexia. However, the vast majority of studies, including those which posit neurological, physiological and genetic routes of causality, are inconclusive. Voluntary organisations such as the British Dyslexia Association and the Dyslexia Institute continue to favour definitions which point to physiological differences. A British Dyslexia Association leaflet published in 1999 notes:

> Dyslexia is thought to be an organic difference in the learning centre of the brain. Dyslexic people experience difficulty in processing language, both written and oral. Many also confuse directions, sequences, verbal labels, letters and words or numbers that may look or sound similar. It tends to run in families.
>
> There is more and more evidence gathered from brain imaging techniques that dyslexic people process information differently from other people.
>
> (www.bda-dyslexia.org.uk)

The definition developed by the British Psychological Society (BPS, 1999) aimed to be inclusive, stating:

> Dyslexia is evident when accurate and fluent word reading and/or spelling develops incompletely or with great difficulty.
>
> (BPS, 1999, cited in Rice and Brooks, 2004: 17)

However, the definition was criticised on the grounds that it focused too narrowly on literacy and failed to distinguish between dyslexics and others with learning difficulties since it avoided the issue of causality.

To summarise, there continue to be major and unresolved debates in relation to what dyslexia is, whether it is caused by single or multiple factors, how it is to be diagnosed and how educators should respond. Given the requirement of the DDA that reasonable adjustments be made for accredited disabled students, there is growing concern about the variability of the criteria and assessments used to identify dyslexia.

Institutional responses

As noted in Chapter 4, higher education institutions have adopted a range of strategies in organising support for disabled students. Some approaches are aimed at specific groups; for example, dyslexia support services could be found in some of our case study institutions. Others had effective learning services, which were open to any student who had difficulty in writing or structuring assignments, including disabled students, those from socially disadvantaged backgrounds or overseas students. There were institutional variations with regard to whether these services were available free of charge, or whether students were expected to make an individual contribution. One of the case study institutions, English University 3, expected dyslexic students to contribute a proportion of their Disabled Students Allowance to pay for a dedicated dyslexia tutor. There was also variation in the extent to which dyslexic students were encouraged to organise themselves into cohesive self-help groups. Scottish University 3 had been particularly successful in establishing self-help groups for a range of students including those with dyslexia, ME and eating disorders. Some universities put considerable energy into the sustenance of such groups, whereas disabled students advisers in other institutions felt that encouraging self-help groups was not part of their remit.

The Teachability Project was set up by the Scottish Higher Education Funding Council to encourage departments to examine their current teaching practice with a view to making it as inclusive as possible. Identifying the core requirements of particular courses or programmes is seen as the first step, because potential students need to know whether there is any conflict between the nature of the subject, programme or discipline, and the nature of their impairment. In addition, clarity on core requirements is needed. The Teachability Project, including the handbook, are regarded as highly successful by the funding councils in both Scotland and England. However, a review of the programme (Edson and Riddell, 2003) indicated that many departments were reluctant to engage with the Teachability Project because it was seen as non-compulsory. In addition, there were concerns about potential conflict between accessibility and academic standards and many departments felt that they did not have sufficient time to devote to the programme. Science and technology subject areas felt that their courses required students to be able to move around laboratory space, thus excluding any one with a mobility difficulty. Finally, staff were uncertain about how they could make the curriculum more accessible for students with hidden impairments, including mental health difficulties.

The handbooks produced by case study institutions for disabled students and institutional policies on assessment rarely mentioned the possibility of making adaptations to the assessment of learning outcomes in class assignments and examinations (although English University 3, which was hosting a HEFCE project in this area, was a notable exception). In the main, the assessment adaptations mentioned were fairly routine, such as extra time, or the option of using a PC or note-taker. Despite the legal requirement to offer alternative forms of assessment in order to prevent disabled students experiencing substantial disadvantage, it appeared that universities did not want to draw students' attention to the possibility of alternative forms of assessment. This contrasts with practice in the USA, where university websites highlight the possibility of reasonable accommodations in all areas. Assessment policies were examined in case study institutions where these were available, and the lack of cross-reference to policies for disabled students was evident, indicating that disability had not yet been fully mainstreamed.

Reasonable adjustments in practice: students' accounts

Liam, Scottish University 2

At the time of the research, Liam was a fourth year student at Scottish University 2 who had just completed his finals. There was a history of dyslexia in his family, which had led to a lot of difficulties, but his own problem was not diagnosed until the start of his third year as a result of an intervention by a lecturer in Media Studies, who recognised a discrepancy between his performance in seminars and in written assignments. Referral to the disabled students adviser led to a psychological assessment. According to Liam, he was assured by the adviser before the assessment was conducted that it was almost certain to be positive:

> I think you have to pay £200, but the disability officer said 'You can get that back if you are dyslexic and we haven't had anyone yet who has been tested who hasn't been and I'm pretty confident you will get it back' so I never ever had to pay the £200.

Liam was delighted to receive the diagnosis, but was advised by the disability officer to be 'as diplomatic in the scenario as possible'. He expected his

English tutors to respond by giving him support with his assignments, and was shocked by the lecturers' reaction:

> You know I went to one guy, in fact the first guy I saw, and said, 'Look, I've been diagnosed as having dyslexia' and I was about to say, 'Who can I go to discuss essays with?' and he said, 'Oh, you know in my experience dyslexics don't spell any worse than the other students'. Afterwards, when I left, and this says everything about the guy, he just said, 'Don't hassle me'. I thought, this guy, he's supposed to be teaching English Literature and doesn't even have a basic grasp of what dyslexia is.

Another lecturer was reported as saying:

> Well I taught students at Oxford who are much more dyslexic than you, you're only moderate.

Liam's experience with a Media Studies tutor was very different. The tutor was aware of Liam's uneven performance, and as someone whose first language was not English, had considerable sympathy. He was also aware that Liam was producing up to 50 drafts of an assignment. He therefore suggested that Liam should limit himself to three drafts before submission, on the understanding that he would be able to re-submit if it was not up to the required standard. In addition, the tutor made special allowances when marking:

> You know if there was an essay from a dyslexic student I tend to try and ignore the kind of structural difficulties and try and see what they are saying and so I tend to mark them on the ideas rather than the actual presentation. But that's totally improvised, that's not because of anything.

In addition to his awareness that the allowances he made were 'improvised' rather than based on sound principles, the tutor also felt uneasy because the support given to dyslexic students was based on the demands they made rather than some more objective judgement of their relative need:

> I felt that in a sense Liam was disadvantaged by his dyslexia but also he was getting all this kind of special attention which I was happy to give. I don't think it was proportional to the attention I had given to other students with dyslexia. So I feel quite uneasy about that as well.

Overall, the tutor felt that Liam had been treated unfairly by the exam system and should have sought an alternative form of assessment, since the only compensation made, additional time, was unlikely to be helpful in overcoming the barriers faced:

> The overall degree he got was not a reflection of his abilities at all as I came to know him. In his exams he was getting a 2.2 and all of his coursework was first class. So even the fact that he had extra time, I don't think that was adequate compensation. So I felt really strongly after that – that here we are assessing a student within a system of assessment that is obviously not giving him a fair deal because he can't really demonstrate what he knows and what he is capable of.

The tutor asked for his concerns to be minuted at the examiners' meeting, but compensatory action was not possible at that point. Liam felt that the award of a 2.1 degree represented a major injustice:

> I applied for funding from the Students Awards Agency for Scotland for a PhD and they said 'Sorry, you don't get funding because you didn't get a first'. And I'm thinking, 'If I was black, this would be racism, blatant racism, but I've possibly missed out on £20,000 worth of funding which everyone says I'm capable of because the system was weighted against me and I was misinformed at the time.

Val: Scottish University 3

Val was a second year student studying German and Social History. She had attended a rural comprehensive school and a severe visual impairment was diagnosed in her early teens. Val was from a middle-class background and had chosen Scottish University 3 because she believed it would provide a calm and supportive environment. Val had great difficulty in reading text and had used her Disabled Students Allowance (DSA) to purchase specialist IT equipment. The adjustments she required were to have handouts enlarged, access to material in electronic format, shorter reading lists, extended library loans and extra time in examinations. In addition, extra tuition was required in German because she had difficulty with the grammar. The disabled students adviser had 'bent over backwards' to help and the Politics department had also been very supportive:

> They did everything that they could. My tutor would give me extra tuition to try and get me through and if he hadn't I wouldn't have passed it. So they did everything they could, they enlarged everything and I got them to record things.

This positive experience contrasted with negative encounters with lecturers in History and German:

History, we kind of drew a blank there, they were very difficult to approach, and they couldn't accept it, they couldn't understand it and therefore they weren't really willing to do anything. They have improved slightly this year, in that my course coordinator was more efficient than last year, it's a different one, and they have on the whole enlarged things for me. German's been a disaster. With German, again they really don't understand and they can't be bothered, they will forget the majority of the time to enlarge things. They don't realise, well they do realise, but they forget that I need extra time in exams than I do in class and it really has been an uphill battle with German.

The reluctance to consider reasonable adjustments was evident in comments made by a lecturer in the German department:

Val's problem is that she is partially sighted so she has trouble reading things and that's a pretty basic problem if you are studying, I guess if you are studying anything at all, but particularly if you are studying a language. Funnily enough in the case of studying a language, we have an oral side and a reading and writing side. So in that sense she has unlimited and repeated access to one side of the subject, she doesn't have easy and accessible access to the other side which is the reading and writing and I'm absolutely amazed that she can get by studying a language given the hindrance that she has. You know, not to be able to pick up a book and read it. When you are studying a subject at university, where half the subjects are literary subjects . . . it comes through in Val's grammar. She does have quite severe problems with this and we have discussed it.

Val accepted that her impairment contributed to difficulties in studying, but felt that departments were wrong to insist that all students should undertake exactly the same work, without considering the learning outcomes they were trying to achieve.

I would certainly say I have struggled with the work and I probably might have struggled anyway but it certainly has been a big drain on me because . . . obviously it takes much longer to read stuff and much longer to gather information and it was often a problem that they didn't realise, they did realise but they wouldn't take that into consideration. For instance, in Politics I told them and one of the things you had to do was read a book every week, and I can't read a book every week as it takes me much longer than anybody else and they didn't accept that and it's put a great strain on my eyes. I can only do a certain amount, and then I've had enough. Normally after I've done a day's lecture I've had enough anyway, but I have to carry on. My mother thinks it's putting a strain on my health, but I'm a nervy person anyway, I'm a tense person and I'm the kind of person who wants to get 100 per cent all the time. Obviously with the added difficulty it does increase the pressure.

Despite acknowledging the difficulties arising as a result of the impairment, Val was in no doubt that the lack of adjustments was a major contributing factor. One department, for example, compiled an introductory reading list with 500 texts on it, although they were eventually persuaded to identify ten of these texts as central. The library borrowing system, organised into general and short-term loans, was also very rigid:

> Obviously most of the books students want are on short loan and I have had a lot of problems in trying to get books . . . we tried to get them to extend it, we said, 'Look, this isn't going to work. I certainly can't just have it for four hours – can you extend it for the whole day from nine to five?' No, they wouldn't do that. 'Would you be able to extend it over a night so that I could have it for two days?' No, it was a completely fixed system and they just said that they couldn't do it and it would be unfair to other students and that they would be put to a disadvantage. I wouldn't want to do that, and I understand from the library's point of view but it doesn't help me. So they were very firm that they wouldn't back down on that.

A key feature of Val's experience was differential practice with regard to the provision of support for learning. A lecturer in Politics provided additional one-to-one support to help Val complete the course. This contrasted with German, where it was believed that any extra tuition should be paid for by the individual student. A lecturer explained:

> Val told me she had put an advert in the staff news for extra help and I was delighted that a retired member of staff contacted her about it and then I was disappointed to hear that Val might not be able to manage it financially. And that's a real shame because she definitely does need extra tuition in German grammar . . . We have a special needs officer in the school and I asked if there was any money available for special needs students and she told me there is no money. She told me she had tried to get money for equipment for Val and had failed even to do that. But when it comes to tuition, all students would want tuition. There are lots of needy cases that would require extra tuition and it would be hard to argue for Val to take priority over other students' needs for extra tuition.

Val's case illustrates the uncertainties over who has responsibility for making reasonable adjustments, which students should receive them and how such adjustments impact on the notion of fairness. Whereas in school it is accepted in principle that pupils should receive however much support is needed for them to learn, in university it appears to be the case that standard provision is available, reflecting the belief that the best students will then emerge. In reality, it is evident that disparate practices emerge in different departments, partly as a result of the beliefs of individual lecturers. Whereas institutions believe that they are moving towards proactive support (see Chapter 3), evidence from the ground suggests that *ad hoc* arrangements often prevail.

Robbie: Scottish College 1

The final student case study presented in this chapter, Robbie, was studying for an HND in Multi-Media Technology in a Scottish college of further and higher education. As noted in Chapter 3, Scotland has far more students studying higher education courses in a further education context than is the case in England (about 20 per cent of all higher education full-time equivalents). Interesting contrasts emerged between university and college understanding and implementation of the concept of reasonable adjustment, and these are highlighted below.

Robbie was profoundly deaf and communicated almost entirely using sign language, although he had some lip-reading ability. His mother and father were also profoundly deaf and his father worked for a voluntary organisation for deaf children. Robbie attended a special unit for deaf children in his local mainstream school and applied to Scottish College 1 because it was an established resource base for deaf students with a reputation which had been established over a 20 year period. In his last two years at secondary school, Robbie visited the college on a number of occasions to meet up with the lecturer with responsibility for deaf students in the Faculty of Learning Support. He finally decided to apply because of the presence of a deaf community, and hoped to transfer to a university to complete a degree programme at the end of the two-year HND:

> I didn't research any other universities or colleges, I just thought this would be the right place for me because of the visit I had been on before, and from talking to deaf friends who knew that interpreters were available.

Robbie was awarded the DSA, which paid for part of the cost of sign language interpreters, a PC and computer software. It was planned that he would receive support from sign language interpreters in most of his lectures at the start of the programme, although a shortage of interpreters meant that this was not always possible. Attendance at lectures without a sign language interpreter was only useful if notes were provided in advance, and this was not always the case.

Unlike the universities, it was expected that all lecturers would be knowledgeable about a range of impairments, and they were encouraged to attend a deaf awareness course at the start of each academic year. The fact that lecturers were not engaged in research left more time for staff development at the beginning and end of sessions. Because of the regular presence of deaf students, most lectures had a good understanding of the adjustments required and learning support staff saw staff development as a key part of their remit:

> We've recently in the college run a deaf awareness session and that's open to any members of staff who want to come in and find out a bit more. And we also through our staff development programmes try and pick up issues that people are wanting some more background on. So I suppose it's like the Chinese drip, though you never reach everybody or sometimes you are putting on training that's not at an appropriate time for people. But it's just a constant keeping it on the boil.

Compared with universities, where first and second year classes were often very large, there were usually only 20 students in Robbie's classes, and therefore individual attention was much more likely. For example, a lecturer described the way in which he encouraged active engagement with deaf students during his class:

> I don't want Robbie to feel he has got to sit back and because he can't hear doesn't mean he can't ask a question in the normal way as everybody else does. Even if his interpreter is not here, he can always write it on a bit of paper and give me it. It might be a stigma that he feels but I try to discourage asking questions at the end or not asking questions at all. I try and get them into the way of interacting with everybody else, I feel that's important.

Recognising the needs of deaf students, lecturers were more likely to use PowerPoint presentations, although the appropriate equipment was not available in all classrooms. Even in this environment, however, basic mistakes in teaching were made. Robbie said:

> If they look at the overheads when they are showing them, and are talking at the same time, that's a problem. I can't look at the interpreter and the overhead at the same time. Sometimes you get interpreters who ask them and they can get a bit nippy.

The learning support lecturer explained that priority was given to finding the optimal environment in which deaf students could learn. At an individual level, that entailed discussing specific needs in depth and putting in rather more support than the student required:

> I tend to say to students at the beginning, look, I'd rather put in too much support at the beginning and then have to withdraw it, than you have to tell me everything is fine, I'm coping, and then at the last minute we discover you are failing. So I would rather put in too much support at the beginning, and then you tell me, 'No, go away, I don't need you'. Fine, we're happy to go away. So I always try to emphasise to them that it will be safety first, if you like. We will put in the maximum, whatever that happens to be. For some, they may want signing in every class. Now, you know for the timetable that there are going to be classes where they don't necessarily need that, because it's a very practical class, so the interpreter is going to be sitting there. But for some of them, they need the security of that until they gain the confidence that the lecturer knows them, they know the lecturer, their classmates know them and then they can relax into it.

This contrasted with many universities, where assessment and support, particularly for students with dyslexia and mental health difficulties, tended to follow a crisis when the student was at risk of quitting the course.

Classes were sometimes rearranged to enable deaf students to learn together as a group. A learning support lecturer in the Scottish college explained the reason for organising some classes separately for deaf students:

> Now communications is always problematic for deaf students because they can't listen, well not can't, but they do have to have alternatives to talking and listening, which means they have to have their certificate adapted and all the rest of it. So we started off when they first came here, the student just went with their own class to the communication class, and it was absolutely diabolical. The students were stressed out, I was stressed out, the lecturer was stressed out. So after a couple of years trying that, at a meeting of the group, I said, 'What do you think? You know, how would you feel about having separate communication classes?' And it was like, 'Yes, we'd much rather do that with other deaf students. That way you would get more time, and it means that the communications lecturer can concentrate more. He would maybe get six students rather than a class of twenty with one deaf student in it. And since then, that is what we've done. So I kind of look at all the timetable and cobble together times when students are free, and then we set up specific communication classes for deaf students.

Despite the provision of sign language interpreters in classes, these were not available to support social activities. However, Robbie did not experience this as a problem:

> Well really a deaf person concentrates on the deaf group anyway and I've met a lot of new deaf people here anyway, if you like, new deaf friends. I'm not bothered about the prospect of not knowing these other hearing people.

If his deaf friends were going to a social event:

> . . . then I wouldn't want or need an interpreter to be there because I wouldn't be mingling with any of the hearing folk.

In Chapter 4, we drew attention to the relatively generous funding of learning support in Scottish College 1, with additional support being paid for directly by the Scottish Executive. Robbie's experience illustrates the positive outcomes of these funding arrangements in a particular context. As a result of this investment in the institution, responsibility for making reasonable adjustments was much more likely to be accepted by lecturers, who did not perceive a gap between their own and institutional priorities and the requirements of anti-discrimination legislation.

Key themes

The limits of reasonable adjustments in the context of the DDA

In most universities, the easiest adjustments to make concerned access to additional aids and services which were paid for by the DSA. Computing equipment was made available for almost all students, and the funds available meant that relatively generous provision could be made for students with lower support needs. However, equipment was often not available until the course had commenced, so that students had no time to familiarise themselves with it. As illustrated in Chapter 6, the provision of personal assistants, note takers and sign language interpreters was more problematic. Difficulties arose with regard to employment, training and supply of suitably qualified individuals. Students with more significant impairments often relied on informal help from friends, family or volunteers.

Adjustments which involved altering policies and practices were perceived as being more difficult. In particular, requests to lecturers to alter their teaching methods were often received unsympathetically. A minority of lecturers, particularly in Scottish College 1, were very keen to make their classes interactive and accessible. In contrast with this, Val described her on-going difficulty in persuading lecturers to provide enlarged handouts:

> I've had several talks with them through the couple of years. They are distressed at the time when they realise that things are not going right and they say, 'Oh yes, we will put that right' but it's just words, it's not actions, and it's not sincere and you just need to keep badgering them. . . . The majority of the time they say, 'Oh I forgot to enlarge that for you' and I think, 'I've been in your class all semester, you should know, you shouldn't have to have me to keep reminding you'.

There were very few examples of the curriculum being modified for disabled students. At Scottish University 3, a lecturer explained that they had adapted field trips to allow students with mobility difficulties to examine rocky outcrops at the side of the road rather than off the beaten track, but other plans to construct virtual field trips had to be put on hold because of other institutional pressures. At some institutions, lecturers had co-operated in identifying key texts for students with visual impairments, but in other institutions this had been more problematic. Adaptations to assessment almost always consisted of additional time in examinations, but there were very few examples of modifications to the mode or content of assessment and students appeared unaware of their right to request alternatives to written examinations or coursework. Even within the same institution, lecturers often had only a hazy understanding of institutional policy on reasonable adjustments in assessment. For example, there was a lack of consistency within and between institutions with regard to making allowance for poor spelling or structuring.

One of the most common adjustments required by disabled students was access to lecturers' notes in electronic format before lectures so that these could be downloaded in the student's preferred format. Lecturers were very unlikely to comply with this request, particularly in pre-92 universities. Reasons given for this were that if notes were available in advance, students would not come to lectures. Furthermore, lecturers felt that notes were their intellectual property and they did not want them to be reproduced without their permission. Finally, a number of lecturers said that they did not have written lecture notes but preferred to lecture spontaneously, pulling together information from a wide range of sources just before their lecture. To have a formal written lecture would take away from the creativity of lecturing and make it more of a mechanical activity. However, it was also evident that, far from constantly revising their notes, many lecturers were using photocopied handouts which had been produced many years before, some of which were scarcely legible. A number of students commented that age was a significant feature here; younger lecturers were more likely to use IT, including PowerPoint, and be less precious about sharing their lecture notes.

A major theme in the accounts of lecturers in the two pre-92 universities was anxieties about the 'dumbing down' of academic work. A lecturer in Scottish University 3 commented:

I think the issue is with academic standards and again this will really only come because as I say people are really sympathetic in Geography anyway. It will come to the fore when we have a lot more students who fall into the disabled group and what we will get is the student who is disabled and a bad student, a student who is disabled and is a bit lazy, and I think people are not quite sure what to do because of the PC nature of it. These are the cases that will be difficult because the question arises, is the student using their disability as an excuse for being lazy? But most of the people we have had so far are here because it isn't yet mainstream and they have struggled so hard to get here and they are willing. As I say, in the past it's been a case of asking the lecturer, 'Can I have this extra thing, can I tape the lecture and go away and rewrite it?' So they are going through all this extra work, so they tend to be the students who are motivated.

A particularly difficult area concerned the adjustments required by dyslexic students who said they were having problems with structuring their work as a result of their dyslexia:

Yes, I had a student who was making this case to me today when he was talking about advising him to honours. He was saying, 'I have problems with the exams because I can't structure'. I always have questions about structure because there are students who are not dyslexic who say that as well.

Generally, adjustments made for disabled students were reactive rather than anticipatory, as the legislation requires. Scottish College 1 provided an example of a more anticipatory approach, having a permanent contract with a sign language interpretation unit, which supplied a set number of interpreters who were then deployed throughout the college.

Implicit understandings of equality

Particularly in the pre-92 universities, there were concerns that making adjustments for disabled students might involve disadvantaging others who might also have pressing needs, but might not have been identified as disabled. With regard to making adjustments for poor spelling, for example, lecturers could not understand why allowances should be made for dyslexic students but not for students from socially disadvantaged backgrounds or overseas students. Other adjustments which were refused on grounds of fairness included extended access to course materials or library books and additional contact hours with lecturing staff. Lecturers in pre-92 universities were resistant to the idea that students from under-represented groups should be admitted with lower grades; the aim, rather, should be to improve state education to erode differential levels of attainment.

As we noted earlier, the DDA is based on the idea that fairness can only be achieved if adjustments are made to equalise the position of those who experience substantial and adverse effects of long-term impairment. There seems to be considerable evidence, however, to suggest that some staff in traditional universities operate with the idea that equality means treating everyone the same. Bourdieu and Passeron (1977) argued that the politics of formal equality, applied in this way, are a robust mechanism for guaranteeing inequality since they assume that all learners come equally equipped for the process of learning. This assumption accentuates the social and cultural advantages already possessed by some learners which educators assume to be normal. In the same way, by expecting disabled students to perform in exactly the same way as every one else, institutions may accentuate their existing disadvantages.

The funding of reasonable adjustments

The ring-fencing of a central resource to fund reasonable adjustments appeared critical to their success. For 20 years, Scottish College 1 had received preferential funding from the Scottish Executive to cater for the needs of deaf students. The existence of a deaf community and the college's ability to organise sign language interpretation services meant that the number of deaf students was growing. Higher education students were taught in small classes and lecturers regarded disabled students as part of their core clientele, rather than a small group making additional demands. They were also able to draw on the expertise of lecturers in the Faculty of Learning Support. Raab (1998) and Gallagher (2002) have noted that Scotland's colleges have attracted a much higher percentage of students from disadvantaged backgrounds to their HE courses compared with universities. However, it should be noted that whilst the culture and ethos of colleges may favour disabled students, these may experience difficulties with modes of assessment, teaching methods and access to staff in the much bigger universities to which they transfer (Gallagher *et al.*, 1997). By way of contrast, funding for disabled students in most universities was patchy, although some universities had found ways of pooling individual DSAs to fund particular posts, such as a mental health support tutor (see Chapter 7).

Academic cultures and the impact of performativity in higher education

As noted earlier, university lecturers believe that there has been a gradual erosion of academic freedom and an intensification of academic work, with a new emphasis on performativity. Many academics in pre-92 universities explained that their efforts had been directed into fulfilling research assessment exercise commitments, distracting attention from teaching:

Well the TQA and the RAE have had a disastrous effect on universities and the reason is really very simple. When the government in the 1990s made our funding dependent on student numbers, that automatically had the effect, when considering students, when doing our job, we have to have at least one eye on the finances. We no longer have both eyes on the ball, education and academic matters, scientific work, we have to have one eye on financial matters. To put it crudely, the new financial system puts pressures on us to pass students who would have previously failed.

  . . . So that's TQA and you mentioned the RAE. The problem with the RAE is that it again, in effect, it's a government scheme. In effect the government tells us academics how often we should put papers out and in what format we should put them out so we get financial support for publishing RAE-type publications which means single-authored monographs and substantial articles but apparently not for student textbooks or review articles for edited books, for attending conferences that won't lead to an RAE-type article themselves yet all those do exist, they are not peripheral, they are essential. . . . And so that's one problem. The second problem . . . is that the RAE forces us to be conservative in our research and not adventurous and not creative and original and indeed not critical. It's much harder with the RAE to engage dialectically in our subjects. That is to say to criticise other people. To go out on a limb and say something different, now again that's fundamental to science. So to answer your question, the RAE and TQA have led to a disastrous situation in our working conditions and I'm afraid that I regret to say that very much but it is a fact and I think the sooner the universities face up to it the better and what I don't understand is why don't the universities tell the government this.

The teaching quality regime in particular was associated in a negative way with managerialist control of universities. Lecturers were generally unaware of the QAA's Code of Practice in relation to disabled students, but given the general opposition to quality control mechanisms among teaching staff in pre-92 universities, they would have been unenthusiastic about compliance. It was pointed out that some practices in universities, which had been introduced on grounds of standardisation of practice, such as anonymous marking, were likely to militate against disabled students because they made informal allowances impossible.

  The RAE was also blamed for prioritising research over teaching, which meant that lecturers had little time to devote to the type of curriculum change activities promoted in the Teachability Project:

As I was saying, everything is being run by the RAE and with your ESRC grant to do this piece of research you're in that game as much as everyone else. . . . So that's your number 1, 2, and 3 priority and every-thing else is done on some relic of professionalism and goodwill and all the rest of it. So I think, I'm sure the RAE will continue but the sad thing about all this is, I'm sure there are people out there that would love to say, 'Right, okay, well what am I going to achieve this semester as well as all my teaching? I'm really going to try and make these courses accessible', but the difficulty is finding the time to do that with the pressures of the RAE so I think it's going to be a longer process than it might have been and a more *ad hoc* process than it might have been.

In post-92 universities, there was less evidence of lecturers feeling pressured to meet RAE targets, and lecturers were more likely to perceive widening access as a central part of the institutional mission, rather than an external constraint.

Conclusion

Disabled students may provide a lens through which universities' capacity to respond and adapt to needs of under-represented groups may be viewed. It was evident that, despite the duty placed on institutions to make anti-cipatory adjustments to meet the needs of disabled students, in practice the nature of the adjustments was very limited. Whilst payments to individual students provided support in the form of equipment, the funds available were inadequate to meet the needs of students with more significant impair-ments. Particularly in pre-92 universities, lecturers used very traditional lecturing methods in many subjects and were often unable or unwilling to make their notes available electronically. College lecturers working with small groups were more likely to be flexible in their approaches to teaching and to have less fixed views about a body of knowledge to be conveyed. Some policies and practices in pre-92 universities reflected the view that equality entails treating all students the same, in direct contravention of the spirit of the DDA. There were also concerns that making adjustments for some students, particularly those with dyslexia, may lead to a reduction of standards generally. Pre-92 universities were particularly likely to believe that academic freedom had been eroded through a range of managerialist measures, giving them less time and freedom to respond to the needs of disabled students. This finding was also borne out by responses to the institutional questionnaire reported in Chapter 3.

Chapter 6

Disabled students' experiences of access and independence

Introduction

In previous chapters we have identified a number of factors which have shaped the wider policy context in which provision for disabled students has developed. Widening access policies, the Disabled Students Allowance, premium funding, the requirements of the Quality Assurance Agency, the Research Assessment Exercise and Part 4 of the Disability Discrimination Act have all been crucial in establishing how diverse institutions have developed support for disabled students. As referred to in Chapter 4, the dominant model of support has been located within a welfare-based discourse, promoting the idea of professionally assessed needs rather than rights. However, as outlined in Chapter 5, the requirement of Part 4 of the Disability Discrimination Act that reasonable adjustments be made to pedagogy and curriculum has added impetus to the need for academic departments to provide ongoing support to disabled students. In this chapter we examine in detail the experiences of three disabled students, Paula, Peter and Shelly, in order to shed light on how current forms of provision for disabled students are impacting on their academic and social experience of higher education. We begin by presenting brief pen portraits of each student, indicating the main difficulties they have encountered in accessing and achieving independence within higher education.

A particular focus of this chapter is the extent to which ideas drawn from the independent living movement are currently being applied in higher education. According to Barnes (2003) independent living is a radical concept providing an ideological and practical solution to the everyday environmental and cultural problems encountered by disabled people. If disabled people are enabled to purchase and organise their own support, they are likely to have a sense of agency and empowerment. The control of assessment and service delivery by professionals, acting as agents of the state, is likely to locate disabled people as the passive recipients of services. The independent living movement has its origins in the campus culture of US universities during the 1960s, when a range of self-help groups were established by and for students with severe physical impairments who were enabled to attend mainstream classes. Activities ranged from wheelchair repair (Watson and Woods, 2005) to the establishment of personal assistance schemes. Subsequently, the idea has been applied through schemes such as direct payments in the UK, whereby cash payments are made to disabled people to purchase the support services they are assessed as needing. Barnes (2003) points out that independent living is the type of concept which is capable of appealing to those on the right and the left of the political spectrum. In its guise of radical consumerism, it offers the possibility of more effective and efficient services, and a reduction in the local state infrastructure. From another angle, independent living may be seen primarily as a tool to empower disabled people by challenging traditional paternalistic notions of dependency and promoting the autonomy of disabled people. In this chapter, we consider the experiences of disabled students with relatively high support needs, with a view to examining the extent to which the Disabled Students Allowance and other state benefits are sufficient to allow the principles of independent living to be put into practice within the context of higher education.

Student experiences of access and independence

Paula, English University 2

At the time of the research, Paula was a 19-year-old blind student attending English University 2. She was completing the first year of a three-year degree in Psychology and Sociology. Paula considered herself to be working class and was financially independent of her family. Her studies were funded through a combination of the Disabled Students Allowance and other disability benefits. Paula was anxious about incurring debt and resisted applying for a student loan to supplement her income. On her initial application to the university, Paula was particularly interested to discover how she could manage the environment and, in particular, her accommodation. The university facilitated this process through a personal interview and assessment which was offered to all students identified by the disability office from their applications as needing extra assistance. The details and anticipated needs of each student were then passed to each of their academic departments. For Paula, this assessment identified a number of support mechanisms, and arrangements were made for these to be implemented. In addition, the disability office arranged for a local organisation to provide Paula with familiarisation training around the campus for herself and her guide dog. This training was important for Paula who wanted to be confident about her surroundings before commencing her course:

> It took a little while to get a little bit organised. I came down for two weeks during the summer to do training with the dog and with the cane and that was because I wanted to come down and get my routes down

before I started and I didn't have to worry about where I was going on my first day, where the shops are, where the station is obviously for travelling back and forward, and where the gym and the library are. I tried to get the room numbers of the lecturers when I started. Things like that, so that I knew where the rooms were.

Paula lived in university accommodation and relied on her guide dog to navigate the campus. She felt that she has had a generally positive experience of university life but encountered some serious difficulties.

Barriers encountered by Paula

Paula's initial difficulties concerned the availability of equipment (including computer, scanner, printer, Braille Lite). Despite the fact that she had made the earliest possible application to her local authority, her equipment was not in place at the start of term:

> I just got grants from [local authority] which obviously they took a while to come through as I had to wait for the scanner and . . . oh the Braille Lite, I had to wait ages on the Braille Lite because of the money.
>
> *How long did it take to arrive?*
>
> Well what actually happened was that because the money was taking so long . . . I was starting university with nothing to take notes on.

In fact in common with almost all other students needing the DSA in order to obtain equipment, Paula was forced to wait until after Christmas in her first year before receiving the full payment of DSA which enabled her to obtain a Braille Lite machine. A second source of difficulty for Paula involved organising and managing the employment of her reader. As she understood it, her initial assessment determined that she had the use of a reader for approximately five hours per day. The tasks of organising reading in time for classes and coursework and maintaining records of time spent by the reader she experienced as very stressful:

> I really do get stressed out but I think that's a personal thing and I think it's because there is so much reading. But I think if you can cut it down a little bit that helps you know and I think I just get stressed out that I will not be able to do all the reading on time. But it is hard work. I think it is because you're always having to think in advance. Like I got a book last week with all the pages that I need to read for each week for like seminars and you're always like 'What are we doing in three weeks time?' because he [the reader] needs to go and do it now so that I can have it on time and it can get quite hectic I suppose.

In her first interview Paula made it clear to the researcher that she was finding managing her reader a difficult process, particularly in terms of knowing how much material she needed to be read or have scanned and converted to Braille:

> You can get some books from the Braille library and you can also get books on tapes which you can use as well and apart from that my reader's big job is to scan in books. Like he finds books and then prints them out in Braille and he has to do a lot of editing as well, pictures and stuff like that. The other thing that struck me actually was that because when you first start uni, you obviously don't know how much work you'll have and all that sort of stuff and it's quite hard to judge you know, how much material you'll need to get . . . and I think that's what the problem was because I just got so inundated with you know, material.

At the time of her second interview in her second year at university it was clear that Paula had accumulated considerable debt. This was entirely due to the fact that she had signed time sheets for her reader which had then cumulatively exceeded her support allowance as determined by the DSA:

> Because you get a certain amount for your readers per year and because my reader has to work like 37 instead of 25 hours a week, he was working more than he should be. I couldn't say to him 'Right you've to stop working' because if I said that I wouldn't have gotten the work done and been able to sit exams and that you know. So he had to like continue doing the work for me and he was quite happy to do that. But at the end of the day I ended up in like three thousand pounds of debt because I went way over what the limit was. I wasn't so bothered in the beginning because I thought, well I'll just write to [local authority] and say what happened and they'll pay it. They didn't, so I wrote to my MP so he tried and they still wouldn't pay it.

In the final interview, Paula explained that she was personally responsible for the debt to her reader which was then in the region of £3,000. Determined not to have the burden of a student loan, she was writing to a number of charitable organisations to see if they would help her pay at least part of this debt. Paula had simply signed her reader's time sheets and was unaware that she was accumulating debt:

> *How do you work with a reader – do you have to pay them yourself and then claim the money back, what way does it work?*

> [Name of reader] actually puts in time sheets and he's entitled to work like five hours a day, so he puts down how many hours he has worked and stuff like that and then they will send him his wages.

So you're not responsible for it then?

No, I just say that he's done the work, but I'm not responsible for his money.

The disability office at the university was equally shocked to learn of Paula's accumulated debt but felt that they had not the resources to manage her funding budget for her.

Paula had mixed experiences of academic support. In her first year, it was not clear to her how much reading she actually needed to do so she opted to do as much as possible. At the end of her first year, aware of her accumulating debt, Paula was beginning to realise the value of discussing and negotiating reading with lecturers on an individual basis. This was something at which she was gradually becoming more adept:

> They are not too bad, some are better than others obviously. I think it depends on what your course is like as well, 'cause I found that I have a History module, which is like optional and the way that was done was that you had to read lots of references for the first assignment and then you had like a second assignment where you had to do lots as well. So things like that I had to look at cuttings 'cause I felt that I was not going to be able to read all these books as well. So I actually had a chat with the guy who was doing it and it worked out that when I was doing my first assignment from books, I could do my second assignment and it would sort of cut the workload down and just practical things like that you can work into your course with the lecturer. About deadlines they have been okay so far but my lecturers have all asked me if I would like to put a couple of weeks on or whatever. They are quite willing so that's quite nice.

While Paula could make effective use of her Braille Lite machine for taking notes in lectures, she was dependent on lecturers providing her with guidelines of the work they would be covering and, in particular, reading lists of material to be covered. This required lecturers to be prepared and able to provide Paula with the appropriate course material in advance. The disability officer felt that it has taken considerable effort to bring this about but that lecturers were now beginning to respond:

> It's a bit of a sea change in this institution to have everything like that so far in advance of a new academic year, for many areas anyhow. So that took some shoving and pushing around in the school by the disability support tutor and ourselves, and a lot of chasing around during the summer. But eventually I think we got there and I've emailed Paula attachments of module guides and so on and so forth.
>
> (Interview with disability officer)

A particular, and very practical, problem was cleaning up after the guide dog. The university disability office managed to provide her with a dog pen in which the dog was trained to go to the toilet. However the faeces then had to be cleaned up. In her first year, cleaning and janitorial staff helped Paula, but this help was withdrawn in her second year. Although somewhat amusing for Paula, it was also a real problem when people complained about the mess and smell:

> I have had a kind of problem with that this year so what I've had to do is because it's like a job that nobody really volunteers to do, I have to like clean it up myself which is quite amusing because it's like well how do you know where the shite is?

At present Paula is in the bizarre situation of having to have a person direct her in terms of cleaning up the faeces:

> They have this policy where the people who are on the precinct, like the cleaners and security guards and all that sort of stuff, they're not allowed to pick up the dog shite which I thought was a bit daft but never mind. They're not allowed to pick the dog shit up so I've got this thing that I get the security guard to tell me where it is and he directs me to it and I pick it up, it's so stupid.

In addition to cleaning the pen, Paula then has the further difficulty of having to have it disinfected. Again there is no help available in this process and Paula finds it difficult:

> The other problem that I had, talking about pens, the other problem that I had was because you have to disinfect it. You have to take the disinfectant out in a bucket with a handle and it takes about four or five buckets to wash it out and all that so the problem I have there is to get from inside my flat to outside. You have to go through about three doors and you know how you don't have a big enough bucket of water, so when you come out of the flat most of the water's over you.

The disability officer made reference to the fact that Paula had received some training in this matter and was now confident in view of fewer complaints that it was no longer a problem:

> The problem was getting someone to clean it and as I said earlier there's two or three times I've just hopped in the car and gone up and done it myself you know, and I think really, talking to [local guide dog organisation], they've subsequently come down and worked with Paula

and trained her and taught her how to do it herself and as far as I'm concerned because I haven't had complaints from the estates now about it not being cleaned out and stuff that appears to have solved the problem.

(Interview with disability officer)

Peter, English University 1

Peter was a first year student studying History at English University 1. He had high support needs and required 24-hour assistance. He was able to move around independently in an electric wheelchair but for the majority of his time he was accompanied by a personal assistant funded by the local education authority. Peter's support was divided into two shifts with cover for the evenings being provided through the Independent Living Fund. Peter ultimately hoped to become a sports journalist. He was happy to acknowledge his impairment and support needs on the UCAS form and felt that this was necessary for him to receive the correct response from the university:

> With the UCAS form they have all these choices of disabilities and obviously I ticked that I was disabled and in a wheelchair and Muscular Dystrophy and all that stuff. But then basically I discussed my needs with people before I started university in good time so that things could be organised.

The disability officer screened the UCAS forms to identify those who declared a disability. She then decided who should be invited for interview with regard to putting in place appropriate support, subsequently making contact with academic departments to inform them of individual students' needs. The disability officer was under pressure to streamline this process as the workload involved in individual negotiations with departments was becoming increasingly onerous. Peter believed that it was absolutely necessary to disclose information about his needs in order to receive the appropriate level of support:

> *Some people might be hesitant about divulging that kind of information [details of impairment] but you seem to be kind of matter of fact?*
>
> Yeah well I am really. It's the only way to deal with it. I don't think that being disabled has affected my life negatively at all. In many ways it has affected it positively, like you get disabled stickers and you can park the car wherever you want. So it hasn't affected my life negatively at all. So I'm quite happy telling people about my condition and it's vital that you do really to get stuff sorted out.

Barriers encountered by Peter

At the time of the research English University 1 had just completed an access audit in order to meet the HEFCE deadline of March 2002 and qualify for disability capital funding (approximately £300,000). The main concern for the disability officer appeared to be the accessibility of university buildings and the access routes between them. The audit involved extensive consultation with a range of different people including disabled students. In very general terms access issues had not been a major difficulty for Peter in terms of preventing or hindering him with his everyday life. However, it appeared that having access to a PA was very significant, for while Peter was able to move around unassisted, a combination of relatively minor access issues had the cumulative effect of hampering his independence around campus. The photographs on the following pages were taken by a researcher working with him and illustrate a number of the barriers facing him on a daily basis.

In lectures Peter took his own notes but with the agreement of his lecturers also recorded lectures onto mini-disc. This gave him the opportunity to go over parts of the lecture which might have been missed or only partially understood:

> I take my own notes but what I usually do is I've got this microphone and I record the lectures. But I do make notes through the lectures as well, then I can listen to it again and add to my notes. I'm probably not much slower at writing than other people but it's other issues like getting a piece of paper when I'm finished with one sheet or dropping my pen. So if I miss it I've got it recorded and I can listen to it again and make sure I catch everything and the lecturers have all been fine about that. There are no problems of it being recorded.

Peter found that lectures being made available online were particularly beneficial but this was only the case for one particular class:

> Oh yeah quite a few lecturers have a lecture structure but you know how that can fall away. There was one lecturer who actually had a website for the course and he put the lecture notes on the website after each lecture and you could use those lecture notes. But most of them just have a handout with the lecture structure.

Rather than more detailed notes?

Well this guy, he provided more detailed notes after the lecture.

Was that something that was particularly useful?

> It was useful certainly because last term there was an open exam at the end of the term so revising for that it was really helpful that I could listen to lectures again and check out the lecture notes online. It was really helpful.

Photograph 6.1 The photograph above shows a double door with a coded entry system on the larger of the two doors. Four bags of rubbish were piled slightly to the right of the main door. It was difficult for Peter to press the coded lock correctly and then manoeuvre sufficiently to gain entry. The bags of rubbish further complicated this process.

Photograph 6.2 Two large swing doors opening outwards are shown in this photograph. The handles were at a height of approximately 1.5 metres and the doors provided access to some of Peter's lecture rooms. Both doors had such a strong spring that it was virtually impossible for Peter to negotiate them by himself.

Photograph 6.3 Peter in his electric wheelchair is positioned in front of a first-floor lift. The lift was narrow and the entrance shielded by two book trolleys positioned at either side. The lift control buttons were located too high for Peter to reach. The presence of other people willing to assist meant that this difficulty was lessened.

Photograph 6.4 The main entrance to the university library is shown here, with a flat paved area with swing doors opening outwards. The volume of student traffic ensured there was usually someone to hold the door open, but the doors represented a major barrier at quieter times.

Photograph 6.5 The photo above shows the door to a lecturer's office. On the right-hand side of the door at a height of approximately 1.5 metres there is a noticeboard for students to see details of and sign up for tutorials. This notice is out of Peter's reach.

Shelly, Scottish University 1

Shelly was enrolled on a four-year course leading to a BSc in psychology at Scottish University 1. She had cerebral palsy, which affected one side of her body and created speech difficulties and problems with walking and balance. A PA supported her movement around the university campus. Shelly attended her local mainstream school and, while this was a positive experience, she felt that she was something of a 'guinea pig' in being the first disabled person to go through both her primary and high schools. On leaving school, Shelly took a gap year in order to work in a small business near her home. She then had a further but unintended year out after access difficulties at her first choice of university meant that she had to withdraw her application. Shelly lived in university accommodation and tried to visit home at least once a term but the length of the journey and the need to arrange for assistance prevented her going home as often as she would have liked.

Barriers encountered by Shelly

Shelly's academic experience had been very mixed. Whilst acknowledging that she required some help, her main wish was to be treated like any other student:

> I found that most lecturers just treat me the same as everybody else, which I'm really thankful for. I wouldn't like my lecturers to make a big issue of me being there. I just try to blend in and you know be like any other student, you know I only speak if I really need to but in saying that they all ask me how I'm getting on and if they can help.

She was confident that, with the use of a PA who also acted as a scribe, extra time in exams and accommodation adaptations, she could manage her university career. However, despite her confidence, there had been several serious difficulties. The first of these involved her first year Spanish class. Four weeks into the module, Shelly was summoned by the head of the Spanish department and told that she was not likely to succeed in the oral part of the module and as a result would be wise to give up Spanish and do another module:

> Last year when I did Spanish they were horrible. Four weeks into the module I was called to the head of Spanish and I wasn't told why. I thought it might have been about the paperwork and when I went in she said that they were worried about my speech and they felt that I wouldn't be able to do the module. So basically she said 'Could you go and do another module?' and it wasn't until that night that I felt 'How can they ask me to do another module when I'm four weeks into the term and I'm going to be four weeks behind, so I can't leave Spanish'.

In the class of about 20 people Shelly felt that she was largely ignored and was given separate work to do rather than joining in with the rest of the class in an oral session:

> I didn't join in with the others. I was set a separate task writing it, . . . writing what you are going to say and stuff like that. I was always made separate from the class.

Shelly was upset by this situation and, during a chance meeting in the corridor, brought it to the attention of the disability officer. The disability officer then made contact with the Spanish department who were upset that Shelly had made a complaint. The resolution of the matter was that Shelly was permitted to sit a written exam in place of her oral examination. The initial confrontation took Shelly by surprise and she obviously felt isolated and discriminated against by the Spanish department:

> You don't learn Spanish just to speak it. I was learning how to write it and read it and to ask me to go, you know! I mean my tutor, if my tutor said to me in the class or discussed it with me before she went to the head and said there was a problem, but she didn't. Well later on

that week I met [disability officer] and I mentioned it to him and he took it up. I don't see Spanish as any different from speaking English, it's a similar language you know ... I merely said that the next time I go to Spain I would just take a note pad and paper, at least I would be able to write and that's what I couldn't understand. There are people in Spain that have a speech problem, ... it's the same as speaking English and I know that I didn't have a problem in high school with languages ...

Shelly received DSA which paid for her laptop and her PA support. In her first year, Shelly's PA was recruited by the university and she had no real say in their appointment. While this enabled Shelly to commence her classes at the start of term, the person appointed was unqualified for the role:

Last year my PA was really, really quiet, painfully quiet and people would hesitate from speaking to me seeing her hanging around behind me. She was really, really shy, no fault of hers, she was only eighteen and had never been to college or university. Last year my PA had no experience of note taking so that it was very hard and that is one of the things I looked for when we were interviewing.

Also in her first year Shelly's PA was reluctant to scribe for her and this caused problems in terms of recruiting another person capable of undertaking both tasks:

In my first year for some reason my PA didn't want to scribe for me.

Was she embarrassed about it?

I don't know. She just said that she hadn't really done it before and she didn't really want to do it.

Not a good speller or something?

I wasn't going to force her so I had an exam in January and that was a disaster because I'd got this guy to scribe and he didn't understand a word I said. So I spent three hours spelling out the words in my essays and it was so disheartening. You know when he couldn't understand a word I said I had to spell it. Even words that were easy I had to spell and that was really hard. Towards the end all I wanted to do was go.

In her second year Shelly brought this situation to the attention of the disability officer and it was agreed that she should draw up an advertisement and select her PA with the assistance of the disability officer. A number of applicants were received and three interviews were conducted.

At the time of the research, Shelly had a PA for a standard 26 hours per week. This allocation of hours was problematic since support only covered her academic activities (usually five hours per day, Monday–Friday) and further assistance outside this period was not affordable. As a result, Shelly relied on the support of friends if she wanted to go shopping or to socialise with other students. On a number of weekends her friends were away and as a result Shelly was unable to leave her flat. This was a situation she was unhappy with but felt she had to accept.

Prompt payment of the PA was an additional problem as a result of delays in transferring the DSA. This caused financial difficulties for the PA and anxiety for Shelly that her PA might be forced to take another job:

> So she comes in and it's very good, but we are finding a big problem in her wages. What happens is we keep a time sheet of the hours and at the end of the month I add up the hours and submit an invoice to the award agency and the award agency sends the money to [PA]. But her wages have always been at least three weeks late and because she is only getting paid once a month, there is a big backlog and because her money is late she can't pay her bills or her rent. You know and it's her main job and nobody else would have been expected to put up with it.

As a result, the PA was forced to cut some of her hours and work in a bar in order to receive at least some wages more promptly:

> We put the last invoice in two weeks ago and there is no sign of any money, and already it's two weeks late. She's actually had to get a part-time job at night just to have money coming in.

Shelly tried to rectify this situation herself but, after constant unsuccessful appeals to the awards agency, she contacted her MSP in desperation. While this resulted in the prompt delivery of the next payment, Shelly remained anxious that subsequent payments would be delayed, with the risk that the PA might leave.

Discussion

Despite the difficulties encountered, each student described their overall experience of higher education in very positive terms. However, this should not mask the fact that each of them encountered significant barriers, which could, in different circumstances or for other disabled students, result in withdrawal from university. Paula's experience of delays in having essential equipment installed prior to commencing her studies was common. Even those who applied to their awarding agency early in the summer faced delays until at least October in their first semester before equipment arrived and was functional. For Paula, this was a major inconvenience which not only compromised her study, but contributed to the debt she accumulated since she was forced to use her reader rather than scanning material herself. No other support was forthcoming, and disability officers could do little to accelerate the process. Individual students were left to put whatever pressure they could on the awarding agencies to speed things up.

Shelly and Paula faced more serious difficulties in dealing with awards agencies and in particular managing the responsibility of staff hours and payments. For both Paula and Shelly this was a new position of responsibility for which they had little preparation. In her first year, Shelly allowed the university to appoint her PA. Although apprehensive at not having been involved in this process, she felt that it would ensure that she could start university with the necessary support in place. The university chose to appoint a volunteer from a national voluntary organisation. This practice was also common in other case study institutions and problems inevitably arose. The voluntary organisation had a responsibility for the personal development of their volunteer, which often focused on developing their confidence and self-esteem. The role of personal assistant for the disabled student was regarded as of secondary importance. In Shelly's situation, the person appointed initially was not equipped for the role and this created significant difficulties. Fortunately in her second year Shelly had the opportunity to advertise and be involved in the appointment of her own PA, which gave her much more of a sense of control.

Unlike Paula, who over-ran her support budget, Shelly managed to avoid debt but only at the expense of limiting her PA support, relying instead on friends to assist in practical outings such as shopping and social events. Clearly Shelly's access to the wider benefits of university life were limited. It was apparent that both Paula and Shelly needed support in managing people and budgets. They both experienced significant emotional stress in dealing with their PAs and readers, to whom they felt responsible as friends and employers.

Problems in dealing with everyday barriers, often arising as a result of other people's carelessness, was evident in Peter's experiences captured in the photographs above. Peter found the entrance to his accommodation difficult to negotiate due to the type of lock on the door and the regular presence of rubbish obstructing the doorway. The library main door, lifts and catalogue were all problematic while his lecture rooms were sometimes difficult to reach and signing up for a tutorial could be impossible. In order to have these difficulties addressed, it was necessary to draw attention to each of them, probably on an individual basis and to a number of different university staff. In isolation, each of the issues illustrated could have been resolved relatively easily, with the exception of the library main door. However, their cumulative effect was significant. Determined to be treated as any other student and to get on with his course, Peter chose not to spend his time drawing attention to various access issues, preferring instead to rely heavily on his PA to overcome them.

While Paula, Peter and Shelly were each making steady academic progress, the support received from academic departments and staff was varied. Paula spoke positively of her lecturers but nevertheless received little initial guidance on her reading lists. Taking the initiative, she had partly resolved this difficulty by approaching individual lecturers to help organise her reading. Fortunately for Paula, these difficulties were recognised by the disability officer and a new system was established to provide her with more detailed module guidance in advance. Peter recorded each of his lectures as well as making notes but benefited greatly from the actions of one lecturer who made his lecture notes available to all students on the web immediately after each lecture. This simple practice made lectures more accessible to Peter and benefited other students. However, such innovative practice was rare across the 48 student case studies and was dependent on initiatives taken by individual lecturers rather than wider change at an institutional level. Shelly's experience in her Spanish class echoes that of Val (see Chapter 5) and illustrates the reluctance of staff to move beyond a focus on individual impairments towards a new focus on reasonable adjustments. Again the onus to resolve this situation fell on the individual student, with the department involved seeking to avoid responsibility for change. As a result of her tenacity, Shelly remained on the course, but the adjustments made were minimal.

Conclusion

The difficulties encountered by Paula, Peter and Shelly reflect the tensions inherent in the current policy environment which sees disability as located within a student welfare discourse, with some limited attempts to increase the responsibility of academic departments. While some specific individual support is necessary in order to deal with DSA claims and the organisation of equipment and resources, the major barriers to inclusion appear to lie in a general disregard for the rights of disabled students to equal access. As discussed in Chapter 5, departments are often reluctant to recognise their responsibility to make reasonable adjustments to teaching and assessment arrangements. In addition, even when adequate support is in place, there appears to be a casual disregard for disabled students' right to access buildings and services, reflected in practices such as stacking plastic bags in front of self-opening doors or pinning a class list at an inaccessible level.

Because academic departments persist in seeing disabled students as the responsibility of the disability officer, barriers are very slow to be addressed and a significant burden is placed on disability services. Even if only one electronic communication per student was required, this would need to be generated by a disability officer, and, in order to be effective, reach all relevant academic staff. This in itself would generate a considerable challenge to communication processes in any institution. It comes then as no surprise that 'fixing' individual students' difficulties as they arise is a particularly difficult task. As a result disabled students are required to address, negotiate and resolve a number of difficulties by themselves. This places considerable extra demands on disabled students and assumes that they will have the necessary confidence and skills to address them. Borrowing from the familiar discourse of 'Person specification' found in many job descriptions, the following table summarises some of the skills and qualities which disabled students need to have for a successful experience of higher education:

'Essential qualities' for disabled students

- Excellent interpersonal and communication skills
- Ability to liaise/negotiate with academic staff
- An understanding of academic practice in higher education
- In addition, must be prepared to work flexible hours including some evening and weekend work (more than non-disabled students)

'Desirable qualities'

- Experience of managing budgets
- Experience of employing staff
- Sound understanding of student learning barriers and strategies to address these
- An ability to work independently as well as in a team in identifying problems and seeking imaginative solutions to them

Shifting from a primarily welfare-based model of student support towards a rights-based approach, which recognises the duty of academic departments to teach and assess in an accessible manner, may not alleviate all of the demands placed on individual disabled students as summarised above. It would, however, lessen the burden of individual responsibility experienced by disabled students challenging the difficulties they encounter. Independent living is based on the premise that basic resources should be made available to disabled people to procure the support they need to achieve autonomy, whilst at the same time the barriers to inclusion are systematically dismantled. It appears that, for students with the highest support needs, the level of resourcing is inadequate and the commitment to a rights-based approach has not yet been achieved.

Chapter 7

Support for students with mental health difficulties in higher education

The students' perspective

Introduction

The number of students in higher education experiencing mental health difficulties is increasing. A recent report from the Heads of University Counselling Services (1999) reports an increase in the number of students with severe psychological problems presenting themselves to university counselling services. Student suicides have increased from 2.4 (1983–4) to 9.7 per 100,000 (1993–4) (Mental Health Foundation, 2001) and official statistics from the Higher Education Statistics Agency (HESA) suggest that the percentage of students declaring a mental health difficulty on entry to higher education rose from 1.8 per cent in 1995–6 to 3.3 per cent in 1999–2000. In reality, the actual percentages are likely to be higher, given that these figures only include students willing to disclose a mental health difficulty on entry to higher education. Many more cases are likely to go undisclosed or to emerge at a later stage.

The world of higher education is beginning to take note of this increase. A number of initiatives have been taken. For example, Universities UK have published a guide to reducing student suicides (UUK, 2002), and the Higher Education Funding Council for England (HEFCE) has funded a number of institution-based initiatives aimed at mapping the extent of student mental health difficulties, raising staff awareness and sharing good practice. In addition, a number of institutions see this as a priority area for development and have appointed specialist staff or committees to develop policy in this area. There is a long way to go, however: management and support staff in the case study institutions made clear that provision for students with mental health difficulties, beyond the provision of counselling services, was an area that they were only just beginning to grapple with at a wider institutional level.

The students with mental health difficulties that we spoke to during the course of our research did not particularly identify themselves as 'disabled', but institutions saw their support as the responsibility of the disabled students adviser. Indeed, Part 4 of the Disability Discrimination Act, which came into force in 2002, covers students with mental health difficulties, making it unlawful for institutions to discriminate against them on the grounds of mental ill-health. The preceding chapters, particularly Chapter 3, show that some progress has been made in improving provision for disabled students generally. However, provision for students with mental health difficulties was seen by staff and students in the case study institutions as a particular area in which staff lacked awareness and in which institutional policy and direction were needed.

Higher education in Britain has been through a period of major upheaval since the mid-1980s, with a massive expansion in student numbers, an overall reduction in funding, increased inter-institutional competition, greater accountability and pressures to widen access to under-represented groups. The increase in student numbers coupled with a drop in funding has resulted in higher staff–student ratios, which Heads of University Counselling Services (HUCS) (1999) relate to the rise in students experiencing mental health difficulties.

> The fact of increasing numbers of both full-time and part-time students since 1992 has created a much busier, less personal study environment which requires that students possess greater degrees of mental robustness and an ability to work independently. For many students, teaching staff are distant people to whom it is hard to gain access and it is possible for students to undertake their studies with few, if any, staff members being aware of their psychological well-being. In many cases this is because the number of students on some courses is very large and the amount of time that academic staff have available to interact with individual students is comparatively small.
>
> (HUCS, 1999: section 16)

HUCS also see the increased pressures on staff to generate income and do research as reducing time available for pastoral duties with students. They argue that, in some institutions, modularisation of the curriculum has led to the loss of stable peer groups and to instability in staff–student relationships, and has generally contributed to greater fragmentation in the student experience. They maintain that government pressure to widen access to higher education to under-represented groups, such as those with no family history of higher education, mature students and those with vocational rather than academic qualifications, has meant greater demands being placed on support services, with no corresponding increase in resources. Indeed there is evidence to suggest that non-traditional entrants to higher education may place greater demands on support services. An Office for National Statistics report on the mental health of children and adolescents (aged 5–15) in Britain (Metzer *et al.*, 2000) makes disturbing reading, showing increased prevalence of mental disorders among children from working-class backgrounds, those with less well-educated parents, larger families, lone parents and those experiencing poverty. Naylor and Smith (2001) in a study of university student withdrawal made a clear link between socio-economic status and 'dropping out'. Those with low socio-economic status were at greater risk of withdrawal, as were younger students, those who were married and those with lower entry qualifications.

Traditionally students with mental health difficulties have been seen as the responsibility of student support services, in particular counselling services. A survey of academic and support staff carried out by the Mental Health Foundation (2001) found a reluctance among staff outside health and counselling services to take responsibility for student mental health. A separate survey of students identified inter-related issues as influencing mental health, including accommodation, fitting in and making new friends, finances and university systems.

> Although staff generally identified the same stressors as students, most made no overt links between such structural issues and their effect on mental health nor did they see it as the university's role to play a part in solving such problems. Many staff saw the causes of student mental health problems as lying within the individual student's behaviour such as being anxious, generally unable to cope, or misusing drugs.
>
> (Mental Health Foundation, 2001: 5)

How a problem is understood has a significant impact on solutions chosen to address it. In the case of student mental health, if a problem is seen entirely as resulting from a deficit in abilities/skills within the individual, then interventions will be focused on assisting the individual to develop the skills that they are perceived to be lacking. In the case of students in higher education, this approach fails to address the wider structural factors identified by HUCS and the Mental Health Foundation as impacting on student mental health, such as the loss of pastoral relationships between staff and students, the reduction in staff time available per student, the general fragmentation in the student experience and increasing financial pressures on students. The need to understand mental health in environmental as well as individual terms is just beginning to take hold in the higher education sector, influenced by ideas in the field of health promotion. The notion of the health promoting university (Tsouros et al., 1998) has been developed, based on the 'settings approach' to mental health.

> The inter-relationship between social, environmental and political influences, and their effect on individual and community health, is increasingly being recognised. As a result mental health promotion requires a co-ordinated approach, bridging these boundaries, directed at specific settings where problems arise, aimed at improving the health of whole communities.
>
> (Department of Health, 2001: 129)

Disabled people have argued for a move away from what they term the medical model of disability, which sees impairment as the main source of disablement, towards the social model, which states that people are disabled by barriers which exist in society. From this perspective, disabled people face barriers because they are negotiating an environment which was not designed for them, and if they are to enjoy equality of access it is this deficit in the environment which must be overcome (Oliver, 1996a). For people with mental health difficulties it is essential to examine how the environment is creating or exacerbating difficulties, as well as looking at ways to support people to deal effectively with the environment within which they are operating.

This chapter draws on case studies of five students experiencing mental health difficulties who took part in our research project to illuminate some of these issues from the student perspective. The students clearly describe how the environment of higher education is creating and exacerbating their difficulties. Three of the students were studying at an institution in which an innovative model of support had been set up, alongside the counselling service, to support students with mental health difficulties. This system is described and discussed. Finally, the chapter draws on the students' experiences and the model of provision described to re-visit the medical vs. social model debate with respect to students with mental health difficulties.

The five students were studying in three different institutions, one of which was in Scotland, the other two in England. The next section introduces the students, whose experiences form the basis of the rest of the chapter. Each student was interviewed in depth for up to an hour and a half in 2002. They were also asked to nominate relevant members of staff, who were also interviewed.

The students

Owen

Owen was repeating his second year of a general arts degree at a traditional Scottish university. He withdrew from the second year of a Geology course after what he described as a 'nervous breakdown'. He was 21 and described himself as having depression. He went to an all-boys private boarding school and said he had a really hard time there. In his own words, he described his experiences as follows.

> I was pretty unhappy in the sixth form at school. I went to an all-boys school and I did quite well and then I got victimised for doing well, I think. And I didn't really fit in with the general ethos of the school . . . it wasn't a very nice place . . . I wouldn't bend. I've never been one to give way. I always tackle all problems head on really. . . . there was no way I was going to give over the ground of what I thought, so I pretty

much made life pretty difficult for myself when I was at school . . . And then when I came to university . . . after being at . . . boarding school for most of my life and I didn't really have any idea who I was and I got a bit of freedom and I lost the plot really. . . . this time last year, I just totally lost it and my parents wouldn't really accept that there was anything wrong with me, so that made it more difficult. And eventually I just had a nervous breakdown. I . . . don't really remember quite large chunks of last year . . . I spent most of my time in bed really. I didn't go to any lectures in the last term . . . which nobody noticed . . . I did the exams, the Christmas exams. I did really badly and then I came back and just tried to struggle on . . . I went home for Easter and it was awful. But my mum and dad just sent me back and then I took, not really an overdose. I took sort of an overdose and then went out to a stag party. At the party I had far too much to drink with the intention of – probably just a cry for help. I wasn't trying to do myself damage. I just wanted people to realise that there was something wrong with me. And I ended up in an ambulance on the way to hospital and my mum and dad arrived the next morning. They drove up from [home town] and said they wanted to take me home and I refused to go home so they tranquillised me, then took me home. So I ended up at home and there I was six months and for the first couple of months at home I didn't really talk to anyone or – I had panic attacks pretty badly like about seven, like five to ten times a day really . . . I was thinking about what I'd say to you today and the only way to describe it is: when there's so much you want to say that you can't open your mouth, like you can't physically do it.

He said he really had to persuade the university to take him back onto a different course, on the strength of his A level performance.

He also had dyslexia and he felt this contributed to his difficulties when he was studying Geology. He got through his A levels on the strength of his ability to learn facts; however, this did not work at university. Also Geology involved a lot of formulae and chemical processes, which he found difficult because of problems with sequencing. With hindsight he believed he was taking the wrong subject. He had come to this university partly because of parental pressure and the only subject he could get into with his grades and subjects was Geology. His predicted grades at school were three Ds and he ended up with an A and two Bs. He had not really considered other alternatives. His reasons for coming to university were to satisfy other people's expectations rather than to fulfil any ambition of his own.

Chloe

Chloe, a mature student, was studying Business Information Technology part time by distance learning at a new university in England. She was provided with module folders which she worked through at her own pace. She had one-to-one tuition once a week at the university through the disability support office and applied to sit the exams whenever she felt ready. She was halfway through her second year and expected to be studying for four and a half years. Chloe was diagnosed as having a borderline personality disorder (BPD) and lived in a supported housing project specifically for people with BPD. She was expected to attend individual psychotherapy once a week, group psychotherapy in the house twice a week and house meetings at the end of every day. She felt this has slowed down progress on her course. Some of the groups had been added since she joined the house and she said she might not have moved in if she had known the extent of the time commitment required.

> Wednesdays I generally go into university. I do tend to go into university on a Monday as well. I don't actually have to go, but I do go in and use the computers in the library and stuff and get, just really to get myself out the house because it can get really sort of stressful in the house, so I try to spend some time away . . . sometimes it helps just to go out for a few hours and have some time to yourself.

Chloe was disenchanted with life in the house because they had asked her to attend more meetings and she felt she did not have time, but was being told that if she did not attend them she would have to leave the house.

> I think it has been helpful but . . . the project's in the early stages now and there's a lot of inconsistencies and problems.

The project had been going about two years and house staff were always available to discuss anything at all that residents might need to talk about. Chloe expected to stay there for two years, and was approaching the end of this period. However, she had been given a month's extension because of exams.

She had problems with concentration and had been advised to do more than one thing at a time. She often studied while watching the TV, which helped her to retrieve the relevant information in exams because she tried to recall what she was watching at the time. She preferred coursework to exams and was allowed extra time in exams, sitting them in a separate room, using a computer. One of her project workers went with her, because she became very anxious.

She decided to study by distance learning, because she felt it would suit her better.

> I have had problems in the past with dealing with having to go into places like college or uni everyday and dealing with people . . . because a lot of personal problems tend to get in the way. I get very angry very

easily and when I get like that I can't learn and . . . when I get in that frame of mind that's it and there's no point . . . rather than finding a hundred and one excuses to not go to lectures or seminars or whatever, I'd rather just do it at home when I feel like I'm up to doing it, which is, it generally works out pretty much all the time now because I really enjoy doing it.

Rena

Rena was in her fourth and final year, studying Microbiology and Computing at a new university in England. She came straight to university from school. Her degree would be a unique combination, because of the flexible range of options available to students. She had a diagnosis of clinical depression.

> The depression is there all the time, but it's not so bad at the moment. It kind of gets worse and then gets better. I've had to go on anti-depressants recently . . . as I had a tiny relapse, nothing so major as it was when it first started.

She fell so far behind in her second year because of depression that she decided to take a year out and repeat the year.

> . . . it was a bit of a trek to get in here to uni and it was just more of the fact that I couldn't really be bothered to get up and take the bus.

Eventually she decided to drop out and repeat the year. The depression had been with her all the way through university, but 'came to a head' about a year ago. Her tutor 'virtually frog marched' her to the doctor, where she was prescribed anti-depressants.

She felt she was expected to go to university by her school and family. She went to an all-girls state school, where most students went to university. Her parents support her financially by paying her rent, food and tuition fees. But she struggled to survive on her student loan, receiving only the minimum. She had recurrent kidney infections, which left her tired, sometimes for months.

She was diagnosed with dyslexia at 8 and formally assessed at 12. She said neither of her schools really knew what to do about this. She did have the support of a specialist dyslexia tutor, however. She was put into the bottom groups for her GCSEs, but when she came to do her A levels, she was in the top group for maths and middle group for English and achieved quite good GCSE grades. She wanted to do Engineering at university, but being in the bottom group for maths meant the best she could hope for was a D. She needed a higher mark than that, so her Mum 'went on the warpath' and got her moved up to the top group and she managed a B.

Ellie

Ellie was studying Conservation and Countryside Management. A mature student with a young daughter, she was repeating her first year at a new university in England. She described her mental health difficulty as:

> I've suffered from stress. I've had a lot of stress in my life over the years. My Dad was an alcoholic and his central nervous system had been destroyed by chemicals earlier on, so he suffered from depression and anxiety quite badly you know and living with that is very hard. So I've always had quite a high level of stress and I do get anxious about being around people and have become quite reserved over the years. I find those kind of things . . . a struggle you know just basically being around people.

Going to university was not expected of her by her family and she was the first generation to do this. She went to 'a standard secondary school', not a grammar or public school, and about half the students from her school went to university. She left school at 16, went back to do re-takes, but dropped out after a month. She then went into youth training to be a mechanic and after that tried childcare.

She said:

> When I went back into education I'd had my daughter and stayed home for the first few years and then decided that I needed to get some qualifications. I ended up taking two A levels and a GCSE with the hope to get into university to do this. I decided that this was my . . . subject area according to what meant most to me and wanting to be able to provide for my daughter and sort of made a plan from there really. After not studying since I was 17 . . . , taking two A levels and a GCSE in one year, was a bit ambitious . . . That year flew by; I knew I couldn't take it all in. . . . so had resigned myself to the fact that a year of retake of one A-level was great as it meant that after all that time not studying, I had achieved an A level and a GCSE in one year. I had no idea that the university would take me on with just this. I didn't think that I would come so I made no plans and then later on it was about two weeks before I was due to be here that they sent me the thing saying 'you're accepted'.

At the time of her acceptance, she was living in her home city. She subsequently tried to find accommodation in the new city, but didn't manage it, so started off staying in a bed and breakfast with her daughter through the week and travelling back home at weekends.

> I moved in November in the end and then there was the move . . . and over Christmas I was sort of settling in and there was just so much

going on that I couldn't keep up and then I lost my father in April and that sort of ended the year really and I sort of suspended my studies from there.

She started the year again, staying in the same place, which was 'quite a trek' every day. She was hoping to move again with her daughter and was finding it easier to keep up this time around. Having some things organised, like being registered with a doctor, had already made life easier.

Pete

Pete was in his final year of a Civil Engineering degree at an English new university. He was supposed to finish the previous year, but had taken an extra year because of difficulties that he had encountered. He transferred from another university in 1999, after taking an HND in Business Finance there. He was a mature student with a diagnosis of depression and was taking anti-depressant medication. He was married and had a family. The reason he transferred to a different university was because his wife had a medical condition and she moved to the city for treatment. He found transferring really difficult because he did not know anybody. He was black and came from what he described as a poor family in Nigeria. He chose Civil Engineering on the advice of a careers adviser, because he had done well in maths previously and had experience of building materials from work in Nigeria.

An innovative model of support

Rena, Ellie and Pete were studying at the same English university, which had an innovative model of support for students with mental health difficulties. In addition to the university counselling service, money from the Disabled Students Allowance (DSA) was being used to fund the post of a mental health support worker (MHSW). He worked with students specifically on how their mental health difficulties affected them in undertaking their education and his focus was on supporting students to get through their studies. He met all three students on a weekly basis and tailored his work to each individual student's needs. His work might involve helping them to develop organisational and time management skills, teaching them assertiveness skills and supporting their communication with staff, either through direct liaison, three-way meetings or generally backing up their requests for extra time or extensions. He helped students to tackle negative thinking, to build and maintain motivation and to identify and build on their achievements and strengths. He encouraged them to look after themselves better, for example tackling fragmented sleep patterns, setting up exercise routines, having rests and taking time out for themselves. He helped them to apply structure to their workloads and provided a continuous point of contact, understanding their mental health difficulties and listening to them without judgement. He also worked with staff to explain the implications of mental health difficulties.

All three students were overwhelmingly positive about their experiences with the MHSW.

> I think it really, really works. I had a really, really hard time – really hard . . . They [MHSW and his predecessor] are people that, even if I leave this university . . . I will never, never, never forget them. . . . These two people they are just great . . . The reason why there is a lot of change for me is just because of . . . [them]. Before these people – even before I come to the university, suffering things I cannot tell anyone . . . they are there to help me, they are there to listen to me. I think this programme is really, really effective. If this programme is being . . . for every university, there would be low drop-out . . . it's given me opportunity to have one to one . . . I'm doing fine. Really, really doing fine. And actually I'm ahead of my dissertation.
>
> (Pete)

> They have helped me realise that the workload isn't the be all and end all you know. If I don't get it done on time or exactly on time it doesn't matter so much that I need to crack up . . . when you're in the throes of a depression you can't see that at all, everything is just ultra-negative.
>
> (Ellie)

Rena said that her work with the MHSW has helped her to organise and structure her work. She felt that, since working with him, she was keeping on top of the work. She felt more confident now to go and discuss her difficulties with her tutors, which she put down to her work with the MHSW.

The MHSW scheme was part of a wider service, which aimed to assist students who faced barriers to academic progression. It did this in two main ways: by assisting students to find ways to manage the difficulties that they faced in the academic environment and by making a large number of observations and recommendations about adjustments which might be made to the environment in order to ensure both that the students were adequately supported and that the university met the requirements of the DDA.

The students' experiences

Stigma and alienation

All five students were well aware of the stigma attached to mental health difficulties and this made them cautious about what they would disclose to people.

It depends who I'm talking to and why . . . if you're just talking to everyday people you don't really let them know the depths of your problems as such do you? . . . I mean I know it's serious but I don't sort of, as I say I don't tell people really, you keep it to yourself.

(Ellie)

I try not to tell anybody, so that they don't go 'oh, she needs special treatment'. Which I suppose is where I've gone wrong as a lot of the time [when] I try to do it on my own, I can't cope.

(Rena)

At the end of the day, my degree's going to say I've actually got an honours degree with whatever grade . . . They're not going to know I did it through flexible learning . . . I hope it hasn't got flexible learning on it because the biggest problem I would have is in jobs. If I explain to someone where I've been for the past few years and why I haven't been working, I'm not going to get a job. But if I say to someone I've been studying part time and I've taken time out to do some study, they're going to understand that but I know they're not going to understand – I've been on a project because I've got a personality disorder. They're going to say, alright then, bye bye, sort of thing.

(Chloe)

Two of the students, Owen and Chloe, also described experiences of social alienation. Owen had a girlfriend before his breakdown, but she left him shortly after it happened. He was then out of university for a while and his ex-girlfriend told a lot of people what had happened to him. So when he came back people kept asking him whether he was 'having a bad day' and, he felt, were quite patronising. This all came to a head when he had had too much to drink at a party and another student made one of these type of comments. He lashed out and punched the student, leading to a complaint being brought against him by his ex-girlfriend's flatmates who said he was a threat to other students because he had 'mental problems'. This was investigated and he was subsequently let off. In addition, the young man he punched subsequently apologised for taunting him. Following this incident, he developed a group of friends and did not socialise much outside that group. He described his flatmate as his best friend because he treated him as a human being rather than someone with a problem.

Chloe, because she chose to do distance learning, had struggled to feel part of the wider body of students.

I never feel like a proper student even though . . . when you've got your student union card you can go anywhere in the university with it . . . but

> I don't feel like a student because I just don't go in and it doesn't feel
> like I'm actually doing a degree.
>
> (Chloe)

Since staying in the housing project, she had begun to feel more like going
out and interacting with people, but because she opted for distance learning, she had not been permitted to sit in on any classes.

> I wanted to sit in on some more lectures sometimes and I don't think
> they're going to be able to let me basically because of the type, unless I
> change my course . . . I'm not going to do that. And I would like to do
> that because that would actually help me and benefit me, and get me
> out the house and things . . . enable you to get out and meet people
> more. Contact with other students as well because I've had no contact
> with any other students unless they live here basically.
>
> (Chloe)

Non-accepting culture

Pete and Owen described how the culture of higher education did not allow
for differences or for students to admit to having difficulties. Owen described how it is 'not cool to care' among students. He thought that people
needed to be more aware that others were struggling and to watch out for
each other more. He thought that student support services needed a change
of image to remove the stigma attached to going there. If students promoted their services that could really help. In his view, they needed to move
from the perception that they were a place where people go who have
mental health difficulties, to a place where all students can get support. He
described a situation in which a student tried to throw herself off a balcony
in a student residence and nobody noticed. He also felt that he more or less
'disappeared from classes' before he temporarily withdrew, which went
unnoticed, and that no support network was available to him.

> . . . a change of ethos. People don't . . . nobody can cope with their life
> by themselves and the sooner people realise this, you know, the better.
> I mean, nobody can go through life being a one-man band . . . everyone
> has a weakness and everyone needs help at [some] point in their
> life . . . it's so frustrating, I mean, yeah, you just need a whole change
> of attitude towards it really but Rome wasn't built in a day, was it?
>
> (Owen)

Pete had difficulties with his eyesight, which means he has trouble seeing
the board in classes. He had been provided with a tape recorder to help him

overcome this, but he had felt very uncomfortable about using it. He attributed this to a culture which did not accept difference.

> This tape recorder is good – but one thing I find out with it is – I can't use it. You know why – I felt like people will be looking at me and thinking 'Oh', you understand . . . it's just not possible for the student to come out with 'hey, this is my problem' . . . it's not really easy . . . This year, my final year – I start understanding this is how things is, because you think that it's you, you are the one who has problems.
>
> (Pete)

Academic experiences

Several of the students described how the academic environment that they found themselves in at university had exacerbated their difficulties. Rena described how the modular system she was part of contributed to her distress.

> And part of the reason I have depression is because I really, really hate the instability of university. Having to move around so much and one week is never the same as the next week. It's taken me a while to realise that's why I'm depressed. Well one of the big reasons . . . and it probably won't go away until I leave and get a stable job.
>
> (Rena)

She liked the fact that the modular system offered a lot of choice, but hated the instability. Meeting weekly with the MHSW helped to overcome this by providing some continuity.

Pete believed that his difficulties had been exacerbated by a badly designed course and incompetent and unsupportive lecturers, some of whom failed to recognise his difficulties; for example, when he asked for extensions these were only sometimes granted. He used to feel put down for asking questions when he did not understand aspects of the course. He said that a lot of the students on his course were having difficulties, finding the workload too high. Lecturers did not communicate with each other to coordinate the workload or the contents of the course and there was no personal contact with the lecturers. Overall, he felt there was a lack of support for learning and realised that this was not a good learning environment. He did a one year placement, which he generally found less stressful than coming to university.

> I went to university not having too much problem, though I did have a bit of a problem . . . but . . . instead of them helping you according to what the rules and regulations they put here . . . they give you more stress . . . at the end of the time you're getting more problems.
>
> (Pete)

Owen described how he lost his role and sense of purpose in the transition from school to university. He had done well at school academically and in sports. At university he was failing academically and had not taken up sports.

> ... when I got to university I was just a nobody and I felt totally lost ... I lost my purpose in the grand scheme of life ... it just seemed that everything was, you know, ebbing away from me.
>
> (Owen)

He described his breakdown as the best thing that ever happened to him, regarding it as something which had to happen. His position was untenable. He realised now that he would rather not have come to university at all, but to have gone straight into the army. However, he believed that he had let other people's expectations of him shape his destiny. He was choosing to finish his degree, to prove to himself that he could do it. He believed that some of the subjects he was studying in first year – Divinity, Philosophy and Anthropology – contributed to his depression.

> ... these subjects ask a lot of questions of you and can, when you're already confused and disillusioned, then it's pretty ... at a vulnerable point in your life, having all these life-changing questions thrown at you ... really shakes your foundations ... So yes, very difficult to remain separate from the subject you're studying. That's what I found anyway. And I know a lot of people have ... agreed with me pretty much on that.
>
> (Owen)

Staff awareness

All of the students described difficult experiences, when staff had dismissed their problems as 'normal stress'. For example, Ellie described how in her first year, her course leader dismissed her worries about getting really behind, in spite of knowing that Ellie had experienced three bereavements, two during her time at university.

> ... it was getting towards Christmas ... and there were ... exams coming up at the end of the year. Well in January the exam comes, the first exam anyway and I'd already had four essays that I hadn't done and I knew that I couldn't do it all and I thought I ought to stop as I'm going to fail this year otherwise and she kept saying 'oh no, you'll be fine, you'll be fine' and it wasn't until Dad died at the end of April that they suspended my studies. So there was nearly four months when I was struggling by, getting extra stressed about being so far behind which could have been utilised sorting out everything. We moved house ... in

a rush, in late November . . . into a new area, 15 miles from college, no personal transport, child in a nursery on the other side of the city to home, and not having had time to familiarise myself to the area. I still feel I should have stopped at Christmas and come back, ready, in September of the next year, as did happen anyway.

(Ellie)

On another occasion a member of staff had completely misunderstood her, when she tried to explain her major anxieties about giving a presentation.

I couldn't stand the thought of presentations and when I did finally have to do one last year, it was terrible, it was awful. I've never had such a terrible experience and that tutor [said] . . . 'oh, you'll be fine . . . you'll get through', but the thought of it was just turning my stomach. I also received a fairly bad mark for it. It wasn't until after the experience that I managed to get my point across. I did try and tell him before the presentation but he took it as a normal nervousness. He's accounted for that now and says he's sorry that he didn't listen in the first place, you know, which was nice to know.

(Ellie)

Now she did personal presentations or a 'viva', which, she said, she 'still stutters over, but not quite as badly'. More generally, the MHSW had now intervened to add weight to Ellie's discussions with her lecturers and to provide staff with information about mental health difficulties in general.

Owen described various experiences with lecturers when he felt badly misjudged. One example was of his final field trip with the Geology department. He had given up Geology the day before, but to avoid causing a fuss had still gone on the field trip, but was not taking notes. A lecturer questioned this.

. . . he asked me why I wasn't taking any notes and I said: well I'm not doing the module any more, and he said: well, why are you here? So I said: I didn't want to cause a fuss, so I came. And he said: well why aren't you doing it any more? And I said: because I didn't do very well on the exam. And he said: why is that? And I said: well just various reasons. And he goes: well it's not because you're bloody lazy is it? And you know that's like people throwing opinions like that at you when they don't know anything about the situation really. And that wasn't the only experience I've had with lecturers here . . . I think that's really ignorant.

(Owen)

Pete felt that some lecturers took no account of his difficulties even though they had been written down and officially recognised. He felt it was a constant battle to get reasonable adjustments, such as extra time, but had been helped by the backing of the MHSW, who wrote letters to lecturers if necessary. When that happened, the lecturers listened.

Conclusion

It is clear that the nature of higher education had exacerbated and even created some of the students' difficulties. Lack of understanding among lecturers, a culture in which it was difficult to admit to having difficulties, a lack of support for learning and badly designed learning experiences had all contributed to the students' distress. Although the chapter is based on the experiences of only a small number of students, their stories accord with the findings of HUCS and the Mental Health Foundation, giving a personal insight into the more general issues raised. Higher education can be a very amorphous experience, with students expected to structure and organise their own time and workloads with little direct support. On top of this, large numbers of students are adjusting to living away from home for the first time, making new friends and dealing with financial difficulties. It is a vulnerable time. As HUCS argued and our case studies show, this is exacerbated by the fact that there is less and less support available to students academically, given mounting pressures on staff within the higher education sector. We would argue that the experiences of students with mental health difficulties simply make the difficulties inherent in the system for all students stand out more clearly. The wider fragmentation of experience caused by modularisation, the general lack of academic support and poorly put-together learning experiences all need to be addressed. The vast majority of students are left to negotiate this system as best they can without support. Tackling flaws in the higher education environment is no mean feat, but we would argue that it would not only help to alleviate demands on student support services, but also improve the quality of the higher education experience for all students.

The social model of disability focuses on the need for environmental and societal change to remove barriers to the participation of disabled people. In the case of people with mental health difficulties, historically the emphasis has been placed on supporting individuals to negotiate whatever environment they find themselves in. For students with mental health difficulties, we would argue that, in fact, interventions at both levels are needed. Higher education institutions should be considering addressing flaws in the learning environment as well as supporting students individually to develop the skills they need to get through their courses. Furthermore, addressing these two factors in isolation is also not an adequate solution, since individual and environmental factors clearly interact.

The model of support described was highly praised by the students and proving an effective means of getting them through their courses. It provides a potentially useful additional service that universities and colleges could consider offering alongside more traditional counselling services.

Chapter 8

Disabled students in higher education
Negotiating identity

Introduction

In Chapter 2, we employed social categories to explore participation rates and characteristics of disabled students in higher education. The analysis in that chapter was based on the assumption that it is possible to measure social characteristics of individuals and that the categories which are used bear some relation to subjective reality. In this penultimate chapter, we draw on recent theoretical developments in the field of disability studies to question whether a simple conceptualisation of disability as a unitary category is empirically sustainable and whether it is supported by the subjective experiences of the case study students.

For many disabled people, such as those labelled as having learning difficulties or mental health difficulties, the category of disability has been assigned to them by others with little or no negotiation. For many, the category signals a spoilt identity and as a result it has not necessarily been incorporated into their sense of self. Indeed, many people with learning difficulties actively reject the label, preferring to see themselves as having a physical impairment or as not being disabled at all (Riddell *et al.*, 2001). Disabled students in higher education are different from this, in that they have chosen to disclose an impairment on their UCAS form or at some time during their studies. For some, the fact that their impairment is visible and restrictive means that declaring it is essential to obtaining the support they require. However, for the majority of disabled students, who have dyslexia or a hidden impairment such as ME, disclosure is less essential to everyday survival and the invisibility of their impairment means that it might be possible to avoid disclosure. Interesting questions therefore arise as to why disabled students choose to disclose an impairment and whether they see this as an essential part of their identity, or whether it is viewed as transient and contingent on the particular context in which they find themselves.

Understanding identity

Watson (2002) notes that identity has become a highly contested field of theorising and research in recent years. According to Hall (1996), there are two distinct approaches to understanding identity. In the first model, identity is viewed as essential, natural or intrinsic. An individual is born with a given identity, which remains with them throughout life, structuring their biography and experience. Much thinking characterised as 'modernist', such as versions of feminism, anti-racism and nationalism, is implicitly or explicitly based on an essentialist understanding of identity. The second model denies the existence of any identity based on a shared origin or experience, suggesting instead that identity is multiple and temporal. Often associated with postmodernism, this version of identity is based on the notion of an evolving and 'endlessly performative self' (Hall, 1996: 1). These multiple selves are viewed as 'incoherently, actively and playfully assembled and negotiated with those relevant at any particular point in time' (Baron *et al.*, 1999). Within the second reading of identity, different views are expressed with regard to the extent of individual agency and external power structures. Riddell *et al.* (2001), in their discussion of people with learning difficulties within the context of a learning society, concluded that the parameters for negotiating identity available to this group were distinctly limited as a result of many factors including the stigma associated with learning difficulties, the lack of financial power and the restrictions imposed by the repertoire of available services. A different vision is presented by Beck (1992) in his discussion of the 'risk society' in late modernity. According to Beck:

> Increasingly everyone has to choose between different options, including as to which group or subculture one wants to be identified with. In fact one has to choose and change one's social identity as well and take the risks in doing so.
>
> (Beck, 1992: 88)

Instead, risks have to be navigated by individuals, and the process of identity construction and maintenance is inextricably linked with the negotiation of risk, with some forms of identity having a privileged social status and others attracting 'an abundance of risks' (Beck, 1992). A paradox in Beck's view of identity is that the act of choosing and changing one's social identity implies an active agent, which might be viewed as approximating to the modernist version of the essential self.

Disability and identity

Early writing in disability studies tended to assume that impairment was a fixed attribute, whereas disability was a relative construct in that it was contingent on the particular environment in which an impairment was experienced. This argument was powerfully set out by Oliver (1990) in his book *The Politics of Disablement*. The front cover exemplified this idea by depicting a wheelchair user attempting to access a polling station, approachable only by steep steps. Whilst the individual was clearly capable of exercising his democratic right to vote, he was prevented from doing so by the physical barrier. Abberley (1987) described impairment as 'the bedrock' which has to be taken into account in understanding the experience of disability. There is a strong current in disability studies and in public policy which continues to see the presence of impairment as the key element in defining who should be described as disabled, and indeed, it is difficult to conceive of a legal definition of disability which could be divorced from the notion of impairment. This type of thinking corresponds with Hall's first model of identity, based on a modernist understanding of the self as fixed and essential, 'unfolding from beginning to end through all the vicissitudes of history without change' (Hall, 1996: 3).

Recently, however, postmodern and poststructuralist writers have mounted serious challenges to the basis of disability studies, critiquing the taken-for-granted distinction between disabled and non-disabled people, which is seen as perpetuating Enlightenment fallacies that social categories and constructions are 'real' (Corker, 2003; Corker and Shakespeare, 2002). Whilst the construction of a binary line between disabled and non-disabled people may be useful politically and legally, these writers argue that such a hierarchy may simply not accord with people's experience, as impairments fluctuate and are experienced in different ways over an individual's life course. In addition, what is constructed as an impairment at one point in time may be viewed differently at another. This is well illustrated by a historical analysis of many categories, such as hysteria, which plagued middle class Victorian females, and dyslexia and attention deficit disorder, which appear to be affecting growing numbers of school children in the western world. These examples suggest that, whilst the reality of some impairments cannot be denied (e.g. a serious spinal injury), others are the product of historically contingent social constructions. Such views are clearly challenging to the development of a movement based on a common identity, but nonetheless have to be addressed in order to develop a better understanding of the relationship between disability, impairment and identity.

Data presented in Chapter 2 underlined the range of associations between social class, ethnicity, gender and disability, indicating that disability should be seen as one of a number of interlocking factors influencing the construction and maintenance of identity. However, the statistical data suggested that disability was unlikely to be the most salient category in all cases. In this chapter, we draw on case studies to understand the way in which disabled students understand disability and reconcile it with other aspects of their identity. Key themes emerging from students' accounts included a critical recognition of the complexity of identity and a deep ambivalence about identifying themselves as disabled, partly as a result of fear of stigma and a rejection of victim status. In the following paragraphs, we illustrate some of the ways in which disabled students made sense of the category.

Disability as an equivocal identity

As noted above, although the case study students were aware that they had voluntarily placed themselves within the category of disability, many continued to express uncertainty about the adequacy of the label to reflect their perception of self. This ambivalence was particularly evident in the case of the dyslexic students, who described their struggle for recognition whilst at the same time questioning the congruence between dyslexia and disability.

Maurice: Scottish University 2

Maurice was a second year medical student at Scottish University 2 who had previously completed a degree in Physiology and Sports Science. His parents were both teachers, but his dyslexia was not formally diagnosed until the second year of his first degree. At school, he was regarded as 'a bit slow':

> I went through school – everything was never fine – I was always slow. Always from the start of primary school, my mother and father would have been brought in because my reading wasn't very good, my reading was always very slow. Both my parents were teachers, so I think what really happened was that they sort of worked with me a bit. Nothing was ever diagnosed except that 'Maurice's a bit slow', do you know what I mean, and I must have just muddled through school to be honest. English was never a strong point and I don't know if that was why I went down the science route, because it wasn't structured essays, factual learning. It was understanding, and I was always better with diagrams and thing like that.

Maurice was prompted to go to the disabled students adviser for a diagnosis because of the problems which emerged in his second year with assignment writing. A lecturer noted the discrepancy between his oral and written performance:

> He stood out from the very beginning in class. He usually led the questioning and in all oral interchange he was outstanding . . . but it wasn't coming through in his written work, that similar ability to construct concepts, to critically handle them.

Just as he had been labelled 'slow' at school, university staff began to see him as a lazy, disorganised student. When he asked why he had been given a poor grade for an assignment, he would be told: 'Well, Maurice, it just doesn't look – it looks like you've done it the night before . . . It doesn't flow, there is not a structure to the essay'.

Following a visit to an educational psychologist, Maurice was told that he was dyslexic, and described a feeling of relief at being able to exchange a negative identity for a more positive one:

> Initially my diagnosis was 'You are dyslexic' and at that time that was a relief to me. I didn't take it to heart, I didn't think I was retarded or something like that. I think some people do take it to heart. I thought, 'Well, that's quite a relief' and I was quite happy with the position that the university was going to give me some extra time in exams and I thought, 'Oh that's good, it will take a bit of the pressure off me a bit more in writing essays'.

In reality, the extra time in exams was experienced as a mixed blessing, but the sense of release from blame meant that Maurice was able to finish his first degree and embark on a second.

However, the negotiation of identity with significant others was ongoing. When he enquired about entering Medicine, he received a slightly frosty response from the medical faculty:

> I came to enquire about it and they were a bit standoffish about the whole dyslexic thing. . . . Their point of view is that they see it as an excuse and they say, 'Why do you want extra time in an exam, you wouldn't get extra time during a surgery or extra time in resuscitation.'

Fellow students were also likely to look down on anyone who might be regarded as less able:

> I know it is better being dyslexic, I can feel my medical friends saying 'And how did you fail that test Maurice?' There are a few people think that.

Whilst having the diagnosis of dyslexia is important to Maurice in bolstering his self-esteem, he is reluctant to discuss this with other students:

> There's about three other people in my year who are dyslexic in Medicine and I've bumped into them as we've arrived at the exam hall 25 minutes early, you can work it out, but that's the only way. Sometimes it comes up in the conversation, 'Where were you?' 'Seeing the special needs adviser.' 'Oh, what's that about?' It never gets brought up in conversation with any academic members of staff.

Maurice continued to struggle with the idea that he shared a common identity with someone with more significant impairments:

> I don't like thinking of myself as disabled, I don't even like, when you started talking, I don't even like that you almost put me in the category with someone in a wheelchair. I almost find that offensive. No. I mean, God, I'm glad I'm not and it's almost a relief that I don't have to deal with a physical or other disability. I really don't like holding it up or shouting about it at all. I like that it's been identified and I'm not stupid, I rather look on it like that.

Despite his ambivalence about the category of dyslexia, Maurice maintained a sense of himself as a person who was discriminated against by the university assessment system, which prioritised mastery of the written word and 'tested my weakness'. Rather than extra time in exams, Maurice considered that an alternative form of assessment based on oral work should be permitted. At the very least, he felt that 'people who are marking my exam scripts or marking my course work should know that I am dyslexic, so that allowances could be made'.

Sheena, English University 1

Sheena was a 32-year-old mature student studying for an MPhil in Psychology following a first degree in Psychology at a post-92 university. She had embarked on a PhD at English University 1, but had been told at the end of her first year that this was not realistic due to her difficulties in writing. This had been a severe blow and she felt that she had suffered an injustice. Sheena's early education involved many changes of school, since her father was in the armed forces. Like Maurice, she grew up with a sense of herself as slow and uncoordinated, although dyslexia was not diagnosed formally until much later:

> No, I didn't know that I had it. I've always had a sense of feeling different. I was the last kid, for example, in my class to move out of pumps because I couldn't tie my bloody laces. I was sixteen before I could use a normal clock. I always knew there were things I couldn't do that other people could, but I always thought I must be horrendously stupid and that. I was also one of three and I was the only daughter to fail my 11 plus and that kind of reinforced the whole idea that I must just be incredibly stupid. . . . I did think, 'Well, why am I good at this and why am I crap at that and why am I so clumsy all the time?'

Sheena managed to get through her first degree without major difficulties as a result of 'over-learning', but 'there were a few times that they had to re-read my exam scripts as my writing is absolutely appalling and for my tutors to allow me to do that was very nice'. Problems became more apparent when she left university to begin work:

> I'm a pretty bright person who had managed to compensate in a variety of ways for these problems but I was very aware of it and I was having a chat with a friend when I was 21 and saying, 'There's something wrong, I don't know what it is, but there is something different and there's something wrong but I just don't know what it is' . . . I went out to work for a while and did very, very well. Kept getting little things on my desk about time management and I thought, 'Cheeky buggers, I'm working my nuts off here, working hard and what's this time management about?' I didn't realise then that I was working hard but working pretty inefficiently as well because of my organisational problems.

The identification of dyslexia seems to have happened in a somewhat roundabout way. Whilst she was working with young offenders, her difficulties with spelling kept on being pointed out to her. Subsequently, a conversation with a young man who had just received a diagnosis made her realise that she had exactly the same set of difficulties:

> I think the boys noticed. 'Miss, how come you spell crap miss, miss, why can't you spell? Miss, why don't you know the correct way round for H, Y and Z?' So in a way the boys picked up on it but nobody else seemed to. But it wasn't until I went to see my supervisor because I met somebody I had been testing and he came in to see me and told me he was dyslexic and I said, 'How do you know you're dyslexic?' and I thought, 'Oh my God, that's what it is, I'm dyslexic'.

Sheena described the shift that happened in her sense of self when it was suggested for the first time that she might have dyslexia:

> You know you have these problems and you suspect that you have these problems but you spend your whole life covering up and compensating for them and you get to a point when you wonder if it's just your paranoia and then somebody goes, 'Yes, you were right, you do have a learning disability or learning difficulty or whatever' and it's like all of those things that you quite suspected but weren't quite sure. All of those things that you thought made you slightly more cracked up than everybody else is true and that was the hard part. I think that was the hard part for me getting the diagnosis and feeling different as well, and all of a sudden I had a legitimate reason.

Like many of the students in our study, the diagnosis of dyslexia was experienced as a form of absolution, altering their self-perception in such a way as to free them from a sense of guilt and failure. However, during the first year of her second degree, disclosure became a major issue. It transpired that her supervisor had discussed the possibility of dyslexia with other people, including the disabled students adviser, without including Sheena in the conversation. As a result, Sheena experienced a sense of betrayal and loss of control over the management of her own identity:

> If you disclose something to one tutor, . . . it then becomes public know-ledge and at some point I think it did. That worried me hugely because it does undermine your confidence in the institution where you study. But yeah, I think there was an element of control there, I don't mind admitting that control is important because control allows you to predict what's going to happen next and give you structure and it gives you some certainty at least.

For Sheena, the diagnosis of dyslexia did not imply an acceptance of dis-ability as an essential part of identity:

> I don't see myself as disabled. I ask myself the question, 'Has it stopped me from doing anything?' and the answer is 'No'. My only worry is that if I had known earlier it would have become self-limiting so I'm very pleased that I didn't find out that I had it before I went off and did things that I found challenging.
>
> I don't identify with the notion of disability, I do identify with the notion of difficulty. Because difficulties can be overcome. Disability, I think it feels much more like a life sentence, do you know what I mean, it seems much worse to have a disability than to have a difficulty that you have some kind of notion, some capacity for overcoming. I don't think of myself as disabled.

One reason for Sheena's rejection of the idea of herself as a disabled person was that it conflicted with her self-image as a determined and competent individual:

> It [being identified as someone with a learning difficulty] just makes me proud or stubborn but I don't want people to kind of think, 'Poor you', because you get on with it, don't you. You don't make a drama out of a crisis, you just get on with it.

The department's refusal to allow Sheena to progress with the PhD had made her very unhappy and she believed this was attributable in part to a lack of support:

> I think it does ultimately affect your relationships, but your mental state and how much support you get affects your mental state as well.

> I think it depends ultimately on how good your self-esteem is as well. A lot of your self-esteem is derived through your ability to be successful and your ability to do a good job, and when you feel that you're failing, that's a huge issue, a huge issue.

Some people in the university continued to have doubts about the validity of a diagnosis of dyslexia, an attitude she had also encountered in relation to ME, which was seen as 'a hysterical hormones thing'. Ultimately, her own ambivalence about dyslexia and disability was reflected in uncertainty about whether to disclose a disability in a job application:

> I wouldn't, I would not tick the disabled box – I think maybe I did actually rein in my pride and tick the disability box and I rang them and said, 'I'm dyslexic and if I'm coming to your centre then I need access to a word processor'. So yeah, I think in that instance I made it work for me and then I thought, well, damn it, why should I handicap myself? In other instances I haven't because I'm very suspicious, despite the fact that the Disability Discrimination Act exists. I'm very, very suspicious of people making a judgement about who you are depending on whether you tick a box or you don't. Because I think people don't understand that you can have dyslexia and be completely, perfectly affable, perfectly bright person who just has a few problems in these areas over here.

Disability as a misplaced identity

Terry, English University 4

Terry was a 27-year-old student studying for an MSc in Deaf Studies at English University 4, an elite pre-92 institution. His father was a physician and he described the family as 'middle class' and 'not rich but privileged'. At the time of the research, Terry was an active member of the deaf community both within and outside the university. He was diagnosed as having hearing difficulties at a relatively early age, but was not allowed to learn sign language or connect with the deaf community:

> As I said before, when I was growing up I was kind of kept separate from the deaf community. I remember growing up and asking if I could learn sign language and kind of being refused time and time again. I remember at the age of 12 and 14 and 16 kind of being insistent about learning sign language and again, as I said, being refused.
> I kind of arrived in the deaf community late and I suppose that was because I grew up in an oral environment and there are quite a lot of deaf people who are like that and they don't identify as deaf people,

you know, they see themselves as a person with a hearing problem, rather than growing up in a deaf community. And you know the oral system can kind of in a way brainwash people into thinking, 'Oh no, no, there is nothing relevant about me being deaf and using sign language'. And if you don't learn sign language the oral system kind of labels you as a failure, or has done in the past, you know, as somebody who can't speak, or somebody who can't lip-read, so it can be quite a negative connotation. So people kind of internalise that so it can be quite difficult to reject that and then actually go out and learn sign language.

On leaving school, Terry went to a university in London and there learnt sign language, which rapidly opened up new possibilities:

So at the end of that course I started meeting more deaf people and I started learning sign language and that was kind of a real epiphany, it was amazing and it was the first time that I could really express myself and just chat in a group and the first time that I really started having complete access to an academic environment. So that was a very positive experience.

After a brief period in another university, he moved to English University 4 and was extremely active in university politics, representing disabled students in the students' union and also for the National Union of Students. However, he continued to experience ambivalence about whether he was primarily a disabled person or a deaf person, and eventually he decided to put his energies into establishing a new union for deaf students.

At University 4, some of Terry's lecturers could use BSL, but others required sign language interpreters and these were not always available. As a result, Terry had taken advice from two solicitors and was planning to bring a case against the university under DDA Part 4, on the grounds that it had failed to make reasonable adjustments. Despite this very high level of involvement, Terry still felt isolated from wider university life:

I feel cut off from university life as though I can't really participate socially within groups. I can't go along to open lectures . . . here at the Centre for Deaf Studies it's easy because there are other deaf students and within the corridors there are academics I can talk to but other students in other departments won't necessarily be able to do that. Even students here might have an informal chit chat when they are having coffee or whatever and talk about the course and obviously as deaf students we are not able to participate in those discussions. So you kind of feel, and I do feel, quite cut off from the wider participation of the university and I think that's an important part of university life.

That was definitely how it felt at [other universities], I just felt really quite isolated from everybody else.

According to the director of the access unit, having a peer group was essential to the building and maintenance of strong identity and sense of self, which might otherwise be undermined by an institution geared towards the needs of 'standard' students:

Deaf students, particularly those students who use sign language, will have a sense of identity with each other but also with the deaf community, so they will have a connection into that community as well as making contact with each other and having a sense of a group of students who actually meet regularly on social occasions. They will often be students who are studying on their own in a department and that's one of the major difficulties, for deaf students in particular, but other disabled students as well, that is often the case, they will be the only deaf student in their year and that does create enormous difficulties of isolation. My own view is that the university, because of its overall ethos, tends to deal better with those students who are nearest to the normal and the further away the student is from the norm the more difficult it is for other students and the more informal university, if you like, to deal with it.

Robbie, Scottish College 1

In Chapter 5, we discussed experiences of pedagogy and curriculum in higher education and, using the experiences of Robbie by way of illustration, noted the emphasis on learning support in the Scottish College of Further and Higher Education compared with the approach in older universities, where learning support was a relatively novel concept. Robbie felt that his college experience had been a positive one partly as a result of the presence and support of a deaf community, reinforcing the points made by Terry. With regard to his identity, Robbie commented:

It's not something that I walk around thinking about, but I kind of know that I'm disabled, but in some recess of my brain I don't call myself disabled. Sometimes you think that this word is more applicable to someone who can't walk properly or maybe they are blind or something. Because you probably know that a lot of hearing people think of deaf people as being stupid or deaf and dumb and things like that, and that's something I don't like.

We [deaf students] don't talk about these sort of issues, about disablement: Are we disabled? Are we deaf? We wouldn't use the word disabled to describe ourselves, the word we use to describe ourselves is deaf. I don't mean that I hate the word or reject it, it's just something that we don't use.

Unlike Terry, who had struggled with significant others, including parents and teachers, to be recognised as deaf, Robbie grew up with a positive sense of himself as a deaf person who was a member of a deaf family and a deaf community. For both, using sign language was essential to the maintenance of this identity. For other case study students who were deaf and were not sign language users, there was a sense of double exclusion both from the hearing community and from the deaf community. The prioritising of a deaf over a disabled identity, described by both Terry and Robbie, is important and resonates with Sheena's and Maurice's view of themselves as people with dyslexia rather than disabled people.

Disability as a resisted identity

Leslie, Scottish University 3

Leslie was in his first year at Scottish University 3 studying History. He had left his local comprehensive school to work as an apprentice fitter and turner. After six years undertaking 'heavy work', including a spell in a restaurant which left him 'hacked off', he decided to come to university and enrolled in an Access course at the local FE college. The university was 'on the doorstep so it seemed straightforward to come here.' However, just before he was due to start, Leslie was involved in a serious accident which left him with major head injuries. The university disability service had provided a very high level of support, ensuring that assessments were conducted quickly, a DSA claim was made and note-takers engaged. Leslie was provided with a small laptop computer and note-takers for each lecture. Overall, he felt that the university had provided him with excellent support. However, he described himself as 'generally quite dull' and his life at university as 'quite boring'. Fellow students were described thus:

> . . . these people are all very clever people, you know what I mean. Which makes them seem a lot older than 18. Especially since they are all the same, you know.

They were contrasted with people from the small town where he grew up and still returned to:

> It's fine when I go home. I still see some people I knew ten years ago, they know what happened to me . . . they make allowances for it anyway.

Overall, Leslie felt alienated from the university. In addition to his head injury, which he recognised had caused him major physical and psychological problems, other factors such as age and social class may have had an effect. Although he had a problem with balance and walking, Leslie did not see himself as disabled, an identity he associated with people who were, in his view, more seriously impaired, such as wheelchair users.

Karla, Scottish University 2

Karla, a mature student, was in the fourth year of a Sociology and Politics degree at Scottish University 2, an ancient institution taking 85 per cent of its intake from state schools or colleges. Karla had a physical impairment, acquired as an adult, which meant that she had difficulty walking and sometimes used a wheelchair. Karla was from a working-class background and left school with no qualifications. After travelling, she spent two years at college before entering university. Karla's perception was that her status as a single parent with money problems was more salient than having an impairment. She complained, for example, that a course in Women's Studies was held from three to five o'clock in the afternoon, which made it inaccessible to those with childcare responsibilities:

> I can't get back to get my little girl after school. Now I pay excessively for the childcare service. Classes that are late I can't do . . . I've had to see lecturers more about asking for extensions and they are never very forthcoming and it's got nothing to do with disability. I've got a child, I get her to bed, I sleep with her from 8.00–10.00 p.m. and I set an alarm and get up and work until two at night . . . I don't believe in the assessment system. I know it's meant to be fair assessment and everyone's got the same chance, but that's rubbish. Some of my friends are out working every hour God will send. Others, their parents pay for everything.

Karla perceived there to be a difference in identity and awareness between those born with an impairment and people like her who acquired it later in life:

> From what I've seen of my friends who are born disabled, they are very comfortable with it and call me a guest sometimes. 'Oh, here's the guest'. And my uncomfortableness is wrong. Well, not wrong . . . it's the whole thing of becoming disabled once you have developed as a person or been born disabled . . . If there was a group, I'm sure that you would find that most people had been born disabled in it.

She particularly objected to being grouped into a special area with other disabled people in cinemas and theatres:

Sometimes when you get out somewhere because it's accessible, you almost feel like it's 'Freakers' Ball'. It's horrible.

Karla was clearly at a critical point in her life, when existing aspects of her identity, such as being working class, were being held up for critical scrutiny and either rejected or incorporated into a new narrative. Being a single parent was regarded as the most important aspect of her identity, which would continue to play a key role in structuring her biography. Reflecting a sense of how disability is socially constructed, Karla tended to see herself as a 'guest' rather than a core member of this group.

Maureen, English University 2

Maureen was a mature student in her 60s who was studying History on a part-time basis. She had spent the majority of her adult life in the home, bringing up three children and undertaking the majority of household work including decorating. When she reached the age of 55 she decided there was a need to 'turn my life around and do something with it, and just set myself a couple of goals'. One of these was to get a degree, and as a first step she enrolled on an Access course. Maureen had a diagnosis of rheumatoid arthritis and was obliged to use powerful drugs to keep the condition under control. She described the way in which she saw the idea of disability as being imposed on her by others:

> *Do you see yourself as disabled at all?*
>
> No, no, not at all. It's weird because the lecturer I was talking about earlier, who was brilliant and helped me through, we were having a chat one day and I said that I had never thought that I was disabled and she said 'Who put the label on you?' sort of thing and I said 'The hospital really'. The hospital and different people at the hospital gave me leaflets and said that I could apply for different things from social security and I was thinking 'I'm not disabled'. But I don't like it, I don't like it at all and I don't think anybody else does really.

Even applying for disability-related benefits had been difficult for Maureen as she felt that disability was a term reserved for people with more severe impairments. When she came to the university, for example, she was reluctant to speak to the disabled students adviser about claiming the DSA:

> I felt I was taking something that I shouldn't be. Like when I go to the hospital, and I go every two weeks because they monitor my blood, I sit there and if you didn't see my hands, you would say, 'What's wrong with her?' type of thing. And I see people who are really fantastic but they are really crippled and I think, 'I'm wasting their time'. So I don't

feel very comfortable, I feel a bit of a cheat, but on the other hand I couldn't have done without it . . . I feel there is someone more worthy than me, you know. It's like my disabled parking bay, I've got my blue badge, I'm registered disabled. I didn't register myself as disabled. There is no way I will go into a disabled parking bay because someone with a wheelchair might need it more than me so if there is another parking bay I will use that. I've talked to [partner] about this and he says, 'Don't be silly, look at the state of your hands'. As I say, I feel there are people a lot worse off than me and I don't see myself as disabled.

Disability as political identity

Phil, Scottish University 1

Phil, at Scottish University 1 (a post-92, inner-city institution), was in the second year of an undergraduate degree leading to a professional qualification in social work. He had a visual impairment from birth which he described thus:

I'm registered blind, macular degeneration, very poor central vision. I have very poor vision generally but I have blind spots in the middle so I do tend to look out of the side of my eyes. But I just have very poor vision and I can get about as long as I cross at the green man and all that kind of stuff. I'm not very good at night and everything I have to read has to be magnified, speech by computer and so on.

Phil had received little support in his mainstream school and left with no qualifications, in large part because of his visual impairment:

So I kind of bluffed my way through school. I couldn't see the board, I couldn't read the books, you know, I just managed to get through it somehow, but I never got any qualifications. I nearly got an O level in English but I didn't pass. I think I left quite disenchanted.

After marriage and a period studying in his local FE college, Phil decided to stay at home to look after his new-born daughter since his wife had a full-time job. He described this time in his life as rather demotivating:

I was in the house . . . I didn't do very much apart from personal reading and playing sports. Not basically doing a lot, I just kind of gave up. I think I was quite disillusioned by the way the various systems act against you. I thought I was missing the educational system, I didn't get any real help.

However, just as educational failure contributed to his low self-esteem and loss of purpose, a later period of education at a local university was instrumental in the development of a much more positive sense of self:

> It's been a gradual confidence-building thing, probably one of the greatest things education has given me is confidence in myself again and obviously enhanced self-esteem.

In part, this positive sense of himself as a disabled person came about as a result of his first encounter with the social model of disability:

> When I came to university I started looking at the social model of disability. We had a lecturer who came in for the day who was blind and he started talking about the social model of disability . . . he went on about the social model of disability and he had a couple of books about it and then I sort of became more aware of it. I always remember one thing which stood out at me when I was reading, it was about the issuing of ramps. You know how that's viewed as a special requirement and the article said, well, stairs are provided for people. If there were no stairs to some buildings no one would get in, but there was nothing about society providing stairs, they are just provided and that's that. And that turned a wee light on in my head, and another one was that people can't do anything without glasses, but because of the cost of them, glasses are widely available to people, but computer equipment is expensive so people don't get it.

At this point in his life, Phil described himself as a highly politicised disabled person who was willing to argue for his rights:

> I probably do think of myself as a disabled person, but disabled in the sense that I'm disabled by society, not by my physical disability. So it's more a kind of political definition I would give. I don't tend to see myself as disabled in the negative sense. But I think a lot of it has come from my education.

Because of his commitment to his course and his young family, Phil was not able to get involved in student politics as a disabled activist, but he believed his understanding of disability infused all aspects of his life, and he intended to develop his thinking further in his future employment as a social worker. At Scottish University 1, there was an established tradition of student activism and another mature student, Fiona, who had a diagnosis of cerebral palsy, continued her earlier work as a disability activist within the university, sitting on the Student Representative Council.

Conclusion

It is evident from the accounts above that the experience of higher education plays a critical part in identity formation. For some people, higher education allows them to shed aspects of their former self. For example, Karla saw university as offering the opportunity to forge a new identity as a middle class person. For others, life as a student requires the melding of existing aspects of identity with emerging aspects of self. For example, Phil had to incorporate his identity as a parent and mature student into his new understanding of disability as a social construction. A striking finding of the research was that the majority of students were ambivalent about owning disability as a key facet of their identity.

Students' relationship with the category of disability was, to some extent, linked with the nature of their impairment. Those diagnosed with dyslexia tended to embrace this category as preferable to the spoilt identity associated with generic learning difficulties, a negative label which had often been attached to them at school. This is consistent with earlier research (Riddell *et al.*, 1994) which described parents' struggles to have their children diagnosed as dyslexic in school in the face of opposition from educational psychologists. In their study of policy and provision for children with specific learning difficulties in Scottish schools, Riddell *et al.* found that parents often insisted that children with dyslexia were a discrete group, whilst educational psychologists maintained that learning difficulties occur on a continuum, and with no qualitative distinction between dyslexia and 'common or garden' types of learning difficulty. Whilst dyslexic students were willing to categorise themselves as disabled in order to obtain support, they found it difficult to identify with others in this group. Deaf students were equally ambivalent about the category of disability, seeing themselves as a linguistic minority and rejecting the deficit connotations associated with the term.

Students who had acquired an impairment as a result of accident, injury or the ageing process saw themselves as qualitatively different from those who were born with an impairment. Those with acquired impairments represent the majority of disabled people, since the incidence of impairment increases with age, and only 17 per cent of disabled people have a congenital impairment (Riddell and Banks, 2001). As a result of the demographic profile of disabled people, the understandings of people with acquired impairments are likely to be particularly salient in influencing future policy. Indeed, a recurring theme emerging from the case studies was that students saw other people as being 'more disabled' than they were, even when their impairments had a significant impact on their daily lives. In the light of the new public sector duty to positively promote equality for disabled people, this ambivalence towards disability as a key facet of identity is important and is discussed further in Chapter 9.

In relation to theories of identity which we outlined at the start of this chapter, it is evident that disabled students' construction of self appears to coincide with Hall's second model of identity as temporal, contingent and negotiated. This is consistent with Watson's (2002) finding that disabled people may not prioritise disability in developing and maintaining their sense of self. Watson suggests that impairment, and hence the fixed identity of being a disabled person, is generally viewed negatively in a society which 'denigrates disabled people'. As a result, people with impairment reject the identity of being a disabled person, since this is experienced as something which others wish to impose, rather than arising as an embedded part of lived experience. This explanation resonates with the accounts given by disabled students in this study.

Chapter 9

Conclusion

Connecting the threads

In this final chapter, we briefly summarise the issues emerging from each of the earlier chapters, before returning to some of the key themes which weave their way through the text. In Chapter 1, we set out the national and international policy context of the study and outlined some of the major theories shaping our research questions. In essence, we were interested in the potential of higher education to reproduce or disrupt existing inequalities experienced by disabled students. Connections were made with initiatives to widen access to higher education for under-represented groups, which have tended to focus on social class rather than other social characteristics. We discussed various understandings of social justice, outlining the ongoing debates between those who prioritise either the economic or the cultural aspects of equality. The importance of the recent legislation prohibiting discrimination against disabled students was noted, and we also drew attention to the use of new public management strategies to promote both quality and equality in higher education.

In Chapter 2, we focused on patterns of participation in higher education by disabled students, drawing on our analysis of HESA statistics. We noted the relationship between a range of facets of identity (disability, social class, gender and ethnicity), and made comparisons between levels of participation by disabled students in different types of institution and different subject areas. In the light of the different approaches adopted by the English and Scottish Funding Councils, we analysed differences between levels of participation and disabled students' characteristics in the two countries. Overall, it was argued that whilst disabled students have benefited from the expansion of higher education, the greatest gains have been experienced by those who were already the most socially advantaged (see below for further discussion).

Based on a questionnaire survey administered to all higher and further education institutions delivering tertiary level education in England and Scotland, Chapter 3 considered the ways in which various institutions were responding to multiple policy pressures and innovations, including the requirement to accommodate the needs of disabled students. Compared with research conducted in 1999, it was evident that much had changed in the sector, and the provision of dedicated support staff was now standard. However, it was evident that widening access was not treated as a top priority by pre-92 institutions; the Research Assessment Exercise was identified by these universities as by far the most important force shaping their direction and activities. Teaching quality assessment was regarded as more important by post-92 institutions, and new universities and FE colleges both placed greater importance on widening access than the older universities. Shortage of funds was also seen as a key issue by post-92 institutions and FE colleges. The picture that emerged was of multiple and potentially competing pressures, with provision for disabled students having to take its place alongside other demands on institutional time and energy. Policies for disabled students were clearly much better developed than they had been five or even ten years earlier, when they had been virtually non-existent, but institutions acknowledged that less progress had been made in altering grassroots academic understanding and practice, reflected in curriculum, pedagogy and approaches to assessment.

The possibility that, in some cases, policy for disabled students might remain at the level of rhetoric was reinforced by the analysis of institutional ethos presented in Chapter 4. Different approaches to learning support were considered and it was noted that in post-92 institutions support for learning was much better established than was the case in their older counterparts. The downside for the new universities was a shortage of funding which restricted some of the investment in effective learning services which they believed would have a positive impact on improving retention rates, a benefit for disabled students and others. In pre-92 universities, learning support was a novel concept, and lecturers were often struggling with the idea that it might, on occasion, be justifiable to provide extra tuition or alternative forms of assessment. Pre-92 institutions were clearly more deeply imbued with notions of meritocracy, which envisaged all students competing within a neutral system, which would allow the best and brightest to flourish whilst the weakest students failed. The idea that the goal of education should be to enable all students to learn was difficult for them to grasp. The Scottish college which featured as one of our case study institutions offered an entirely different model, having major investment in learning support and an underlying commitment to the idea that, within certain broad boundaries, teaching and support should not be rationed, but delivered according to need.

The construction of the concept of reasonable adjustments in the areas of curriculum, pedagogy and assessment was further explored in Chapter 5, with a particular focus on understandings of learning difficulties in relation to students with a diagnosis of dyslexia. Whereas the websites of US universities often advise disabled students of their right to request alternative forms of assessment, institutions in Scotland and England were cautious about making adjustments at all. In the light of the emphasis on quality assurance and 'product standardisation', there was a common view that *ad hoc* adjustments were inherently risky, and formulaic adjustments, such as extra time in examinations, were the most that students should expect. Students with a diagnosis of dyslexia were often frustrated at the reluctance of lecturers to find ways of teaching and assessing which played to their strengths rather than their weaknesses, whilst, particularly in pre-92 universities, misgivings were often expressed by lecturers that making reasonable adjustments in teaching and assessment was a form of 'dumbing down', allowing lazy students to obtain dispensations by hiding under the cloak of disability.

The gap between rhetorical policy and practice was also abundantly clear in the academic and social experiences of students with higher support needs, which were explored in Chapter 6. Whilst some institutions went to great lengths to make accommodations, others were very reluctant to alter standardised provision. The rhetoric of empowerment and independence was often used to justify placing the onus on the individual disabled student to organise all aspects of support, including the employment of workers and the negotiation of physical obstacles. Drawing on case studies of particular students, we illustrated the incremental nature of the barriers encountered. In order to survive the course, disabled students were often required to make super-human efforts which most other students would find quite unreasonable. The ideology of independent living, strongly promoted by the disability movement, makes clear that financial and practical support are essential to the achievement of autonomy, which inevitably involves relationships based on inter-dependence (Shakespeare, 2000). Within higher education, independence was often misconstrued as a regime based on ideas of the survival of the fittest.

Chapter 7 draws attention to the experiences of students with mental health difficulties, who are often struggling to survive at the institutional margins. An unintended consequence of higher education expansion and the intensification of academic work may have been the creation of a far more anonymous environment, in which students experience a loss of structure and identity. Faced with overwhelming and conflicting pressures, staff may find it difficult to recognise that an individual is experiencing mental health difficulties, which may be misconstrued as disorganisation or lack of application. As a result of these pressures, institutions may unintentionally exacerbate, or even create, significant mental health difficulties. In this chapter we presented examples of the pioneering work which is taking place in some institutions, as disabled students advisers find ways of using premium funding and individual funds channelled through the Disabled Students Allowance to employ dedicated workers offering students direct support.

Finally, in Chapter 8 we considered the iterative relationship between disabled student identity and institutional policies. Whilst much policy creates a binary divide between the disabled and non-disabled population, discussions with students revealed that a unitary identity based on disability rarely accorded with their experience and sense of self. The category of disability was experienced equivocally, sometimes to be used for pragmatic purposes to obtain support, but rarely as an individual's defining characteristic. Sometimes, the category was resisted or rejected, and at other times it was seen as irrelevant, for example by deaf students who regarded themselves as a linguistic minority or by dyslexic students, who acknowledged their learning difficulty, but saw themselves as having little in common with students who were wheelchair users or had severe visual impairments. A conscious political identity was embraced by a small minority, who had often come to university as mature students and described their earlier encounter with the social model of disability as a revelatory experience.

Disability, social justice and higher education

A major concern of the research was to consider the extent to which widening access policies have indeed contributed to social justice goals. According to one interpretation, social justice is concerned with the way in which social goods, which may be economic or cultural, are distributed between different groups. Given that graduates earn considerably more than non-graduates, and have access to the wider benefits of higher education such as intellectual development, personal growth and access to social networks, higher education must clearly be regarded as a social and positional good. The most socially advantaged groups have traditionally dominated higher education, particularly gaining privileged access to the elite institutions. The question then arises: to what extent have widening access policies challenged this dominance? Data from the Higher Education Statistics Agency presented in Chapter 2 demonstrates that disabled students have increased numerically and as a proportion of the student body, suggesting that some redistribution has taken place in their favour. However, disabled students are more likely to come from middle-class backgrounds, and are less likely to be drawn from minority ethnic groups. A greater proportion are male, due to the preponderance of students with dyslexia, a syndrome more commonly diagnosed in men than women and in middle class than working-class students. Disabled students, particularly those with dyslexia, are more likely to be studying art and design subjects rather than science, social science, engineering or subjects leading to professional qualifications such as law, medicine, social work and education. This raises questions about what is being accessed, and the extent to which art and design courses have similar exchange value in the labour market compared with the subject areas where disabled students are less well represented. Whilst the growing number of disabled students in higher education is to be applauded, it is important that questions are asked about which groups are included and which continue to be excluded or cooled out. Furthermore, there is an ongoing need to monitor which universities and subject areas are including a more diverse range of students, and those which are continuing to draw from a narrow sector of the population.

Disabled people have particularly high rates of economic inactivity. For example, in Scotland, only 50 per cent of disabled people of working age are employed (Riddell and Banks, 2005). Questions therefore arise about whether disabled graduates are able to benefit from their qualifications when they move into the labour market. A HEFCE funded project (Evans and Farrar, 2003) has begun to explore the outcomes of disabled graduates in the labour market using HESA first destination survey data. The findings of the destination survey in 2002, which looks at outcomes six months after graduation, found that 48 per cent of disabled graduates with a first degree and 53 per cent of non-disabled graduates were in full-time employment. Disabled graduates were more likely to be employed in clerical and secretarial, craft, personal services and sales jobs, as well as in part-time and unpaid work. They were less likely to be embarking on careers in health and education. Further work is needed to explore the fortunes of disabled graduates as their careers develop. Evidence suggests that significant differences between disabled and non-disabled graduates exist, but nonetheless this group is performing markedly better than disabled non-graduates. In the post-university labour market, therefore, it appears that disabled graduates are likely to enjoy the benefits experienced by others with tertiary level qualifications. The importance of ensuring that more disabled students have the opportunity to access higher education is therefore underlined.

Whilst the distribution of economic resources is a key component of social justice, the importance of the related concept of respect or cultural validation has been increasingly emphasised over recent years. The research presented in this book makes clear that many disabled students in higher education struggle with the consequences of a spoilt identity, which they understand to be a consequence of the way in which society continues to denigrate disabled people. The experiences of our case study students demonstrate that many have severe difficulties in accessing 'normal' student experiences and often experience social isolation. As noted earlier, it has been argued that horizontal links, sometimes described as bonding social capital, are essential to getting by, whereas vertical or bridging forms of social capital are vital for getting on. Disabled students may have strong links with a disabled students adviser, a personal assistant, a mental health support tutor or a small group of friends, but they often lack the myriad loose connections which are a vital part of the higher education experience for many students. The full benefits of higher education may therefore be elusive.

In many ways the position of disabled students is contradictory. On the one hand, they may be seen as a highly privileged group of disabled people, with enhanced earning power and social status. On the other hand, they continue to be deeply disadvantaged by the negative social connotations which continue to be associated with disability. The experiences of students diagnosed with dyslexia illustrate these tensions. In order to obtain the support they require, they actively seek a diagnosis, but at the same time they resent and reject the stigma associated with the category of disability. Efforts of voluntary organisations for people with dyslexia have actively sought to destigmatise the condition, with celebrities such as Jackie Stewart or Susan Hampshire testifying to the creativity of people with dyslexia. Underlying these advertising campaigns is the message that a clear distinction must be drawn between people with dyslexia and those with non-specific learning difficulties, who cannot claim the special qualities and talents exhibited by those with dyslexia.

Overall, it is evident that whilst disabled people have benefited from the expansion of the higher education sector, they have also suffered as a result of the expansion, which has led to more standardised working practices and a less enthusiastic academic workforce. Whilst many disabled students experience a sense of dislocation in anonymous institutions, lecturers may resent further calls on their time to produce accessible curricula or individualised forms of assessment, maintaining that non-standard provision is incompatible within a mass higher education system.

New public management and social justice

New public management, inherited by New Labour from the previous Conservative government, has its origins in a neo-liberal philosophy which holds that all human behaviour can and should be measured and, in order to achieve efficiency, effectiveness and value for money in the public sector, all activity should be measured against agreed targets. New Labour attempted to adapt this strategy to achieve not only a more efficient public sector, but also one which was better able to achieve pre-specified social justice goals. The higher education sector exemplifies this approach, where targets were set by HEFCE in relation to, for example, student retention and completion rates, but also widening access objectives, both of which feature in league tables compiled by the press to inform student choice of institution. Summarising the complex reworking of new public management thinking by New Labour, Newman (2001) comments:

> In the UK, it [the Third Way] can be understood as an attempt to retain the economic gains of Thatcherism, while invoking a set of moral and civic values through which Labour sought to reshape civil society. A new emphasis on citizenship, democratic renewal and social inclusion appeared alongside a continued emphasis on economy and efficiency.
>
> (Newman, 2001: 2)

The question arises as to whether there is justification for New Labour's belief that new public management may serve social justice as well as public efficiency objectives. In relation to disabled students in higher education, a number of tensions emerge in efforts to achieve these diverse goals. According to the accounts given to us by institutional senior managers, benchmarks published by HEFCE in order to promote the widening access agenda have certainly had an impact, incentivised through premium funding. Similarly, the precepts set out in the QAA's Code of Practice in relation to disabled students has also had some effect. However, the impact of these measures appeared to have been greater in post-92 compared with pre-92 institutions. Within post-92 institutions, the RAE was seen as of much greater importance than the quality assurance regime, which was resisted within this sector and, it was believed, had become less powerful over time. The RAE, on the other hand, was seen as being very strongly incentivised both financially and in terms of prestige. It was believed by lecturers in pre-92 institutions that chances of promotion were tied more strongly to RAE than teaching performance, and the rational response was therefore to invest in developing a strong research profile. Clearly, this illustrates the way in which a proliferation of performance targets may generate internal friction. Furthermore, it was evident in the pre-92 institutions that lecturers resented the regime of performativity which they felt curbed their individual autonomy and creativity. Given that many reforms aimed at enhancing the position of disabled students have been couched within a new public management discourse, there is a danger that academic staff will resist such initiatives as yet another assault on their autonomy.

As Power (1997) pointed out, the promotion of an audit culture is likely to produce a range of adaptive behaviours which may work against the ends which the targets are trying to achieve. As noted earlier, premium funding in relation to disabled students is based on the number of students within an institution claiming the Disabled Students Allowance. The funding does not take into account the nature of the student's impairment, and therefore it is possible that institutions may be tempted to encourage students with less significant impairments to claim the DSA, rather than seeking to recruit students with higher support needs, for example those requiring 24 hour personal assistance. It is evident from the statistics presented in Chapter 2 that the expansion in participation by disabled students is largely accounted for by the growth in number of dyslexic students, with a small decline in the proportion of students with major sensory or physical impairments. It was also evident that institutions with a more socially advantaged student body attracted a large number of students who had been given a diagnosis of dyslexia at school, and they were more likely to come to university with a psychologist's report already completed. By way of contrast, institutions attracting students from less socially advantaged backgrounds tended to have fewer students identified as having dyslexia. It is likely that the continued emphasis on the widening access agenda, incentivised by premium funding, will encourage institutions to strategise in order to maximise funding in this area, and it will therefore be important to monitor the impact of benchmarks and premium funding in order to avoid the creation of perverse incentives.

Overall, it is evident that aspects of the new public management agenda in higher education have benefited disabled students, forcing institutions for the first time to monitor recruitment and retention in this area. However, the effects of managerialism have been mixed, with contradictions emerging between different audit regimes, the emergence of some unintended consequences and a general resentment of performance management across the sector.

The impact of anti-discrimination legislation

Throughout the various stages of the research, we looked for evidence of the extent to which higher education institutions were gearing up to meet their new responsibilities under Part 4 of the Disability Discrimination Act, which was about to come into force. In this area, too, findings were equivocal. On the one hand, institutions were aware of their legal obligations and had policies in place and there was clear evidence that they were anxious not to openly flout the law, resulting in cases being brought to court. However, discrimination may take more subtle forms, and students' accounts of admission procedures indicated that a cooling out process might occur, whereby applicants with higher support needs were being advised that another institution would be able to meet their needs more easily. It was also evident that changes in deeply ingrained aspects of institutional culture, such as established practice in relation to pedagogy, curriculum and assessment, were much less susceptible to change.

At the time of writing, further changes are underway. The Disability Act 2005 places a duty on all public sector bodies to positively promote equality for disabled people, both staff and students. This measure is in line with European Union equality treatment principles and mirrors the provisions of the Race Relations (Amendment) Act 2000. Further legislation is likely to extend the public sector duty to cover gender and, further down the line, other equality strands. In order to demonstrate compliance with these new duties, institutions will be expected to monitor and report on the proportion of disabled staff and students in the institution.

An interesting feature of these measures is that, like the widening access targets, they require a clear division to be drawn between the disabled and non-disabled population, a distinction which may not accord with disabled students' sense of self (see above). This highlights a core tension for the disability movement, which recognises that disability is a socially relative concept, but at the same time draws strength as a political movement from the idea that disabled people are essentially different from the non-disabled population. There is clearly a need for further research to explore the impact of social audit on institutional ethos and the negotiation of individual identity.

Mainstreaming equality: new challenges for higher education

Over recent years, widening access policies in higher education have been targeted at specific groups, primarily students from socially disadvantaged backgrounds, but also those from minority ethnic backgrounds and disabled students. In future years, it is likely that the sector may be increasingly influenced by the European Union's equal treatment principles, which recognise six equality strands (gender, race, disability, sexual orientation, age and religion), but also promote the idea of mainstreaming equality. Mainstreaming equality implies that equal opportunities principles, strategies and practices should be integrated into all aspects of the work of government and public bodies. The strategy is supported by the United Nations, the Commonwealth governments, the Council of Europe and many governments world-wide. Mainstreaming also has implications for participative democracy, since it implies that wide consultation of individuals and groups should take place before legislation is passed to ensure that it is 'equality proofed' (Rees, 2002; Breitenbach et al., 2002). The UK government has announced its intention to move towards a mainstreaming approach, on the grounds that individual identity is complex, not unitary, and it may be difficult to know whether discrimination has occurred as a result of an individual's gender, disability or ethnicity. In addition, it is argued that the principles which underpin equality in relation to all aspects of identity are fundamentally similar.

If mainstreaming becomes established as the new orthodoxy, it is likely to have major implications for the management of policy for disabled students in higher education, which has often been insulated from other widening access programmes. A mainstreaming approach to equalities might mean that targeted provision for disabled students becomes less common, and services would be delivered through generic learning support and student welfare provision. This might have the effect of removing the stigma, which is clearly still felt by some disabled students, but on the other hand it might lead to fewer resources being targeted on those grouped under the category of disability. At the time of writing, the Commission for Racial Equality has registered strong objections to the government's proposal for a single Commission for Equality and Human Rights, so progress towards a mainstreaming approach may be slower than anticipated.

Future policy trends

Looking towards the future, it is evident that inclusion policies for disabled students will inevitably be shaped by changes in the higher education system. The experiences of disabled students in higher education illustrate the tensions which have emerged as the UK higher education system transforms itself from an elite to a mass system. There is considerable evidence that academics are finding it difficult to adapt to the challenge of educating a much more diverse group of students, but there is also evidence of innovatory work in particular contexts. Disabled students advisers, despite the structural problems they encounter, have often acted as change agents, creatively using the funds available to provide disabled students with the support needed to survive in large and anonymous institutions. There are also important lessons to be learnt from the management of learning support in some post-92 institutions and further education colleges, where support for learning is likely to be regarded as part of mainstream provision rather than an add-on extra. Such thinking is far removed from the meritocratic principles persisting in the pre-92 sector, which appear increasingly anachronistic as participation rates approach 50 per cent of the age group.

Over the next decade, much will depend on the emerging political context. New Labour is likely to persist with its attempts to harness new public management strategies to the attainment of social justice goals, and is unlikely to deviate from its goal of including more of those at the margins. A future Conservative administration, on the other hand, would be unlikely to promote a widening access agenda and might allow institutions much more freedom to determine their own priorities. Overall, it is evident that the strategies pursued over the last decade have produced major changes in the position of disabled students within higher education. It is also clear, however, that some of the approaches adopted have produced unintended consequences, and there is still a long way to go before the culture of British higher education could be described as fully inclusive.

Appendix

Table A.1 Summary of disabled student case studies

1 Andy
Aged 17, English University 1, Year 2, English

Impairment
Illness/heart condition.

Application issues
Discomfort with 'special needs interview' – felt admission should have been on academic grounds.

Assessment
DSA assessment – laptop and software provided by LEA. Disabled students accommodation dingy and isolated – ground-floor accommodation with non-disabled students preferred.

Access issues
Some lectures too far from each other and upstairs, so inaccessible. Problem building social networks.

Teaching and learning experience/DDA awareness
No specific problems, but difficulties accessing some teaching accommodation.

Financial situation
Receives DSA and otherwise supported by professional parents.

Engagement with institution/Social experience of university
Virtually no social involvement – argues illness responsible for this but disappointed by university response – very reluctant to disclose and seek support – not active in disability movement. Spends much time watching TV in room. Many visits home.

Identity
Preferred to be seen as ill rather than disabled due to fluctuations in condition. Wanted to merge with others. Referred to 'rubbish body'. Saw disability as signalling spoilt identity. Unaware of DDA Part 4.

2 Peter
Aged 18, English University 1, Year 1, History

Impairment
Mobility difficulties as result of progressive condition. Peter uses a wheelchair and has weakness in his muscles.

Table A.1 (continued)

Application issues
Positive experience of university accommodation service. But spends all leisure time with PAs rather than other students – disappointed that this is the case.

Assessment
DO preliminary interview.

Access issues
Extensive use of two PAs to avoid difficulties. One PA paid for by LEA, one funded through ILF.

Teaching and learning experience/DDA awareness
Positive – primarily lectures and seminars. Personal assistance essential to allow participation.

Financial situation
Mixture of ILF and DSA funds full-time personal support.

Engagement with institution/Social experience of university
Involved in different social groups – university newspaper. Not active in a disability organisation (but father very involved in voluntary organisation for condition). Spends much time with PAs.

Identity
Having impairment has not had negative effect on life. Some advantages, e.g. orange parking badge. Vital to tell people about it and 'to get stuff sorted out'. Not aware of DDA.

3   Clare
Aged 18, English University 1, Year 3, Chemistry

Impairment
Mobility difficulties. Initially walked with splints – now uses wheelchair.

Application issues
Primary reason for application was academic status of university. Didn't get in to first choice. Another university tried to get her to withdraw application.

Assessment
Early assessment by disability officer and close involvement by department.

Access issues
Physical access problematic, especially library. Labs do not have wheelchair-accessible benches. Clare notes that neither would future employer.

Teaching and learning experience/DDA awareness
Mixed experience of lecturers, difficulties with note-takers. Withdrawn from labs due to illness and health & safety implications of fainting. Some lecturers refused to give notes or asked her to pay. Considering taking leave of absence from course for further assessments.

Financial situation
Difficulties in affording university accommodation – solely reliant on benefits. Disabled students accommodation is in highest price bracket. Wrote to DRC to question whether this was lawful.

Table A.1 (continued)

Engagement with institution/Social experience of university
Involved in a number of social groups, active in student union as disabled students representative. Confident in seeking support, but disheartened by obstacles. Does not get support from family.

Identity
Comfortable with being 'disabled' but feels it is label given to her by others. Engages in political struggle within university because feels personally responsible and no one else will. Aware of DDA but does not think university will be able to anticipate full range of individual needs.

4   Ronald
Aged 19, English University 1, Chemistry, Year 1

Impairment
Severe visual impairment.

Application Issues
Chose small friendly university – impressed by initial response of disability office.

Assessment
Effective in terms of support identified – some reservation by student in identifying himself to lecturers. Initiated assessment before arrival.

Access issues
Difficulty studying lab based subject. Some mobility difficulty due to building works on campus.

Teaching and learning experience/DDA awareness
Some academic staff had awareness of Ronald's needs and adapted their teaching methods to accommodate him (notes in advance etc.). But generally mixed experience. Health and safety concerns in lab – danger of spills. Supported by PA with knowledge of subject area (MSc student).

Financial situation
Supported by professional parents for rent – no student loan but works in bar part-time.

Engagement with institution/Social experience of university
Involved widely in social activities but not active in disabled people's organisation – reluctant to draw attention to impairment but felt it necessary to gain support.

Identity
Doesn't identify as 'disabled' – pragmatic approach to seeking assistance. Wants to pass as 'normal'. Unaware of DDA Part 4.

5   Sheena
PhD student, aged 32, English University 1, MSc Psychology, Year 1

Impairment
Dyslexia. Problems with short-term memory, spelling, writing.

Application issues
Keen on university due to closeness to home. Initially more important than its reputation.

Table A.1   (continued)

Assessment
Student had grave concerns about assessment process – angry at how she was informed about her dyslexia. Lecturers did not involve her in discussions.

Access issues
Access to subject hindered by dyslexia – advised she lacked appropriate analytical & verbal skills to tackle PhD.

Teaching and learning experience/DDA awareness
Staff awareness of dyslexia poor – supervisor inexperienced. Improved after supervisor started writing notes. Student felt insufficient allowances made for dyslexia.

Financial situation
Self supporting having saved prior to study.

Engagement with institution/Social experience of university
Finds social life of university difficult – more established outside university – not active in a disabled persons organisation. Angry at disclosure of her impairment within department without her consent.

Identity
Relieved to be diagnosed as dyslexic but does not see it as disabling in relation to other impairments. Feels some stigma still attached to disability and dyslexia. Unaware of DDA Part 4.

6   Rosie
Aged 65, English University 1, Year 3, Applied Social Science

Impairment
Illness/Arthritis. Fluctuating condition.

Application issues
Access route. Academic preference for university.

Assessment
DSA assessment satisfactory but difficulties due to changing nature of illness.

Access issues
Assumed newness of university meant it was accessible. Difficulty with walk across campus. Now has PC in room.

Teaching and learning experience/DDA awareness
Difficulties with written work eventually solved by technology/extensions. Student reluctant to seek assistance from lecturers. Support for Disability Officer – 'absolute gem'.

Financial situation
Financed course by re-mortgaging her house. Reliant on benefits/hardship loan and student grant which was initially withheld due to her age. 'Peculiar' financial difficulties for over-55s.

Engagement with institution/Social experience of university
Sees herself as too old for such involvement. Slight isolation due to age. Regular weekends at home to care for partner – not active in disabled people's organisation – initially reluctant to seek support as 'disabled person'.

Table A.1 (continued)

Identity
Preferred 'damaged' to term 'disabled'. Unaware of DDA Part 4.

7   Maureen
Aged 67, English University 2, part-time History, Year 2

Impairment
Chronic rheumatoid arthritis.

Application issues
Access route. Reluctance to seek special assistance.

Assessment
DSA assessment. Heavy reliance on technological support.

Access issues
Some problems with mobility around campus.

Teaching and learning experience/DDA awareness
Process of meeting student needs dependent on weak communication
system between disability office and lecturers. Lecturers largely not aware of
necessary adjustments to be made to their own practice. Friend assists with
note-taking. Strong praise for efforts of DO.

Financial situation
Reliant on DSA and state benefits. Partner also a student.

Engagement with institution/Social experience of university
Some social involvement with other students. Reliance on fellow student for academic
support – not active in disabled people's organisation – reluctant to disclose
impairment.

Identity
Not willing to see herself as 'disabled' – term for more severely impaired people.
Unaware of DDA Part 4.

8   Paula
Aged 19, English University 2, Psychology and Sociology, Year 2

Impairment
Blind.

Application issues
Impressed with support offered by university. Several interviews before arriving.

Assessment
DSA assessment. Provision of familiarisation training with guide dog and
technological assessment. Initial assessment under-estimated number of reader
hours required.

Access issues
Insufficient LEA/SAAS funding for necessary equipment. Reader available at
start of term, but equipment arrived after Christmas of first year. Guide dog
vital to access but problems cleaning up dog mess – security staff would point
out where mess was, but not help with clearing up.

Table A.1   (continued)

Teaching and learning experience/DDA awareness
Generally OK but access to visual material before lectures patchy. Heavy
course reading not broken down to essentials hence reader difficulties.
Course texts required 3 weeks in advance – organisational difficulties.
Impeded by problems mastering technology, slow arrival of equipment
and limited reader hours.

Financial situation
DLA plus parental support and DSA. Unwilling to take student loan – serious
personal financial problems incurred by exceeding DLA allowance for reader
hours – charity responded positively.

Engagement with institution/Social experience of university
Not active as 'disabled person'. Confident approaching lectures on an individual
level – flat situation not ideal due to need to remain in same building in year 2.
Much involvement in extra-curricular activities (e.g. swimming, gym).

Identity
Mixed – more strongly Scottish in England than disabled – primarily 'blind'. Describes
family as coming from working class, but not rough, area. Aware of DDA in general
but not new Part 4 provisions.

9   Roland
Aged 18, English University 2, Psychology, Year 3

Impairment
Dyslexia.

Application issues
Keen on specific course and impressed by support offered in university.

Assessment
DSA assessment. Assessment by psychologist conveyed to academic staff. Student
concerned that it referred to 'dyslexic-type difficulties' rather than dyslexia.

Access issues
Lectures were 'a bit of a sensory assault'.

Teaching and learning experience/DDA awareness
Positive experience of psychology department – offers of tutorial support. Lecture
notes in advance. Extra time for assignments 'double edged sword'. Benefit of
one to one support from dyslexia unit. Dyslexic students meet once a week as
supportive 'workshop group'. Questions about whether other students could benefit
from this level of support – issue of fairness.

Financial situation
Parental support and DSA. Has student loan, but tries not to worry about debt – will
pay off quickly once working.

Engagement with institution/Social experience of university
Not affected by impairment beyond extra time needed to study – confident
approaching lecturers individually. Used to be reserved socially but now more
outgoing.

Table A.1 (continued)

Identity
Preferred 'minor disability'. Positive view of dyslexia – aware that dyslexics may be very creative. Describes family as middle class and supportive. No awareness of DDA Part 4.

10   Dermot
Aged 27, English University 2, Year 2, Psychology, Course suspended

Impairment
Chronic pain syndrome.

Application issues
Positive impression of department and their response to disabled students.

Assessment
DSA assessment. Did not identify himself early enough to disability office. Long delays in getting internet connection at home.

Access issues
Problems getting to lectures because of fluctuating condition.

Teaching and learning experience/DDA awareness
Some difficulty attending other tutorials/seminars than those designated due to lecturers' attitude. Difficulties with inflexibility of assessment process – no extensions in Psychology, cf. dyslexic student's experience. Good availability of notes/handouts – use of web-based materials.

Financial situation
Reliant on DLA and other state benefits – DSA.

Engagement with institution/Social experience of university
Not strong due to absences but friendly with other disabled students – reluctant to 'play disability card' when negotiating with lecturers.

Identity
Can identify with disabled people but not strongly. Individual view of impairment. Sees himself as mixture of identities with gay community and church etc. Describes self as 'mildly disabled' but would be 'silly' to say everything is 'perfectly normal'. Vague awareness of DDA.

11   Chloe
Mature student, English University 2, Business Information Technology by distance learning (part time), Year 2

Impairment
Borderline personality disorder (+ unassessed visual dyslexia).

Application issues
Distance learning offers the flexibility she needs.

Assessment
She didn't tell the university about BPD until her first exam. She needed extra time and a support person. This led to an assessment at an access centre, an application for the DSA and one to one study skills support.

Table A.1 (continued)

Access issues
Her main needs are flexibility, computing equipment, extra time and personal support in exams.

Teaching and learning experience/DDA awareness
This seems to be going OK. She enjoys her course and gets on with the work at her own pace. Recently she's felt better and wanted to attend some classes but this has been refused because she is a distance learning student. A study skills class for students with dyslexia has proved more useful than her one to one tuition because it's more structured. She has taken someone to court in the past and would only do this if she felt sure that she could prove her case, because she felt she was treated like a liar even though she was the victim.

Financial situation
It took 4 months for her LEA to provide DSA for computer equipment. She is still waiting for money for books, special glasses and internet access.

Engagement with institution/Social experience of university
She doesn't feel like a 'proper student' because she does not attend classes and lectures. She is resident in a supported housing project for people with BPD. This requires her to attend individual and group therapy and house meetings. It is an intensive therapy experience in itself. The time commitment required has slowed down progress on her course.

Identity
She is aware of stigma attached to BPD and will not disclose it to future employers. Not aware of DDA Part 4.

12   Mark
Aged 23, English University 2, Accountancy and Business, Year 2

Impairment
'Eyesight problem' (central vision blindness) developed after his A levels.

Application issues
Applied through clearing after period of employment in a supermarket.

Assessment
Contacted by student support services and met with them few weeks before start of course. Needs were assessed, DSA applied for, extra time in exams arranged.

Access issues
Difficulties using library by self, needs enlargement equipment for text/books. Needs copies of overheads/handouts in advance.

Teaching and learning experience/DDA awareness
Email from SSS failed to produce handouts from lecturers. He now tells them himself, having to remind them constantly because they 'forget' his copies/handouts in advance: a constant bugbear.

Financial situation
DSA provided computer, enlargement software, CCTV, opti (hand-held enlarger), laptop. Fund built up by his work and mum's work when he developed disability also supplied some of this equipment. Still has lot of money in fund.

Table A.1 (continued)

Engagement with institution/Social experience of university
Engaged to be married; has part-time job. Has friends at university.

Identity
Likes to pass as non-disabled, tells people when necessary if he cannot do something. Disability still stigmatised. Likes them to know him first to overcome prejudices. Says he doesn't have a problem with his 'eyesight problem'. Doesn't mind being classed as disabled but doesn't like to draw attention to it. Unaware of DDA
Part 4.

13   Ellie
Mature student, English University 3, Conservation and Countryside Management, repeating 1st year

Impairment
Depression and anxiety.

Application issues
Found out had a place 2 weeks before start. Has 4-year-old daughter, single mum. Stayed in temporary accommodation, got very behind, dad died, eventually dropped out. Repeating 1st year.

Assessment
Tutor referred her to mental health support service.

Access issues
Difficulties with concentration, motivation, attendance, memory and anxiety in groups. Accessing library/computer facilities difficult because of this.

Teaching and learning experience/DDA awareness
Main problem lecturers' lack of understanding. Dismissed as experiencing 'normal stress'. Doing a presentation was a 'terrible experience'. Can now give presentations to the lecturer only. Staff have better understanding now because of intervention of MHT.

Financial situation
Longwinded process to get DSA for computer to avoid using library/computers at uni. Application finally rejected. Mother loaned her money for it – a big help. Receives mature students' grant and allowances and loans. Help from financial services at uni. Support of MHT weekly through DSA.

Engagement with institution/Social experience of university
Initially reluctant to discuss difficulties with tutors because of their lack of understanding – she travels far to university on public transport, has a 4-year-old daughter to get to and from childcare. Therefore no time for socialising. Accommodation services were not helpful in finding her child-suitable accommodation. With support from MHT, now more open. Also 3-way meeting between MHT, herself and course leader established responsibilities and made it easier for Ellie to approach course leader.

Identity
First generation to go to university. Half the students at her school went. Doesn't consider herself disabled. Not heard of DDA, would bring legal action as a last resort.

Table A.1 (continued)

14 Rena
Straight from school, English University 3, Sciences and Computing, Year 4

Impairment
Dyslexia, clinical depression, intermittent kidney infections.

Application issues
Chose this institution because of the dyslexia support available and because liked city and course.

Assessment
Dyslexia assessment early on, but no support other than computer, because 'not available to first years'. Repeated 2nd year due to depression. Tutor 'frog-marched' her to doctor in third year when depression came to a head.

Access issues
In first year, difficulty taking notes in lectures and meeting deadlines. One lecturer refused to give out lecture notes because it would disadvantage other students. She then got note-taker and study skills support.

Teaching and learning experience/DDA awareness
Gets the support of a mental health tutor, once/week who helps her to organise and structure her work, sets short term goals and just listens if necessary. This has been invaluable. She attributes her depression largely to the instability and lack of routine at university.

Financial situation
Has a computer and software, a note-taker, a book allowance, the support of a mental health tutor and study skills support through the DSA. Parents pay for her rent, food and fees. Receives minimum student loans and 'struggles'.

Engagement with institution/Social experience of university
Felt isolated in the past because she lived out of town. Now lives in town, but doesn't have much time to socialise because of workload. Has been very reluctant to tell lecturers about difficulties. However, with the support of the MHT, has now told most of them. Hates asking for extensions, but MHT does this for her sometimes.

Identity
Hates to tell anyone about her difficulties because she doesn't want 'special treatment'. In the past has tried to cope by herself and sees this as her downfall. Now realises she needs support. She was expected to go to uni by school and family. Unaware of DDA Part 4.

15 Joan
Aged 42, English University 3, Human Services, Year 3

Impairment
Arthritis.

Application issues
Application determined by location and specific interest in course offered. Has 4 children – youngest still at home. Worked as aerobics instructor prior to onset of arthritis. Ambition – to be accepted for teacher training. Invited in for discussion with DO following application – unclear if academic & access issues treated separately. After acceptance, DO liaises with academic department.

Table A.1 (continued)

Assessment
Uncomfortable with disclosure but encouraged to 'tell truth' by access tutor.
Required note-taker and lift keys offered.

Access issues
Physical environment tiring due to distances, doors, etc.

Teaching and learning experience/DDA awareness
Generally OK but anxiety in telling lecturers of her difficulties – failure of
communication process. Positive experience of support – note-takers and technology
particularly helpful. Standard 2-week extension on all assignments.

Financial situation
Struggling financially – unable to balance need to work with adequate study time.
Husband is also a student. Receives DSA. University invoices her for note-taker – she
passes invoice to LEA. Paid by cheque which is passed to university. Requires taxi to
get to university but not reimbursed.

Engagement with institution/Social experience of university
Positive – use of fellow students in taking notes and accessing missed handouts.

Identity
Aware of effects of impairment but no association with disabled identity. Finds
condition difficult and frustrating. Unaware of DDA Part 4.

16 Jill
Aged 23, English University 3, Photography, Year 2

Impairment
Dyslexia.

Application issues
School only noticed dyslexia at final exam time – too late. Turned down for
physiotherapy (believed as result of dyslexia). Then studied radiotherapy &
worked abroad. Decided to do course based on visual/creative rather than
linguistic skills.

Assessment
Standard university response to dyslexia – DSA application and personal
support. Dyslexia assessment test used in university – but questions raised
about validity.

Access issues
Final year dissertation problematic for dyslexic students. Longer loan for library books
& free photocopying. Some photography tutors dyslexic – sympathetic.

Teaching and learning experience/DDA awareness
Mixed impression of academic staff. Some give excellent consideration to difficulties,
others poor. Argue that allowing dyslexic students to have notes would breach
copyright and disadvantage other students. Heavy reliance on one-to-one support
of dyslexic tutor. Difficulties in coping with 10,000-word dissertation at end of
2nd year in otherwise practical-based course.

Financial situation
DSA. Financial support from parents. Part-time job in holidays.

Table A.1 (continued)

Engagement with institution/Social experience of university
Confident addressing academic staff – positive social experience.

Identity
Positive attitude to dyslexia, but regards it as pigeon-holed in disability category. Sees self as having learning difficulty, not disability. Disability includes students with sensory and physical impairments. Perceives self as very intelligent person 'who can't bloody write'. Unaware of DDA.

17 Mike
Aged 24, English University 3, Agriculture, Year 3

Impairment
Dyslexia.

Application issues
Left school and did BTec in Agriculture at college. Then National Certificate and National Diploma. College became part of university. Application influenced by location and high level of support.

Assessment
DSA assessment. Long delay in psychological assessment causing hold up in supply of PC and software.

Access issues
Finds course quite demanding & needs support.

Teaching and learning experience/DDA awareness
Individual lecturers have assumed considerable responsibility for adapting teaching/teaching materials – may be a legacy from more intimate previous FE college structure. PowerPoint seen as helpful for all students. Student had heavy reliance on one-to-one support of dyslexia tutor and learning support. Entitled to one hour additional support per week from dyslexia support tutor. Extra time in exams (25% extra). Scribe available if required.

Financial situation
DSA, works part time and supported by parents.

Engagement with institution/Social experience of university
Shy in declaring dyslexia but feels it necessary – positive social experience not significantly impacted by dyslexia. Mum corrected work at college and he still likes to be close to home.

Identity
Was 'tormented' at school and would be reluctant to 'broadcast' dyslexia, but friends know. Was in bottom set at school but knows he is 'not thick'. Sees 'disabled' as term for people with severe physical impairment. No awareness of DDA.

18 Tony
Aged 19, English University 3, Accountancy and Finance, Year 3

Impairment
Dyslexia.

Table A.1 (continued)

Application issues
Application determined by grades. Not first choice university.

Assessment
Reading/behavioural difficulties at school. Assessed as dyslexic. University psychologist assessed him as not dyslexic – reassessed by school psychologist
and university accepted this diagnosis.

Access issues
Difficulties with essay writing – mainly structuring ideas & using correct grammar and syntax.

Teaching and learning experience/DDA awareness
One-to-one support with dyslexia support tutor considered essential to coursework. Some lecturers particularly considerate in their practice, others not. Handouts provided prior to most lectures but little on web. Limited number of essays set in exams to reduce time pressures.

Financial situation
DSA, financial support from parents.

Engagement with institution/Social experience of university
Confident addressing academic staff but unsure as to their capacity to help. Limited impact of dyslexia on social life.

Identity
Confident declaring as dyslexic. Doesn't identify as disabled – confused over terminology, but forced on occasion to use the term for administrative purposes. Not aware of DDA Part 4.

19   Pete
Aged 38, English University 3, from Nigeria, married with family, Civil Engineering, Year 3

Impairment
Depression. Problems with eyesight.

Application issues
Applied because his wife needed to move to area for medical reasons. Only applied to one university, liked 2 people he met there and decided to come.

Assessment
Struggled in his first 2 semesters, failed one exam 3 times, was getting more and more vocal and angry. This led him to be put in touch with the MHT.

Access issues
Needs extensions/flexibility, used to panic in exams. Needed individual support to organise work, manage time, cope with stress.

Teaching and learning experience/DDA awareness
Some lecturers have failed to recognise his difficulties even when the university officially recognises them. The MHT is the only reason he has got this far. He describes a very poor learning environment which he feels has exacerbated his difficulties.

Table A.1 (continued)

Financial situation
DSA pays for MHT support every week. He has a tape recorder. Receives mature
student's grant with dependants' allowance. Cannot afford university accommodation,
so lives in council flat.

Engagement with institution/Social experience of university
Used to struggle to speak to his lecturers because he felt the culture was not one in
which it was OK to be struggling. With backing of MHT now speaks to them and
feels entitled to extensions although he rarely takes them now. Felt racially
discriminated against by one lecturer.

Identity
Sees himself as disabled and as black man. Feels it is a culture which does not
accept difference and this has made it really hard for him. He used to feel it was
all his own fault. The MHT has helped him to see that it is cultural. Unaware of
DDA Part 4.

20 Eve
Late 20s, English University 4, PhD student, Geography

Impairment
Deaf, but not diagnosed till after school.

Application issues
After school worked as gardener. Applied to this university because of support for
deaf students. Lived nearby and had family commitments. Social Policy degree, PhD.

Assessment
Not identified as deaf till after school. At university open day, needs assessed –
received DSA from LEA. Paid for person to type lectures.

Access issues
Seminars continue to be a problem. Has tried teaching but difficult to lip-read so
many students (example of impairment effect linked to disability).

Teaching and learning experience/DDA awareness
Most lecturers helpful. But in seminars questions not repeated. Radio aid draws
attention to self – not always welcome. Conferences difficult – can't hear question
so answer makes no sense.

Financial situation
DSA relatively generous (£10,000). Looking forward to earning after PhD – has
2 children and mortgage.

Engagement with institution/Social experience of university
Doesn't engage with student group – has independent friends in village. Mature
student – relates less to younger age group. Can lip-read on one-to-one basis, but
large groups difficult.

Identity
Has only recently learnt sign language – only partially relates to deaf community in
city. Not aware of changes to DDA, but was told about developments to Geography
curriculum to make it more accessible.

Table A.1 (continued)

21   Nancy
English University 4, Maths, Year 3

Impairment
ME – occurred after gap year. Took 15 months to realise that not well.

Application issues
Applied to this university because good for Maths – not ill at this point.

Assessment
Found out about access unit by chance. Had been elected disabled students
officer on students union – was seeking disabled parking space. Directed to
access unit.

Access issues
Individual learning support not available. If morning lectures missed, no way of
catching up.

Teaching and learning experience/DDA awareness
Some lecturers allow for absence and late submission – others don't. Not allowed to
do degree part time. Support limited – lecturers refuse to 'teach course twice'.

Financial situation
Got DSA for part of final year – paid for computer, printer and adapted chair.
Has note-taker's allowance for lectures, but doesn't often use it. Middle-class
background and parental support.

Engagement with institution/Social experience of university
Became involved in students union by chance – friend pointed out vacancy for
disabled students officer. Difficult relationship with access unit – refused to help her
make contact with other disabled students.

Identity
Has only recently identified with disability issues, but relieved to get diagnosis of ME.
Doesn't define herself through condition, but doesn't keep it hidden. Aware of DDA
because of role in students union.

22   Terry
Aged 27, English University 4, MSc Deaf Studies

Impairment
Deaf.

Application issues
Previous university experience poor – straightforward.

Assessment
Assessed by signer of low grade which led to inaccuracies in assessment despite
having requested signer of higher grade.

Access issues
Availability of signers extremely poor – difficulties concerning payment of signers and
DSA support.

Teaching and learning experience/DDA awareness
Some course assessments to be made in sign language – major concession by
university.

Table A.1   (continued)

Financial situation
Describes himself as 'privileged' class wise but determined to be self-sufficient –
works part time to pay for studies – major financial worry over having to pay for
signers before assurance of extent of DSA support.

Engagement with institution/Social experience of university
Very active politically as representative of deaf students – prepared to challenge
university on a number of issues – social life restricted by availability of signers
to mostly deaf community only.

Identity
Primarily seen as deaf – but 'disabled' in certain circumstances – recent member of
deaf community by learning sign language – currently pursuing legal action against
university under DDA Part 4.

23   Fiona
Aged 34, Scottish University 1, Social Sciences, fourth year out of 5¹/₂

Impairment
Mobility, speech difficulties.

Application issues
Applied very late. This university her first choice. She would have started a year later,
but got in before the end of student grants. Wishes she'd waited so that more was in
place.

Assessment
DO invited her for chat very early on. But this did not prevent severe access issues
in first year.

Access issues
Severe in first year. Lecture theatre inaccessible. Almost gave up. Low attendance,
but compensatory pass because her work was fine and university admitted it
was their fault. Library difficult to access, limited toilet facilities, difficulties
with parking.

Teaching and learning experience/DDA awareness
Main issues around PAs – had 20, many difficulties because of unsocial hours,
difficulties of finding suitable people, keeping them over summer break. PA involved
in all aspects of study. Difficulties with one lecturer, others OK. Sociology 'great' –
doing teachability, disability aware. Psychology 'terrible' – deny knowledge of her
continuous extensions. Issues about over-long exams with extra time. Aware of DDA
and would take action if necessary although sees no need at moment.

Financial situation
Getting cheques from SAAS to pay PAs an issue. Received computer, laptop, tape
recorder, money for PA. Funding may become an issue as she's taking longer to
complete.

Engagement with institution/Social experience of university
Very proactive. She says: 'if you shout, you get' at this university. Disabilities officer
with SRC. Difficulty making friends because of low attendance in first year. Bonded
with two students last year who completed course before she did.

Table A.1 (continued)

Identity
Describes self as activist. Used to be active in disability movement. Proud to be a disabled person. Fighting for rights of other disabled students through SRC.

24 Danny
Aged 22, Scottish University 1, Occupational Therapy, Year 3

Impairment
Dyslexia.

Application issues
None related to dyslexia.

Assessment
Discovered dyslexia in first year after failing first 2 assessments. Guidelines for academic staff drawn up by disability service not followed by academics.

Access issues
Difficulty taking notes in lectures, accessing books in library because of numerical system. Describes lot of stress at university.

Teaching and learning experience/DDA awareness
Doing really well on placement. Received excellent support from dyslexia support tutor. Academic departments not recognised/understood dyslexia, not provided e.g. handouts in advance. Extra time in exams but not assignments. Complained about one lecturer. Very difficult getting through course. Had not heard of DDA.

Financial situation
Received DSA, computer, software, extra time in exams. Has been refused extensions on assignments. Says computer not really useful. He can't use some of the software and received no training.

Engagement with institution/Social experience of university
Very vocal about his dyslexia. Feels he's had to 'shout' to get things. Not ashamed to tell anyone about it. Already complained and would use grievance procedures.

Identity
Proactive and unashamed of dyslexia. Gay and positive about that. Sees stigma but refuses to take it on board. Would take legal action. Wants to promote positive dyslexic role models, will appear on uni website as case study.

25 Jan
Aged 19, Scottish University 1, Electronic Business, Year 1

Impairment
Illness: lupus (sore joints and tiredness).

Application issues
Took gap year due to illness. Came through clearing. Chose course, illness not a factor.

Assessment
Proactively contacted disability service, discussed needs, had assessment. No problems.

Table A.1 (continued)

Access issues
Easier to type than to write. Missed an exam through illness, got doctor's note and re-sat. Unpredictable tiredness the main issue.

Teaching and learning experience/DDA awareness
Disability service lent her a laptop, until she got the DSA. Only in 2nd term of 1st year. No problems so far.

Financial situation
Laptop through DSA, which she finds very useful. No problems getting DSA. Extensions: not used yet. Very positive about disability service. Had not heard of DDA.

Engagement with institution/Social experience of university
Disability service wrote a letter for lecturers. She took it to head of department. Doesn't know who else knows.

Identity
Does not consider herself disabled. Would not use legal action.

26 Phil
Aged 35, Scottish University 1, Social Work, Year 2

Impairment
Visual.

Application issues
Left school with no qualifications. When daughter went to school, did Access course, then HNC, then won place at university.

Assessment
DO preliminary interview. Involved in arguments with SAAS re having his equipment paid for and in place in time for the start of his course.

Access issues
Difficulty reading overhead projector slides. Lecturers don't cover all points on acetate. Needs much support from fellow students and help from reader in accessing articles/books from library. Access assisted by improvements in voice recognition software and scanning.

Teaching and learning experience/DDA awareness
Primarily lectures and seminars. Reliant on other students for access to material presented during the class. Placements not willing to provide technological assistance. Access to course material limited by poor technology on campus and poor quality of handouts. SAAS unwilling to pay for reader in holiday period.

Financial situation
Supported by DSA and partner working.

Engagement with institution/Social experience of university
Negotiated difficulties directly with tutor – confident in doing this. No organised involvement as 'disabled person' but frequent casual coffee and drinks with fellow students.

Identity
Awareness of social model, gained through contact with visually impaired lecturer in Year 1. Has political & social relational view of disability. Expectation that environment can and should change.

Table A.1 (continued)

27   Shelly
Aged 19, Scottish University 1, Psychology, Year 2

Impairment
Cerebral palsy/mobility difficulties.

Application issues
Took 2 years out after leaving mainstream school because initial choice of university turned out to be inaccessible.

Assessment
DO invited her to preliminary interview. Reliance on self rather than disability office to keep lecturing staff informed of her needs.

Access issues
Restricted use of PA. One PA (from CSV) couldn't take notes and hadn't been to university. Also needed scribe. Problems with new scribe in exam – couldn't understand her. Spanish department found speech difficulties difficult to deal with – set separate work.

Teaching and learning experience/DDA awareness
Primarily lectures and seminars but some labs. Participation in Spanish classes restricted. Lab classes difficult – lack of lecturer awareness.

Financial situation
Financed by student loan and parental contribution. Receives DSA. Incurred serious difficulties in paying PA due to slow processing of claims by SAAS.

Engagement with institution/Social experience of university
No organised involvement as 'disabled'. Reluctantly assertive in academic environment – positive experience socially but restricted by limited use of PA – cost issue.

Identity
Desire to be seen as an ordinary student but comfortable with disclosing impairment when necessary. Was seen as 'guinea pig' in mainstream school.

28   Ricky
Aged 22, Scottish University 1, Information Technology, Year 4

Impairment
Hearing impairment. Uses lip-reading.

Application issues
Aware that with support he could succeed at university. Attended post-92 university in England and then Scottish college prior to starting present course. Benefited from greater maturity.

Assessment
Relied on advice and support of RNID as to needs re technology, note-taker, etc.

Access issues
No support till after first term. Poor availability of note-takers. Lacked subject knowledge. Now other students think he has an advantage!

Teaching and learning experience/DDA awareness
Generally good. One lecturer pioneering voice recognition software giving live subtitles to lecture. One lecturer's notes available on web. Prefers to get notes at start of class.

Table A.1 (continued)

Financial situation
Financed by student loan and parental contribution – DSA for laptop and note-taker.

Engagement with institution/Social experience of university
Assertive in dealing with academics and DO – close network of established friends. Little obvious impact of impairment. Travels from home 20 miles away each day.

Identity
Lip-reader with no strong affiliation to deaf community or disabled people. Likes to be seen as 'just one of the guys'.

29 Liam
Aged 22, Scottish University 2, Film and TV Studies, Year 4

Impairment
Dyslexia.

Application issues
Dyslexia not diagnosed till university – felt annoyed that school had not acted.

Assessment
Psychological assessment after referral to disability officer in Year 2.

Access issues
Great difficulties writing consistently high-standard essays – sometimes attempted 20 drafts.

Teaching and learning experience/DDA awareness
Mixed. Some lecturers refused to make accommodations (e.g. looking at draft essay) on academic grounds, others extremely helpful. English department staff unfriendly – Film and TV helpful. Difficulties with assessment process – disappointed with exam result (2.1 rather than 1st). Felt he should have asked for oral assessment rather than exam.

Financial situation
DSA – parental support and student loan.

Engagement with institution/Social experience of university
Assertive in academic situation – only evidence of impairment is extra time needed to study and problems with structuring ideas, leading to need for multiple drafts.

Identity
Relief at diagnosis. Didn't adopt disability identity. Likened discrimination he had experienced as dyslexic to racism – felt he'd been cheated of opportunity to do funded PhD. Wrote letter to university castigating unfairness of exam system, which structurally disadvantages dyslexics.

30 Sally
Aged 24, Scottish University 2, French and German (changed from Marine Biology after stroke), Year 4

Impairment
Physical – stroke.

Application issues
No illness on initial application. Checked out quality of courses in prospectuses and compared. Wanted to go to a high status institution. ('I'm a bit snobby really'.)

Table A.1 (continued)

Assessment
DSA assessment. Disability office assessment with help of Rehab (voluntary organisation).

Access issues
Changed course after stroke – felt languages less problematic than lab-based subject.

Teaching and learning experience/DDA awareness
Withdrew from original course due to nature of impairment. Access assisted by IT and library staff.

Financial situation
DSA – parental support and student loan.

Engagement with institution/Social experience of university
Reasonably assertive in seeking support initially but does not identify strongly as disabled person. Friends were curious, but now treat her as normal. Some people don't notice she has an impairment. No obvious impact of impairment on social life in university.

Identity
Feels disability category is for more severely impaired people. Spent first 22 years of her life as non-disabled person. Has had to cope with sudden change in status and identity.

31   Christine
Aged 21, Scottish University 2, General Science degree (several course changes), Year 3

Impairment
Mobility – wheelchair user requiring PA.

Application issues
Not interested in open day. Wanted personal negotiation with DO.

Assessment
DO preliminary interview. Encouraged by DO to delay application.

Access issues
Access to classes problematic due to times/distances/lift operator. Said that she was an anxious person and worries about accessing courses made her more anxious. Asked to choose CSV on basis of a number of CVs – not a good way of doing it. CSV highly problematic and excessively priced – but no other organisation around to provide that level of support.

Teaching and learning experience/DDA awareness
Primarily lectures and seminars – PA difficulties due to lack of experience. Field trip not accessible/little assistance. Problems with technology – not available till Christmas. When PA sick, Christine misses university or supported by mother. Demonstrators assisted with labs and operation of lift (janitors said it was not included in their job description). Some lecturers won't hand out notes (believed to encourage non-attendance at lectures). Very able student (top 20%) but restricted by access difficulties.

Financial situation
No particular issues – DSA and parental support.

Table A.1 (continued)

Engagement with institution/Social experience of university
Reluctant to be active in asserting needs resulting in difficulties, e.g. field trip – strict commuting schedule (1 hour each way from home) hindered social life. Not involved in disabled students' group or any other extra-curricular activity.

Identity
Strong perception of self as 'different', isolated, unable to discuss issue with researcher. Went to special needs secondary school, because thought she would be dependent on help from others in local mainstream school. Unaware of DDA Part 4.

32   Maurice
Aged 25, Scottish University 2, Medicine, Year 2 (previously completed degree in Physiology and Sports Science)

Impairment
Dyslexia.

Application issues
Not diagnosed prior to university, but difficulties in reading at school. Helped by mother (a teacher).

Assessment
In Year 2, professor recognised discrepancy between written and oral work. Professor approached DO and suggested psychological assessment. Relieved by diagnosis.

Access issues
Very good oral work but problems with written work, particularly structuring ideas.

Teaching and learning experience/DDA awareness
Experienced some negative attitudes to dyslexia but supervisor supportive. Thought dyslexia was 'fashion' but recognised problem. Innovative problem-based learning of medical faculty more accessible. Some suspicion of request for extra time in exams – dyslexia seen by some medics as 'excuse'. Suggestion that many students would benefit from oral examination.

Financial situation
No particular issues – DSA and parental support. Works in hall of residence and is financially independent.

Engagement with institution/Social experience of university
Confident in seeking support – no significant impact of impairment on social relationships. Friends mildly curious.

Identity
No association with 'disabled', relieved not to be wheelchair user. Being bracketed with wheelchair user is 'almost offensive'. But label 'dyslexia' shows he is not thick and brings advantages, e.g. extra time in exams. Thought allowance should have been made in finals – almost got a first but was not allowed viva – a bit bitter about this.

33   Karla
Scottish University 2, Sociology and Politics, Year 4

Impairment
Acquired physical impairment – restricts mobility. Sometimes uses wheelchair.

Table A.1   (continued)

Application issues
Travelled after school. Did two-year course at college before coming to this university – long access route. Chose university because of desire to become 'more middle class'. Had to prove ability before admission.

Assessment
Discussion about physical access needs before coming to university.

Access issues
Only issue is accessible rooms. Secretary in Politics phones up to check with K that rooms are accessible. Handrails fitted to assist access to old building – done quickly.

Teaching and learning experience/DDA awareness
Major problem – child and mortgage. Assessment favours middle-class students who don't have to work and people without family commitments. Disability not major problem.

Financial situation
Difficult – child and mortgage. Works at museum during holidays. Sometimes regrets time spent travelling after school.

Engagement with institution/Social experience of university
Mature student – has friends outside university. Can't get out at night.

Identity
Disability not main part of identity – being single parent, working class, more salient. Doesn't identify with disabled people's groups. Thinks she would feel differently if born disabled. Hates being placed with other disabled people in theatre. Knew about DDA but would be reluctant to bring case – premised on US view of individual rights which she questions.

34   Kirsty
Aged 20, Scottish University 2

Impairment
Visual/hearing.

Application issues
Influenced by need to be close to home/support of mother.

Assessment
DO preliminary interview. Disagreement with disability officer re use of signer. Extensive student involvement in this process.

Access issues
Able to access teaching easily.

Teaching and learning experience/DDA awareness
Primarily lectures and seminars – lack of staff awareness in labs and lectures. Would have preferred viva but university prevented this happening. Use of demonstrator in labs very limited, not a positive experience. Course material available and not a problem.

Financial situation
No particular difficulties – DSA and parental support.

Table A.1 (continued)

Engagement with institution/Social experience of university
No real problems socially – desire to meet other disabled students but could not find avenue for organised involvement as 'disabled person' – confident addressing academic staff.

Identity
Particular association with similarly (genetic) impaired individuals.

35 Lynne
Aged 19, Scottish University 2, Law and Spanish, Year 1

Impairment
Blind – Braille user.

Application issues
Wanted to live at home. Could choose between 2 local universities. Chose this university after visit – seemed eager to discuss and negotiate. No assistance offered to attend open days. Sister worked at university and could act as travel companion.

Assessment
Preliminary interview with DO. Meeting with Law admissions tutor. Extensive faculty involvement.

Access issues
Difficulties moving round campus – assisted by school friend and sister. Faculty suggested she attend seminar groups in most accessible location, but idea rejected by student. Preferred to choose seminar on basis of friendship group/topic/tutor.

Teaching and learning experience/DDA awareness
Preliminary lectures and seminars positive – communication by email. Essential texts downloadable or emailed in advance. One lecturer caused difficulties. But Brailling of essential course materials not completed – extra work resulting.

Financial situation
No particular difficulties – DSA and parental support. DSA did not fully cover cost of Braille Lite machine.

Engagement with institution/Social experience of university
Confident addressing difficulties and seeking their resolution – no problems socially but restricted by travel – no organised involvement.

Identity
Self-perception as ordinary student. Wanted to 'pass' as normal and move round campus unassisted. Admissions tutor comments that L makes 'no fuss' – some students don't know she is blind.

36 Robbie
Aged 18, Scottish College 1, HND Multi Media, Year 2

Impairment
Deaf.

Application issues
Straightforward – only 1 college applied to. Scottish College 1 has reputation for working with deaf students – particularly 'clever' ones. Funded as resource for deaf students. Important to have peer group. Seen as half-way house between school and university.

Table A.1 (continued)

Assessment
Preliminary interview with special needs adviser.

Access issues
Good coverage of interpreters (2 full time), although national shortage creates difficulties. Policy – to put in plenty of support and then withdraw it gradually. Departments very supportive – deaf students seen as part of mainstream clientele – not special. All staff invited to deaf awareness classes.

Teaching and learning experience/DDA awareness
Primarily lectures and seminars but small (<20) classes. Positive experience. Adaptation of communications classes. Staff informed of accommodations required informally. Problem – interpreters have to leave class promptly – doesn't allow for questions. Difficulties – lecturers talk whilst writing on board. Small classes help.

Financial situation
No particular problems. DSA, supported by parents.

Engagement with institution/Social experience of university
Confident addressing lecturers but limited by interpreter availability – no problems socially but limited to deaf community only. Problems communicating with hearing students.

Identity
Not aware of social model of disability. Strong association with deaf community. Identified as deaf rather than disabled – latter term not used. Both mother and father deaf – father works for deaf voluntary organisation. Disabled refers more to people who have mobility impairment or are blind. People think of deaf people as stupid – dumb.

37 Megan
Aged 18, Scottish College 1, HNC Health, Fitness and Exercise (previously NC in advanced sport & performance)

Impairment
Dyslexia.

Application issues
Application determined by location/nature of course. Wanted small, friendly college – no specific regard to support.

Assessment
Originally diagnosed in primary school. Had record of needs. Student reluctant to disclose – assessment by learning support but lecturers largely unaware. Assessment for DSA at another college.

Access issues
Chose course because mostly practical. Writing is very difficult – has scribe in exams. One lecturer doesn't know she has dyslexia – gets nothing from these lectures. Notes are unreadable. Meetings with dyslexia support tutor used to plan when scribe will be needed.

Teaching and learning experience/DDA awareness
Student very reluctant to disclose, leading to difficulties – lecturers who knew provided notes, etc. Main form of support from college learning support – visit every 2 weeks. Extra time awarded in exams. Mother helps with reading.

Financial situation
No particular problems – works part time and supported by parents.

Engagement with institution/Social experience of university
Very reluctant to declare dyslexia to academic staff – some staff still unaware of it – no evidence of effect of impairment in social situation.

Identity
Aware of significant impact of dyslexia but not sure whether this is 'disability' – term refers to people with more significant impairments. No awareness of DDA Part 4.

38 Catherine
Aged 45, Scottish College 1, HND Administration and Information Management (previously HNC)

Impairment
Visual impairment from birth.

Application issues
Entered college after 20 years working in leisure centre. Disclosed impairment on application form – college telephoned to arrange meeting. Known level of support from previous course studied – college was local.

Assessment
Intensive early assessment by college and VST – student confident in level of support. DSA provides laptop, minidisk player and 10 hours of reader services.

Access issues
Excited by potential of new technologies to improve access to education and employment. Uses range of software, e.g. Zoomtext and Jaws. Lecturers who talk a lot and are easy to understand are best. Doing own research is difficult.

Teaching and learning experience/DDA awareness
Each student has individual learning support plan. High level of support from visual support tutor (VST) – lecturers' material adapted, e.g. figures redrawn, large font size, etc. Difficulties with part-time staff. Hope to make lecturers more responsible. Extra time awarded. Curriculum made accessible largely by work of VST rather than lecturers.

Financial situation
No particular problems – receives DSA and is supported by partner.

Engagement with institution/Social experience of university
Reliant on visual support teacher – socially 'the best time in her life', happy with support and meeting other visually impaired people for first time.

Identity
Initially reluctant to declare impairment now comfortable identifying as 'disabled'. Recognises impact of impairment – eye strain in lectures. Necessary to obtain support. Believes mother has difficulty recognising impairment. Attended mainstream school. Being student is 'best time in her life'. Has developed strong affinity with other visually impaired people. Would like to work in this area.

Table A.1 (continued)

39   Donny
Aged 34, Scottish College 1, HNC Multi-media Computing, Year 1

Impairment
Acquired physical impairment – motor cycle accident.

Application issues
Made redundant from job after accident. College known to student as 'accessible' and taught course of interest – wanted local college.

Assessment
Frontline lecturers expected to identify students needing support – not applicable to Donny in academic terms.

Access issues
Building generally accessible but series of irritating difficulties – lifts, parking, keys to toilets. Student has individual learning plan which identifies individual learning needs.

Teaching and learning experience/DDA awareness
Student had excellent experience of course but some access difficulties re bench heights. Plays active role in class.

Financial situation
Advised by DEA that course counted as Training for Work – could therefore claim JSA. Qualified for DLA plus other disability benefits. Travel expenses are paid. Wife works full time.

Engagement with institution/Social experience of university
Confident addressing staff and raising issues. Break times and meal times difficult but enjoying student company. Students make sure he's included in outings to pub.

Identity
Active in disabled issues – director of voluntary organisation for people with spinal injuries – talks to people in hospital. Aware of political nature of disability. Rejects personal tragedy view.

40   Carly
Aged 34, Scottish College 1, HNC Business

Impairment
Mobility – adult-onset arthritis, uses crutches.

Application issues
After school, undertook voluntary work. Hip replacements meant she could consider more ambitious goals. Location crucial factor – close to home. Felt college would offer accessible environment.

Assessment
Frontline lecturers expected to identify students needing particular support – not applicable to Carly in academic terms.

Access issues
Building generally accessible but series of irritating difficulties – lifts, parking, keys to toilets.

Table A.1   (continued)

Teaching and learning experience/DDA awareness
Student had excellent experience of course.

Financial situation
Receives state benefits – course fell within remit of Training for Work – qualified for JSA plus £10 and travel expenses.

Engagement with institution/Social experience of university
Declared impairment on application otherwise little need to address it – cautious of socialising with other students due to painful problems in walking, moving around – embarrassed to ask location of meetings and request changes.

Identity
Some discomfort with declaring herself 'disabled' particularly in company of more severely impaired people. In 20s had denied impairment and withdrawn from social life. Now accepts she has to use crutch, but would rather pass as normal. Has empathy with other disabled people.

41   Lucy
Aged 19, Scottish College 1, HNC Web Development

Impairment
Hearing impairment – partially deaf, uses lip-reading and BSL.

Application issues
Local college and identified in deaf community as accessible.

Assessment
Initial assessment by dedicated learning support tutor – high level of support advised in early stages. DSA provides home PC, software and video camera.

Access issues
Interpreter in class – they may take notes if lecturer is too fast.

Teaching and learning experience/DDA awareness
Generally good in terms of lecturer awareness and use of visual material – availability of signers good but occasional non-appearances – assisted by small class sizes. Problems with slow delivery of equipment.

Financial situation
Receives DLA, DSA and other state benefits but not particular problem.

Engagement with institution/Social experience of university
Confident in declaring impairment but would not request lecturers to change practice – e.g. face her to assist lip-reading – strong social life with other deaf students. Has recently moved out of parental home and into flat with other deaf students.

Identity
Prefers to be called deaf rather than disabled. Grew up in deaf family – strong connections to deaf community. Attended mainstream school with unit for deaf children. Chats to deaf people on internet – the local deaf community is a bit small. Made aware of DDA through local deaf forum.

Table A.1 (continued)

42   Sara
Scottish University 3, Scottish History and Classics, Year 2

Impairment
Dyslexia – diagnosed at local primary school. Contacted psychologist through Dyslexia Institute – paid for assessment.

Application issues
Helpful response to initial approach. Given lower offer because of dyslexia.

Assessment
Went to Access Centre at Dundee for assessment. Computer arrived at Easter, 6 months after starting university.

Access issues
DSA pays for PC and special software. Voice recognition software doesn't work very well. Also entitled to scribe and extra time in exams. Feels dyslexia affects performance in many ways – can't express subtle ideas.

Teaching and learning experience/DDA awareness
Some tutors much more helpful – want to be told what allowances they should make. Others not interested. PhD students may lack knowledge and confidence to make reasonable adjustments. Lecturers don't know whether they should adjust marking. Concern in university about 'dumbing down'.

Financial situation
Middle-class background – supported by family. DSA sufficient to meet support needs.

Engagement with institution/Social experience of university
Lives in women's hall – quiet, domestic life. Enjoys traditional aspects of student life. Very involved in Christian Union.

Identity
Doesn't conceal dyslexia, but doesn't draw attention to it. Not involved in dyslexia support group. Considers herself as 'person with dyslexia' – not disability.

43   Lara
Scottish University 3, Social Anthropology and History of Art, Year 2

Impairment
Diabetes since age 3. Gap year – picked up virus and became ill with ME in first year.

Application issues
Straightforward – did not have ME at time. Had friends and family at this university.

Assessment
Had to leave university because of illness – contacted ME society.

Access issues
Has to miss many lectures – some lecturers reluctant to accept late work or give out handouts.

Teaching and learning experience/DDA awareness
University is 'nothing special' – will leave with ordinary degree. Great variation between departments – some unhelpful. Student support services very understanding.

Table A.1 (continued)

Financial situation
Family financial difficulties – has been awarded grants from university hardship fund in addition to DSA, which pays for dictaphone and laptop.

Engagement with institution/Social experience of university
ME has had impact on involvement – has missed a lot of time. Involved with local Christian group. Lives out of town with small group of friends.

Identity
Doesn't relate to university disabled students groups. Thinks ME self-help group would be depressing experience. Officially disclosed disability, but generally associates disability with physical or sensory impairment.

44 Sheila
Scottish University 3, Geoscience, Year 2

Impairment
Severe congenital visual impairment – identified when very young.

Application issues
Strong learning support at school. Met with special needs support officer before applied – reviewed support needs. Small town better for orientation. Family had house in town.

Assessment
As result of specialist assessment, has magnifiers, special software, telescope for looking at overheads.

Access issues
Enlarged handouts generally supplied. Geoscience particularly supportive – interested in making curriculum notes more accessible.

Teaching and learning experience/DDA awareness
Geoscience supportive but some aspects of course very difficult, e.g. close examination of fossils. Many lecturers want to help but don't understand nature of difficulties.

Financial situation
Support from middle-class family. Income from sub-let rooms in family house. DSA pays for equipment.

Engagement with institution/Social experience of university
Involved with Christian group (father is a vicar). Involved in university working group on disability. Wants to make things better for disabled students who come to university later.

Identity
Identifies as disabled and committed to making things better for others. Wants to engage with institution and work for change within it.

45 Val
Scottish University 3, Modern History and German, Year 2

Impairment
Visual impairment. Neurological, not physical problem.

Table A.1 (continued)

Application issues
Received support at open day from special needs adviser. Lot of contact through email prior to arrival.

Assessment
Assessment at Dundee – great parental effort to have support in place for start of term. Took a lot of nasty letters and emails.

Access issues
Physical environment reasonably accessible because of small town atmosphere. Year abroad very difficult – going to school for children with visual impairment.

Teaching and learning experience/DDA awareness
Problems with German department. Promises of adjustments, e.g. enlarged text, not delivered. German lecturers say disabled students cannot have special learning support because this would give them unfair advantage. Has struggled with the work. German lecturers believe problems with foreign language due to visual impairment may be insurmountable. Reading is very slow – no allowances made. Library will not allow longer loans.

Financial situation
Support from middle-class parents. Has to pay for additional German grammar lessons – may have to stop because of cost. DSA pays for specialist equipment.

Engagement with institution/Social experience of university
Lives in women's hall and socialised with small group of students. Little engagement with wider university life.

Identity
Not involved in disabled students' groups – not very sociable. Doesn't like groups. Tries to minimise significance of impairment – doesn't want to be labelled – 'just try to blend in, you don't try and make yourself special'. Would be reluctant to bring case under DDA – father has pushed on her behalf.

46   Owen
Aged 21, Scottish University 3, repeating 2nd year, started Geology, now General Arts

Impairment
Depression and dyslexia.

Application issues
Applied because of parental expectations, later decided at wrong university on wrong course.

Assessment
Was being assessed for dyslexia, when MH difficulties developed. Breakdown and drop-out in 2nd year. On return disability adviser (DA) has regular meetings with him to monitor progress.

Access issues
Difficulties getting motivated, used to lead to absences and failure academically. Since return to university, doing well and keeping up. Coped with dyslexia at school by good memory, strategy didn't work at university.

Table A.1 (continued)

Teaching and learning experience/DDA awareness
Misjudged by some lecturers as 'lazy'. He puts this down to ignorance of MH issues.

Financial situation
Regular support from DA, describes her as a 'god-send'. DSA for computer and software – very helpful, means can study in room when feeling depressed.

Engagement with institution/Social experience of university
Some difficulties through students being patronising on his return. Complaint brought against him for hitting another student under provocation.

Identity
Breakdown because of existential crisis: loss of identity following transition from school and following parents' wishes rather than his own. Hates lack of class mix at this university, even though from private school himself. Finds it too narrow. Not aware of DDA.

47 Mary
Aged 19, Scottish University 3, Classics, Year 2

Impairment
Partially deaf, cannot hear high frequencies, lip-reads.

Application Issues
Met with student support services (SSS) at an open day and was reassured that support would be in place and that class sizes would be small enough. But chose the university on academic grounds and because based in town rather than city.

Assessment
Spoke to SSS once received offer, to check things would be in place. They also helped get suitable accommodation. Also discussed needs with department disability contact (DC) in first week. He passed on information to other staff. SSS been very helpful she says.

Access issues
She has difficulty lip-reading and taking notes in lectures, so has a note-taker (fellow student). It's easier if seats in horseshoe in tutorials. She accepts she won't always hear everything.

Teaching and learning experience/DDA awareness
Generally positive. Staff are very willing to help. They forget to look at her when they talk, but the note-taker helps with this. A couple of minor difficult experiences due to lecturers' lack of awareness.

Financial situation
DSA paid for note-taker, computer equipment, recording equipment, touch-typing course. She may get hearing aids too. There was a delay in receiving DSA from her LEA. She feels it is adequate for her needs.

Engagement with institution/Social experience of university
She prefers not to draw attention to her impairment. But would tackle a lecturer if an issue arose because of it, because they should know about it anyway. She prefers not to tell other students until she knows them. She doesn't want to be singled out.

Identity
Doesn't think of herself as disabled. Went to private school. This university was first choice.

Table A.1 (continued)

48   Leslie
Scottish University 3, History, Year 1

Impairment
Left school 8 years ago. Accident 2 years ago damaged his brain. He has difficulties with balance, walking and writing.

Application issues
Was on an Access course when accident happened. In hospital for a year, advised to do Access summer school, then started university Chose this one for geographical reasons.

Assessment
He was in contact with university while still in hospital – his mum made most arrangements with DA, re DSA for example.

Access issues
He has not experienced any barriers to physical access. The DA advised that he would not manage a spiral staircase, of which there are a few.

Teaching and learning experience/DDA awareness
He gets scribes, a computer, a special chair, an organiser, extra time in exams, and speaks exams. With that in place, he has no problems academically. Says things are working out well and he did well in his exams.

Financial situation
DSA provides things listed under TLA. University organised employment of scribes including payment.

Engagement with institution/Social experience of university
Not really integrated socially. Puts this down to being 'quiet' and 'boring'. Describes fellow students as very clever.

Identity
Says he has problems with balance and walking and is not disabled. Vaguely aware of DDA. Would bring legal action if it suited him.

Bibliography

Abberley, P. (1987) 'The concept of oppression and the development of a social theory of disability', *Disability, Handicap and Society* 2: 5–19.

Abberley, P. (1992) 'Counting us out: a discussion of the OPCS Disability Surveys', *Disability, Handicap and Society* 7 (2): 139–55.

Adams, M. (2001) 'A postcard from Australia', *National Disability Team Magazine*, 3, Coventry University.

Archer, L. (2003) 'Social class and higher education', in L. Archer, M. Hutchings and A. Ross (eds) *Higher Education and Social Class: Issues of Inclusion and Exclusion*, London: RoutledgeFalmer.

Archer, L., Hutchings, M. and Ross, A. (2003) (eds) *Higher Education and Social Class: Issues of Inclusion and Exclusion*, London: RoutledgeFalmer.

Ball, S.J. (2003) *Class Strategies and the Educational Market: The Middle Classes and Social Advantage*, London: RoutledgeFalmer.

Barnes, C. (1991) *Disabled People in Britain and Discrimination*, London: Hurst & Co.

Barnes, C. (1999) 'Disability studies: new or not so new directions?', *Disability and Society* 14: 577–81.

Barnes, C. (2003) 'Independent living: politics and implications for the 21st century', in J.V.C. Alonso (ed.) *El Movimiento de Vida Independiente*, Madrid: Luis Vives.

Baron, S., Field, J. and Schuller, T. (eds) (2000) *Social Capital: Critical Perspectives*, Oxford: Oxford University Press.

Baron, S., Riddell, S. and Wilson, A. (1999) 'The secret of eternal youth: identity, risk and learning difficulties', *British Journal of Sociology of Education* 20 (4): 483–99.

Beck, U. (1992) *The Risk Society*, London: Sage Publications.

Bennett, N., Dunne, E. and Carre, C. (1999) 'Patterns of core and generic skills in higher education', *Higher Education* 37 (1): 71–93.

Blackburn, R.M. and Jarman, J. (1993) 'Changing inequalities in access to British universities', *Oxford Review of Education* 19 (2): 197–215.

Blaxter, L. and Hughes, C. (2000) 'Social capital: a critique', in J. Thompson (ed.) *Politics and Practice of Widening Participation in Higher Education*, Leicester: NIACE.

Bourdieu, P. (1972) *Current Research*, Paris: Centre for European Sociology, Ecole Pratique des Hautes Etudes.

Bourdieu, P. (1986) *Distinction: A Social Critique of the Judgement of Taste*, London: Routledge.

Bourdieu, P. (1989) 'Social space and symbolic power', *Sociological Theory* 7: 14–25.

Bourdieu, P. (1990) *The Logic of Practice*, Cambridge: Polity Press.

Bourdieu, J.P. and Passeron, C. (1977) *Reproduction in Education, Society and Culture*, London: Sage.

Breitenbach, E., Brown, A., Mackay, F. and Webb, J. (eds) (2002) *The Changing Politics of Gender Equality in Britain*, Basingstoke: Palgrave.

British Psychological Society (BPS) (1999) *Dyslexia, Literacy and Psychological Assessment, Report of a Working Party of the Division of Educational and Child Psychology*, Leicester: BPS.

Brown, S., Duffield, J., Sutherland, L., Phillips, R., Riddell, S., Cox, A. and Amery, P. (1997) *Scottish Higher Education Funding Council Initiatives in Support for Students with Disabilities: Evaluation Report*, Stirling: Education Department, University of Stirling.

Clarke, J. and Newman, J. (1997) *The Managerial State*, London: Sage.

Clarke, J., Gewirtz, S. and McLaughlin, E. (eds) (2000) *New Managerialism, New Welfare?*, London: Open University Press.

Coleman, J.S. (1988–9) 'Social capital in the creation of human capital', *American Journal of Sociology* 94 (Supplement): 95–120.

Conlon, G. and Chevalier, A. (2002) *Financial Returns to Undergraduates and Tuition Fees*, London: CIHE.

Corker, M. (2003) 'Deafness/Disability – problematising notions of identity, culture and structure', in S. Riddell and N. Watson (eds) *Disability, Culture and Identity*, London: Pearson Education.

Corker, M. and Shakespeare, T. (2002) 'Mapping the terrain', in M. Corker and T. Shakespeare (eds) *Disability/Postmodernism*, London: Continuum.

Crow, L. (1996) 'Including all of our lives: renewing the social model of disability', in C. Barnes and G. Mercer (eds) *Exploring the Divide: Illness and Disability*, Leeds: The Disability Press.

Department for Education and Employment (DfEE) (1998) *The Learning Age: A Renaissance for a New Britain*, London: HMSO.

Department for Education and Employment (DfEE) (1999a) *From Exclusion to Inclusion: A Report of the Disability Rights Task Force*, London: DfEE.

Department for Education and Employment (DfEE) (1999b) *Learning to Succeed: Coherence and Diversity for Adult Learners*, London: HMSO.

Department of Education and Science (DES) (1963) *Report of the Committee on Higher Education* (the Robbins Report), London: HMSO.

Department for Education and Skills (DfES) (2003) *The Future of Higher Education*, London: The Stationery Office.

Department of Health (DOH) (2001) *Making It Happen: A Guide to Delivering Mental Health Promotion*, www.doh.gov.uk/pdfs/makingithappen.pdf

Disability Rights Commission (DRC) (2002) *Code of Practice Post-16: Code of Practice for Providers of Post-16 Education and Related Services*, London: DRC.

Dunne, E., Bennett, N. and Carre, C. (1997) 'Higher education: core skills in a learning society', *Journal of Education Policy* 12 (6): 511–25.

Edson, J. and Riddell, S. (2003) *An Evaluation of the Teachability Project*, Glasgow: Strathclyde Centre for Disability Research.

Egerton, M. and Halsey, A.H. (1993) 'Trends in social class and gender in access to higher education in Britain', *Oxford Review of Education* 19 (2): 183–96.

Eggins, H. (ed.) (2003) *Globalization and Reform in Higher Education*, Maidenhead: Society for Research in Higher Education and Open University Press.

Evans, M. and Farrar, V. (2003) *What Happens Next? The Destinations of Disabled Graduates*, London: Association of Graduate Careers Advisory Services.

Exworthy, M. and Halford, S. (eds) (1999) *Professionals and the New Managerialism in the Public Sector*, Buckingham: Open University Press.

Farwell, R. (2002) 'Higher education provision and the change to a mass system', in A. Hayton and A. Paczuska (eds) *Access, Participation and Higher Education: Policy and Practice*, London: Kogan Page.

Field, J. (2003) 'Getting real? Evidence on access and achievement?', in M. Slowey and D. Watson (eds) (2003) *Higher Education and the Lifecourse*, London: Society for Research in Higher Education and Open University Press.

Fine, B. (1999) 'The development state is dead – long live social capital?', *Development and Change* 30: 1–19.

Finkelstein, V. (1980) *Attitudes and Disabled People: Issues for Discussion*, New York: World Rehabilitation Fund.

Fraser, N. (1997) *Justice Interruptus: Critical Reflections on the Post-Socialist Condition*, London: Routledge.

Freedman, S. (1999) *A Critical Review of the Concept of Equality in British Anti-Discrimination Legislation*, Cambridge: University of Cambridge, Centre for Public Law.

Furedi, F. (2004) *Therapy Culture: Cultivating Vulnerability in an Uncertain Age*, London: Routledge.

Furlong, A. and Forsyth, A. (2003) *Socio-economic Disadvantage and Experience in Higher Education*, Bristol: The Policy Press.

Gallagher, J. (2002) 'Parallel lines? Higher education in Scotland's colleges and higher education institutions', *Scottish Affairs* 40 (Summer): 123–39.

Gallagher, J., Leahy, J. and MacFarlane, K. (1997) *The FE/HE Route: New Pathways into Higher Education*, Research Report for SOEID, Glasgow: Caledonian University.

Glass, D.V. (ed.) (1954) *Social Mobility in Britain*, London: Routledge and Kegan Paul.

Gooding, C. (2000) 'Disability Discrimination Act: from statute to practice', *Critical Social Policy* 20 (4): 533–49.

Goodlad, R. and Riddell, S. (2005) 'Social justice and disabled people: principles and challenges', *Social Policy & Society* 4 (1): 45–54.

Hall, S. (1996) 'Introduction: who needs identity?', in S. Hall and P. Du Gay (eds) *Questions of Cultural Identity*, London: Sage.

Hall, J. and Tinklin, T. (1998) 'Students first: the experiences of disabled students in higher education', Edinburgh: Scottish Council for Research in Education.

Halsey, A.H. (1995) *Decline of Donnish Dominion: The British Academic Professions in the Twentieth Century*, Oxford: Oxford University Press.

Hayton, A. and Paczuska, A. (eds) (2002) *Access, Participation and Higher Education: Policy and Practice*, London: Kogan Page.

Heads of University Counselling Services (HUCS) (1999) *Degrees of Disturbance: The New Agenda*, Rugby: BAC.

HEFCE (1998) 'Widening participation: special funding programme 1998–99', *Invitation 98/35*.

HEFCE (1999) 'Improving provision for disabled students: invitation to bid for funds for 1999–2000 to 2001–02', *Invitation 99/08*.

HEFCE (2001) *Performance Indicators in Higher Education in the UK, 1998–99, 1999–2000*, Bristol: HEFCE.

HEFCE (2002) *Performance Indicators in Higher Education in the UK, 1999–2000, 2000–2001*, Bristol: HEFCE.

HEFCE/HEFCW (1999) *Guidance on Base-Level Provision for Disabled Students in Higher Education Institutions*, Bristol, HEFCE (www.niss.ac.uk/education/hefce/pub99/99_04.html).

Hurst, A. (1996) 'Equal opportunities and access: developments in policy and provision for disabled students 1990–1995', in S. Wolfendale and J. Corbett (eds) *Opening Doors: Learning Support in Higher Education*, London: Cassell.

Hurst, A. (ed.) (1998) *Higher Education and Disabilities: International Approaches*, Aldershot: Ashgate.

Hurst, A. (1999) 'The Dearing Report and students with disabilities and learning difficulties', *Disability and Society* 14 (1): 65–83.

Hurstfield, J., Meager, N., Aston, J., Davies, J., Mann, K., Mitchell, H., O'Regan, S. and Sinclair, A. (2004) *Monitoring the Disability Discrimination Act (DDA) 1995*, London: Department for Work and Pensions.

Jenkins, R. (1992) *Key Sociologists: Pierre Bourdieu*, London: Routledge.

Lash, S. and Urry, J. (1993) *Economies of Signs and Space*, London: Sage Publications.

Leicester, M. and Lovell, T. (1994) 'Race, gender and disability: a comparative perspective', *Journal of Further and Higher Education* 18: 52–6.

Macrea, M. and Maguire, M. (2002) 'Getting in and getting on: choosing the best', in A. Hayton and A. Paczuska (eds) *Access, Participation and Higher Education: Policy and Practice*, London: Kogan Page.

Meager, N. and Hurstfield, J. (2005) 'Disabled people and the labour market: has the DDA made a difference?', in A. Roulstone and C. Barnes (eds) *Working Futures: Disabled People, Policy and Social Inclusion*, Bristol: Policy Press.

Mental Health Foundation (2001) 'Promoting student mental health', *Mental Health Foundation Updates* 2: 11.

Metzer, H., Gatward, R. with Goodman, R. and Ford, T. (2000) *The Mental Health of Children and Adolescents in Great Britain: Summary Report*, London: Office for National Statistics.

Miller, D. (1999) *Principles of Social Justice*, Cambridge, MA and London: Harvard University Press.

Modood, T. and Acland, A. (eds) (1998) *Race and Higher Education*, London: Policy Studies Institute.

Morris, J. (ed.) (1996) *Encounters with Strangers: Feminism and Disability*, London: The Disability Press.

Morrow, V. (1998) 'What is social capital and how does it relate to children and young people?' paper presented at the meeting of the Social Capital Empirical Research Group, London School of Economics, Gender Institute, London, 15th July.

Morrow, V. (1999) 'Conceptualising social capital in relation to the well-being of children and young people: a critical review', *Sociological Review*, 744–65.

Naylor, R.A. and Smith, J.P. (2001) 'Schooling effects on subsequent university performance: evidence for the UK university population', *Warwick Economic Research Papers*, Warwick: Department of Economics, University of Warwick.

NCIHE (1997a) *Higher Education in the Learning Society* (the Dearing Report), London: HMSO.

NCIHE (1997b) *Higher Education in the Learning Society: Report of the Scottish Committee* (the Garrick Report), London: HMSO.

Newman, J. (2001) *Modernising Governance: New Labour, Policy and Society*, London: Sage.

Oliver, M. (1990) *The Politics of Disablement*, Basingstoke: Macmillan.

Oliver, M. (1996a) *Understanding Disability*, London: Macmillan.

Oliver, M. (1996b) 'Defining impairment and disability: issues at stake', in C. Barnes and G. Mercer (eds) *Exploring the Divide: Illness and Disability*, Leeds: The Disability Press.

Osborne, R.D. (1999) 'Wider access in Scotland?', *Scottish Affairs* 26: 36–46.

Paterson, L. (1997) 'Trends in higher education participation in Scotland', *Higher Education Quarterly* 51: 29–48.

Phillips, A. (1999) *Which Equalities Matter?*, Cambridge: Polity Press.

Poussi-Olli, H.-S. (1999) 'To be a disabled university student in Finland', *Disability & Society* 14 (1): 103–13.

Power, M. (1997) *The Audit Society*, Oxford: Oxford University Press.

Preece, J. (1999) 'Families into higher education project: an awareness raising action research project with schools and parents', *Higher Education Quarterly* 53 (3): 197–210.

Priestley, M. (ed.) (2001) *Disability and the Life Course*, Cambridge: Cambridge University Press.

Putnam, R.D. (1995) 'Bowling alone: America's declining social capital', *Journal of Democracy* 6: 65–78.

Putnam, R.D. (2000) *Bowling Alone: The Collapse and Revival of American Community*, New York: Simon & Schuster.

Raab, G. (1998) *Participation in Higher Education in Scotland*, Edinburgh: SHEFC.

Reay, D. (1998) 'Rethinking social class: qualitative perspectives on class and gender', *Sociology* 32 (2): 259–75.

Reay, D. (2001) 'Finding or losing yourself? Working-class relationships to education', *Journal of Education Policy* 16 (4): 333–46.

Reay, D. (2002) 'Class, authenticity and the transition to higher education for mature working-class students', *Sociological Review* 50 (3): 396–416.

Reay, D. (2003) 'Shifting class identities? Social class and the transition to higher education', in C. Vincent (ed.) *Social Class, Education and Identity*, London: RoutledgeFalmer.

Reay, D., Ball, S.J., David, M. and Davies, J. (2001) 'Choice of degree and degrees of choice', *Sociology* 35 (4): 855–74.

Rees, T. (2002) 'The politics of "mainstreaming" gender equality', in E. Breitenbach, A. Brown, F. Mackay and J. Webb (eds) *The Changing Politics of Gender Equality in Britain*, Basingstoke: Palgrave.

Rice, M. and Brooks, G. (2004) *Developmental Dyslexia in Adults: A Research Review*, London: National Research and Development Centre for Adult Literacy and Numeracy.

Riddell, S. (forthcoming) 'Disability and social class', in G. Albrecht (ed.) *Encyclopaedia of Disability Studies*, London: Sage.

Riddell, S. and Banks, P. (2001) *Disability in Scotland: A Baseline Study*, Edinburgh: Disability Rights Commission.

Riddell, S. and Banks, P. (2005) *Disability and Employment in Scotland: A Review of the Evidence Base*, Edinburgh: Scottish Executive.

Riddell, S. and Watson, N. (eds) (2005) *Disability, Culture and Identity*, Harlow: Pearson Education Ltd.

Riddell, S., Brown, S. and Duffield, J. (1994) 'Conflicts of policies and models: the case of specific learning difficulties', in S. Riddell and S. Brown (eds) *Special Educational Needs Policy in the 1990s: Warnock in the Market Place*, London: Routledge.

Riddell, S., Baron, S. and Wilson, A. (2001) *The Learning Society and People with Learning Difficulties*, Bristol: Policy Press.

Riddell, S., Tinklin, T. and Wilson, A. (2002) 'Disabled students in higher education: the impact of anti-discrimination legislation on teaching, learning and assessment' (published on ESCALATE website: www.escalate.ac.uk/exchange/resources/Key%20Skills/index.php3).

Riddell, S., Pearson, C., Jolly, D., Barnes, C., Priestley, M. and Mercer, G. (2005) 'The development of direct payments in the UK: implications for social justice', *Social Policy & Society* 4 (1): 75–85.

Scottish Executive (1999) *Implementing Inclusiveness: Realising Potential* (the Beattie Report), Edinburgh: HMSO.

Scottish Executive (2000) *Social Justice: A Scotland Where Everyone Matters: Annual Report 2000*, Edinburgh: Scottish Executive.

Scottish Executive (2003) *A Framework for Higher Education in Scotland*, Edinburgh: The Stationery Office.

Scottish Office (1998) *Opportunity Scotland: A Paper on Lifelong Learning*, Edinburgh: HMSO.

Shakespeare, T. (2000) *Help*, Birmingham: Venture Press.

Shakespeare, T. and Watson, N. (1997) 'Defending the social model', *Disability and Society* 12: 293–301.

Shakespeare, T., Gillespie-Sells, K. and Davies, D. (1996) *The Sexual Politics of Disability: Untold Desires*, London: Cassell.

SHEFC (1998) *Funding for the Future: A Consultation on the Funding of Teaching*, Edinburgh: SHEFC.

Shevlin, M., Kenny, M. and McNeela, E. (2004) 'Participation in higher education for students with disabilities: an Irish perspective', *Disability & Society* 19 (1): 15–30.

Slowey, M. and Watson, D. (eds) (2003) *Higher Education and the Lifecourse*, London: Society for Research in Higher Education and Open University Press.

Stanovich, K.E. (1988) 'Explaining the differences between the dyslexic and the garden-variety poor reader: the phonological core variable-difference model', *Journal of Learning Disabilities* 21 (10): 590–604.

Stein, J.F. (2002) 'Commentary: the dyslexia ecosystem', *Dyslexia* 8: 178–9.

Teachability (2002) *Teachability Project: Creating an Accessible Curriculum for Students with Disabilities*, Glasgow: University of Strathclyde.

Thomas, C. (1997) 'The baby and the bathwater: disabled women and motherhood in social context', *Sociology of Health and Illness* 19 (5): 622–43.

Thomas, C. (1998) 'Parents and families: disabled women's stories about their childhood experiences', in C. Robinson and K. Stalker (eds) *Growing Up with Disability*, London: Jessica Kingsley.

Thomas, C. (1999) *Female Forms: Experiencing and Understanding Disability*, Buckingham: Open University Press.

Thomas, C. (2002) 'Developing the social relational in the social model of disability', paper presented to the ESRC seminar services, the Social Model of Disability: Theoretical Considerations and Concerns, Leeds, October 2002.

Thusing, G. (2003) 'Following the U.S. example: European employment discrimination law and the impact of Council Directives 2000/43/EC and 2000/78/EC', *The International Journal of Comparative Labour Law and Industrial Relations* 19 (2): 187–218.

Tinklin, T. and Hall, J. (1999) 'Getting round obstacles: disabled students' experiences in higher education in Scotland', *Studies in Higher Education* 24: 183–94.

Tinklin, T. and Raffe, D. (1999) *Entrants to Higher Education*, Edinburgh: Centre for Educational Sociology, University of Edinburgh.

Tinklin, T., Riddell, S. and Wilson, A. (2002) *Disabled Students and Multiple Policy Innovations in Higher Education: Report of the Questionnaire Survey of Institutions*, Edinburgh: University of Edinburgh (www.ed.ac.uk/ces/Disability/Papers/QuestRep.pdf).

Tinklin, T., Riddell, S. and Wilson, A. (2004) 'Policy and provision for disabled students in higher education in Scotland and England: the current state of play', *Studies in Higher Education* 29 (5): 637–57.

Tsouros, A.D., Dowling, G., Thompson, J. and Dooris, M. (1998) *Health Promoting Universities: Concept, Experience and Framework for Action*, Copenhagen: World Health Organisation, Regional Office for Europe.

United States Congress (USC) (1990) *Americans with Disabilities Act*, Public Law No. 101–336, 104 STAT. 327.

Universities Scotland (2000) *Access to Achievement: A Guide to How the Scottish Higher Education System is Promoting Social Inclusion*, Edinburgh: Universities Scotland.

Universities UK (UUK) (2002) *Reducing the Risk of Student Suicide: Issues and Responses for Higher Education Institutions*, London: UUK.

Watson, N. (2002) 'Well, I know this is going to sound very strange to you, but I don't see myself as a disabled person: identity and disability', *Disability & Society* 17 (5): 509–29.

Watson, N. and Wood, B. (2005) 'No wheelchairs beyond this point: a historical examination of wheelchair access in the twentieth century', *Social Policy and Society* 4 (1): 97–105.

Williams, R. (1961) *Culture and Society 1780–1950*, Harmondsworth: Penguin.

Williams, R. (1977) *Marxism and Literature*, Oxford: Oxford University Press.

Wilson, A., Riddell, S. and Tinklin, T. (2002) *Disabled Students in Higher Education: Findings from the Key Informant Interviews*, Glasgow: Glasgow University (www.ed.ac.uk/ces/Disability/Papers/KeyInfrm.pdf).

Woessner, B. (2004) *Higher Education, Disability and the Labour Market*, London: Society for Research in Higher Education.

Wolfendale, S. and Corbett, J. (eds) (1996) *Opening Doors: Learning Support in Higher Education*, London: Cassell.

Index

Page numbers in *italics* refer to figures, tables and photographs.